D1179565

The Bible in the Sixteenth Century

Duke Monographs in
Medieval and Renaissance Studies 11

DAVID C. STEINMETZ, Editor

The Bible in the Sixteenth Century

Duke University Press
Durham and London
1990

Printed in the United States of America
on acid-free paper ∞
Library of Congress Cataloging-in-Publication data
appear on the last printed page of this book.

Contents

The Bible in the Sixteenth Century

Introduction

The essays in this volume were written for the Second International Colloquy on the History of Biblical Exegesis in the Sixteenth Century held at Duke University on September 23–25, 1982. The colloquy was sponsored by the Duke Divinity School in cooperation with the Institut d'histoire de la Réformation of the University of Geneva, which sponsored the first (1976) and third colloquies (1988).

The colloquies themselves grew out of the recognition that the intellectual and religious life of the sixteenth century cannot be understood without comprehending the preoccupation of sixteenth-century humanists and theologians with the interpretation of the Bible. Commentaries on Paul's Epistle to the Romans may serve as a case in point. In the fifteenth century relatively few commentaries on this epistle were written, and many of those that were circulated were reissues of earlier works. In the sixteenth century, however, well over seventy new commentaries on Romans were published, excluding fresh editions of older commentaries by patristic and medieval authors. The list of commentators on Romans includes not only such important and obvious scholars as Erasmus, Luther, and Calvin, but also such lesser figures as Alesius, Guilliaud, Grimani, and Brucioli.

This burst of commentary writing has been largely ignored by older scholarship, which regarded biblical commentaries as theological essays in unsystematic form, and therefore less accessible to historians than more systematic theological treatises. Little effort was made to treat the commentaries as a distinct genre of religious literature, different in scope and form from systematic theological treatises. Historians felt, for example, that everything worth knowing about Calvin's religious thought could be found in his *Institutes of the Christian*

Religion. His commentaries, structured by the unfolding details of the biblical text rather than by the great themes of Calvin's theology, were ancillary to his principal systematic writings.

The fact remains, however, that the bulk of Calvin's writings consists of biblical commentaries and sermons. Even Cardinal Cajetan, whose earlier career was devoted to the interpretation and promotion of the writings of Thomas Aquinas, spent his later years commenting on the literal sense of the Bible. Secular priests like Jean de Gagny, Franciscans like Nicholas le Grand, Dominicans like Ambrosius Catherinus Politus, Jesuits like Alfonso Salmeron, Augustinians like Girolamo Seripando, and Capuchins like Francis Titelmans joined Protestants like Martin Bucer, Philip Melanchthon, Peter Martyr Vermigli, and Konrad Pellican to make the sixteenth century a golden age of biblical interpretation.

While not an introduction to the study of the Bible in the sixteenth century in the strict sense of the term, the essays in this book nevertheless illuminate a broad spectrum of themes and problems in the history of biblical interpretation. The first three essays deal with the relationship between the Bible and social, political, and institutional history. H. C. Erik Midelfort reexamines a thesis from his 1972 study *Witch Hunting in Southwestern Germany, 1572–1684*, in which he argued that witchcraft reflected tensions in the community and in the family. Later study convinced him that sixteenth-century Germans would not have understood such a formulation, "for they had no clear notion of community, family, or witchcraft as we conventionally use the terms. . . . We might get further by looking at changes in household (*Haus*) and congregation (*Gemeinde*) in order to understand the fear of hidden evildoing, of pollution, that witchcraft seems to have become." Johann Weyer, physician to the duke of Jülich-Cleves, provides Midelfort with a particularly good illustration of the use of the Bible, especially Exodus 22:8, to redefine the crime of witchcraft and defend people who had been wrongfully accused of committing it.

Guy Bedouelle devotes his attention to the role played by biblical exegesis in the divorce of Henry VIII from Catherine of Aragon. Henry had appealed to Leviticus 18:16 and 20:21 to support his contention that he should never have married his brother's widow, even though Deuteronomy 25:5 and Matthew 22:24 appear to sanction the marriage of widow and brother-in-law. Bedouelle demonstrates how issues of biblical exegesis, canon law, and political necessity were intertwined in the decisions of the English, French, and Italian universities Henry consulted for an endorsement of his position.

Scott H. Hendrix examines the role the Bible played in the institutionalization of the Reformation in northern Germany by focusing on the career of Urbanus Rhegius, superintendent of the Lutheran church in Lüneburg from 1530 to 1541. While Rhegius used the Bible polemically to defend Lutheran teaching against its Catholic detractors, he stressed as well the catechetical use of the Bible in the education of laity and clergy alike. Because he was concerned that Lutheranism in Lower Saxony present a consistent message from its pulpits, he could not support the sole authority of Scripture for the catechetical activity of the church, if the principle of *sola scriptura* were understood to mean that the Bible should be interpreted apart from the hermeneutical structure provided by church doctrine and the testimony of the early Fathers.

The essay by Kalman P. Bland provides a counterpoint to the other ten by exploring issues in sixteenth-century Jewish exegesis. Bland selects three commentators: Rabbi Isaac Karo, who "demonstrated the Bible's high density of philosophic, scientific, and religious enlightenment and guidance," Rabbi Moses Alsheikh, who "unraveled the keen machinations that motivate and serve human behavior," and Rabbi Moses Cordovero, who embraced a transcognitive mysticism that interpreted "biblical allusions as constituting the hierarchical unfolding of God Himself," transcending "the limitations of ordinary language." Bland illustrates the method of each rabbi by providing citations from Karo's exegesis of Genesis 28, Alsheikh's exegesis of 1 Samuel 15, and Cordovero's systematic treatise entitled *Paradise of Pomegranates*.

Protestant theologians like Hans Joachim Kraus have attempted to distinguish Calvin's interpretation of the Bible from medieval exegesis by stressing his interest in the grammatical meaning of a text, its historical context, and the intention of its human author. Richard A. Muller attempts to correct the misconceptions created by such characterizations by arguing that they do justice neither to medieval exegesis nor to Calvin's working hermeneutic. By examining Calvin's exegesis of selected passages from the prophets, Muller shows that while "Calvin's exegesis does represent a more textually, grammatically, and historically ordered hermeneutic" than the exegesis of his medieval predecessors, his exegesis, like theirs, nevertheless "remains within the bounds of a hermeneutical approach in which the final implication of any text is determined by the broader context of promise, fulfillment, and the ongoing history of God's people."

R. Gerald Hobbs's essay deals with a problem that was by no means new in the sixteenth century but was sharpened for the church by the growing number of Christian Hebraists: namely, how should one account for the disquieting discrepancy when the New Testament gives a reading of an Old Testament passage that is not the reading most readily suggested by the Hebrew text itself. Hobbs focuses on Paul's use of the Psalms and the treatment of the issues raised by his use in the commentaries, translations, and paraphrases written between 1500 and 1560.

David C. Steinmetz attempts to clarify Calvin's relationship to the Pauline interpretation of the early church by comparing his exegesis of Romans 8:1–11 with the exegesis of the same passage by Ambrosiaster and Chrysostom. In this passage Paul raised four interrelated issues—law, anthropology, Christology, and ethics—that are explicitly discussed by all three commentators. While Calvin accepted Chrysostom and Ambrosiaster as interpreters of Paul whose views must be taken into account, and while he used them as exegetical partners and guides with whom he frequently agreed, he did not feel himself obligated to accept their conclusions and often pursued a different exegetical agenda.

John B. Payne examines Erasmus's interpretation of Romans 9:6–24 before and after his debate with Luther. In his early exegesis Erasmus argued that Paul in Romans 9 was not so much interested in the salvation and damnation of individuals as in the rejection of the Jews as God's people and the election of the Gentiles as the new people of God. Insofar as Erasmus was interested in the doctrine of predestination at all, he based it on foreseen merit: "salvation is granted only to those who deserve it by the merit of faith." In his later revision of the *Paraphrases,* however, Erasmus accepted a more Augustinian reading of Paul.

Jean-Claude Margolin offers a detailed and nuanced analysis of the exegetical work of Valla, Colet, Lefèvre, and Erasmus on Romans 11. All four attempted to disentangle the Pauline text from philological corruptions and to provide more adequate texts and better translations. Valla was the most detached of the four commentators, the one most devoted to purely philological and grammatical questions. Colet and Erasmus were intensely interested in the religious and theological issues raised by Paul and their relevance for the reform of European society in the sixteenth century. Lefèvre, who shared with Colet and Erasmus an appreciation of the normative role of Paul's letters, was more mystical and philosophical in his exegesis, and less interested in "sociohistorical contingencies."

Martin Bucer's commentary on John went through three editions (1528, 1530, 1536) before the author's death in 1551. Because the exegesis of John 6 is crucial for the intra-Protestant controversy over the Lord's Supper, and because the second and third editions of Bucer's commentary appeared after two crucial moments in that controversy—the Marburg Colloquy of 1529 and the conclusion of the Wittenberg Concord in May 1536—Irena Backus attempts "to trace the textual changes introduced by Bucer between 1528 and 1536 into his exegesis of John 6:52, 53, and 64." After careful and sustained analysis, she concludes that by 1536 Bucer had abandoned his earlier polemic against the Lutherans but did not alter his fundamental exegetical position, especially on the question of the distinction of the two natures in Christ. Bucer refused in his last revision, as in his first edition, to accept the doctrine of the ubiquity of Christ's body so crucial to Luther's eucharistic theology.

Kenneth G. Hagen explores the exegetical method of the Danish Lutheran theologian Niels Hemmingsen in the context of the discussion of theological method by his contemporaries. He attempts to demonstrate Hemmingsen's independence from his teacher, Philip Melanchthon, who was also concerned with questions of theological and exegetical method, and argues for the importance of Hemmingsen's contribution to the development of historical criticism. Throughout his essay Hagen is concerned to guard against an anachronistic reading of Hemmingsen and his contemporaries that ascribes twentieth-century meanings to sixteenth-century texts and technical terms.

Special thanks are due to the Divinity School of Duke University and to Dean Thomas A. Langford and the late Dean Jameson Jones, who underwrote the costs of the colloquy. John L. Farthing of Hendrix College translated the essay by Margolin and revised the translation of the essay by Bedouelle. Edward P. Mahoney, the editor of this series, enthusiastically attended the sessions of the colloquy and encouraged the publication of the papers by Duke University Press. Eugene F. Rice, Jr., of Columbia University and Heiko A. Oberman of the University of Arizona also spoke at the colloquy, though their contributions could not be included in this volume. Without the assistance and encouragement of these colleagues and the patient perseverance of the contributors, the present volume could not have been completed.

H. C. ERIK MIDELFORT

Social History and Biblical Exegesis: Community, Family, and Witchcraft in Sixteenth-Century Germany

It is not often that social historians are given a formal reason to reflect on the biblical exegesis of the age that they study. Even social historians hardy enough to concede the general importance of ideas are likely to shrink from the daunting task of dealing with a subject so obviously bristling with technical difficulties. But a prejudice was common enough in the not-so-distant past to further guarantee that social history and biblical studies would remain separate. This was the assumption, on both sides, that we/they alone were dealing with timeless truths. Biblical scholars do not need to be reminded of this assumption on their part, but it was no less common among social historians who dealt not with "mere events" and mere personalities but with the "longue durée"—the glacial shifts in social and economic structure, the vast continuities that seemed to signal the reality beneath the apparent flux of everyday experience.[1] In grasping imaginatively after comparative methods and interdisciplinary tools from anthropology, sociology, economics, and the experience of peoples from around the world, social historians often proclaimed, at least implicitly, the timelessness of their subjects—subjects such as the peasant economy, the village as a legal or political unit, the moral economy of the crowd, and the sense of time, or of space, or of work and play among "preindustrial" peoples. These subjects were not, of course, literally timeless. They showed characteristic shifts under the impact of industrialization, secularization, and urbanization, of "modernization" as it was once naïvely called. Few doubted, however, that the experiences of peoples in similar circumstances were fundamentally comparable because fundamentally similar. This assumption still undergirds a good deal of innovative work in social history today. I do not intend to claim that all such work suffers from a single, serious flaw, but it does seem important to me that social historians, even in France, are returning, haltingly and awkwardly, to narrative and events, if not yet to biography.[2] For events, especially if they are "mere" events, are unique, unrepeated, and time-bound, not easily assimilated or even compared to presumably similar events in other times and places. In this shift biblical scholars may notice a similarity to what has happened in their own field. Whereas it was once common to search out those exegetes of the past with whom one agreed, calling them profound or brilliant or even inspired—men in whom the timeless spirit moved—it now seems easier to examine the peculiarities of biblical understanding in a given age without having to praise or blame, without holding up our own understanding of the truth of Scripture as an eternal standard by which the earnest efforts of earlier generations could be measured. My point is simply that in a certain sense both social historians and biblical scholars have recovered a sense of time and change, of disorientation and incommensurability.

With these remarks as a preface, I should like to engage in an illustration of what I mean drawn from my own work—a sort of *retractatio,* although not a retraction. I am inspired in part by the recent article by John Bossy entitled "Some Elementary Forms of Durkheim," an article that asks not whether Durkheim was right or how he came by his ideas but *how anyone could have said* what he said about religion and society.[3] Some years ago in a book on witchcraft I argued, among other things, that witchcraft in the sixteenth century responded to tensions and changes in the family and the community.[4] Although I was aware of how flexible the concept of witchcraft was, I was less careful with "community" and "family." I have come to conclude that, like witchcraft, these concepts must be understood in the context of the sixteenth century rather than from a modern or even comparative perspective. Whatever light these comparisons may ultimately shed, we must begin with the ideas of sixteenth-century contemporaries. But whose ideas exactly? It would be an odd apologist who argued that biblical ideas, even in the sixteenth century, were basic, popular, or common to all. Yet it is not so odd to argue that biblical ideas did represent, for at least the literate Christian, a set of idealistic concepts that enjoyed unique authority. To the extent that ordinary people respected this authority (and it was clearly not universal or absolute), and to just that extent, the social historian must interest himself in the biblical exegesis of the sixteenth century.

Let me begin with a few remarks on community, a subject that has been overwhelmed by sociological theorizing for over a century. It is perhaps not surprising that there is no single word in the Bible for what we often mean by community: the Vulgate does not even contain the medieval word *communitas.* There are, of course, words for town and village and settlement, but there is no general term for a union of settlers bound together by ties of neighborhood, cooperation, interdependence, friendship, or relatedness. Sixteenth-century Germans did not use *Gemeinschaft* as a social term, and Luther explicitly rejected the word when it was used by others as a translation of *communio.*[5] *Genossenschaft* and *Gesellschaft* were both specialized abstractions.[6] The closest word in Germany may well have been *Gemeinde,* but that word raises some interesting problems.

When Luther undertook to translate the Greco-Latin term *ecclesia* into German, he might have chosen *Kirche,* just as the King James translators chose *church* seventy years later. But *Kirche* seemed to convey too much of the institution dominated by clerics and too little sense of the congregation. He could have chosen to invent a German word *Ekklesia,* just as Saint Jerome had done in turning the Greek into Latin; but Luther did not believe in neologisms, at least when borrowed from foreign languages. And so he regularly translated *ekklesia* with *Gemeinde,* a word that seemed to catch both the secular and the sacred aura of the Greek. *Gemeinde* had an additional advantage in German: it was already a venerable old word. William Tyndale had tried to accomplish a similar anticlerical feat in his English translation of *ekklesia,* avoiding the term *church* in favor of *congregation,* but he was bitterly and effectively attacked by Thomas More for distorting the sense of Scripture and the shape of the English language.[7] And so *congregation* dropped out as the general term for the church in England. In Germany, *Gemeinde* stuck.

Luther's Bible speaks of the man who strays from the way of wisdom: he will remain in the community of the dead. "Ein Mensch der vom wege der klugheit irret, der wird bleiben in der Todten gemeine" (Proverbs 21:16). The Book of Acts describes the assembly of the Jewish synagogue in Antioch. After listening to the preaching of Saint Paul, the assembly (*Gemeine;* Acts 13:43) broke up and went their separate ways. Similarly, when Paul's teaching caused disruption in Ephesus, the pagans gathered in a disorderly assembly (*ecclesia confusa, Gemeine;* Acts 19:32) and were told to settle their disputes either in court or in a regular assembly (*ecclesia, Gemeine;* Acts 19:39–40). In other words, Luther's translation used a word that easily covered secular assemblies. In his *Vermanung zum Sacrament* (1537) Luther even remarked that the *Gemeine* were the "people who came together in a group at the market": "die gemeine oder das volck so zu hauff auff den marckt gelauffen war."[8] In an extended sense *Gemeinde* could mean the civil community in general: "Just so a citizen is insufferable if he wants to be helped, protected, and liberated by the community [*Gemeine*] without doing anything in return for the community [*Gemeine*]."[9] In reference to John 18:36 ("My kingdom is not of this world") Luther contended that in these words Christianity was "separated from all civil communities" ("die christenheit wirt aussgezogen von allen weltlichen gemeynen").[10]

In addition to these secular meanings for *Gemeinde,* Luther's Bible regularly used the word to describe the people of Israel (Exodus 12:3, 19; Numbers 1:2, etc.), the body of Christians, the church in general ("and on this rock I will build my *Gemeine,*" Matthew 16:18), and the individual churches as well (as, for example, the persecution of the *Gemeine* in Jerusalem [Acts 8:1], or the letters to the seven churches (*Gemeine*) of Asia in Revelation, chapters 2–3). Examples are numerous, but the point is surely clear. By avoiding *Kirche* as often as possible, Luther found a way of interpreting *ekklesia* with a word that emphasized the fact that the Greek word had originally meant both sacred and profane assemblies and that it was not primarily a building or a clerical organization but a community.[11] This was a remarkably happy translation in many ways, but it did carry with it the danger that regardless of what Luther and other theologians might try to teach explicitly, it was very difficult to distinguish the church from the local community. Whether as an institution or as the body of the faithful, it was natural for German readers and listeners to confuse the two.

Social historians need to know, therefore, that there was no clear word for and no distinct concept of secular community in sixteenth-century Germany. Biblical language almost seemed to require the confusion of church, community, congregation, and assembly. As a practical matter, then, secular historians of Germany need to look into the *ecclesiae* of village life when they try to say something about changing conceptions of community in centuries past.

I should like to make a similar point with respect to the idea of family. The word *Familie* was surprisingly late in getting to Germany. It was borrowed in the sixteenth century from French and seems to have been pronounced in French fashion (*famille*) through the seventeenth century; it became common only in the eighteenth century.[12] Drawn as it was from the Latin *familia,* it originally meant household, and especially servants. Indeed, the Vulgate regularly used *familia* for *oikos* (household), as Reformation scholars know from the difficulty the orthodox had in proving that infant baptism was practiced by the primitive church. When a father was baptized with all his *familia* it might mean only that his wife and household servants were baptized with him, without implying that infants were included. In any event, my point is somewhat different. When Luther came to translate the words that the Vulgate took as *familia,*[13] he yielded to no temptation to invent a new German word by adapting *familia* to German usage. And so he got by with *Gesinde, Haus,* and *Geschlecht,* words meaning roughly "servants," "household," and "kindred." Close as these words are to what the Bible may have meant, they are all far from what we mean by family, especially in its warmest emotional settings.

Social historians need to know that sixteenth-century Germans had words for and concepts of kindred, lineage, household, and servants, but no word for the nuclear family, nor one for the extended family, either, unless by that term we mean to include all of one's relatives. When *Familie* finally did enter the German language with a rush in the eighteenth century, it displaced *Haus,* which was gradually reduced to merely architectural dimensions.[14] If historians knew something of these changes, we might recognize another indication that households regularly included servants in the early modern period, and we might be even more inclined to agree with theorists who have pointed to the invention of the family as a modern nuclear nest for the nurture of children and a refuge from the world for husbands who have come increasingly to work far from home.[15] Certainly the spread of thc word *Familie* in German tells us something important about the way Germans were coming to conceive of the domestic unit.

As Otto Brunner pointed out long ago, the basis of the early modern economy (*oikonomia*) remained the *oikos* (household) right through the seventeenth century. When Germans thought of *Wirtschaft,* therefore, they had no vision of a national or regional abstraction, but only the experience of the domestic economy at their fingertips.[16] *Economy* was infused with moral and emotional implications largely because it was primarily a domestic metaphor. Here is the reason why the Bible seemed to provide adequate guidance even in economic matters: the economy had its base in domestic relations that the Old and New Testaments were keenly interested in shaping. What can seem like the naïveté of economic writers in the sixteenth century, then, is not just a matter of their ignorance. In our terms they hardly knew they had an economy, just as they lived out their days without a "family" in the sense described above. Of course, the realists may say that the people of the sixteenth century did have an economy, a community, and a family in our sense of the terms, regardless of whether or not they had words for these things. Objects exist whether we know their names or not; but concepts are not things, and we run a real risk if we treat concepts as things. The nominalists among us, at any event, may gladly sacrifice synthetic power for the historical insight that comes from treating ideas in their own words—literally, in their own terms. Our conceptions depend largely on the words we use for them.

This becomes even clearer when we turn to the subject of witchcraft. Surely no one would argue that all peoples have witches, whether they think so or not. *Everything* in this case rests on what people thought, and in few other cases is it clearer that biblical exegesis made a real difference. In the Old Testament sorcery was first and foremost among the "abhorrent practices of the nations," a contamination to be rooted out as an act of fidelity to God alone (Deuteronomy 18:9–14). Judaism apparently recognized something dangerously religious in the rituals of magic, necromancy, divination, healing spells, and harmful sorcery, and as such they were regarded as surviving elements of paganism, akin to idolatry and human sacrifice and fully worthy of the severe penalty meted out to them (stoning to death).[17] It is easy to see why some of these practices were regarded as abominations—forecasting the future, for example, seemed to infringe on God's sovereignty—but other offenses are harder to understand. The apodictic command in Exodus 22:18 states: "Thou shalt not suffer a witch to live." The

Hebrew term for witch here is *mekhashepha,* but it is not a common word in the Old Testament.[18] As a result, there are real difficulties in construing its original meaning as well as in translating it economically into other languages. At its root was *kshp,* a word that occurred in Akkadian, where it always meant black magic (harmful magic), but in Hebrew the distinction between black and any other magic was not so clear, for all magic was an affront to God.[19] In its Hebrew form, as in Exodus 22:18, it referred to women, so that it is clear that at least in this form it was a magic associated more often with women (and perhaps practiced more often by women) than the other forms of witchcraft, idolatry, and sorcery that have masculine endings. Because the nature of the crime remained obscure, however, it is not surprising that Talmudic commentators tried to distinguish actual witchcraft committed by some charm or act of sorcery and resulting in harm (and therefore punishable) from the mere pretense of witchcraft, which despite its illegality was not really punishable.[20] Although the Jews rarely conducted mass witchcraft trials, Simeon ben Shetah of the first century B.C. is reported (in Sanhedrin 6:4) to have ordered some eighty witches executed in Ashkelon on a single day as an emergency measure. During the Middle Ages, Jewish commentary on witchcraft drifted ever further from the ideas of the Pentateuch. Medieval Hebrew literature used the words for magic (*kishuf*), magician (*mekhashef*), and witch (*mekhashefah*) rarely, but when used they meant the wicked in general: both sinners and Gentiles. *Mekhashepha* itself came to denote "cannibal" or "vampire" as well.[21] This is of interest because the same medieval process may be observed independently among Christian commentators on this verse.[22]

The first major change in the Latin West was the peculiar translation of *mekhashepha* as *maleficos,* changing the gender from feminine to masculine. It was a significant change, one that dominated the medieval understanding of witchcraft right down to the fifteenth century. It was only then that writers began to refer regularly to *maleficae* (feminine), and even so the Vulgate continued to use the masculine ending. Commenting on that text in the ninth century, Hrabanus Maurus stated that "typologically we may understand *maleficos* as meaning heretics, instigated not by the spirit of God but by the wicked spirit; they introduce perverse sects in order to deceive men, which the law of God orders to be abolished, that is, separated and anathematised from the community of the faithful, who live a true life in God, so that *maleficium,* which is error, shall be extinguished."[23]

We find here a dramatically figurative or spiritual reading of the text. Witches were primarily heretics, and their sects were to be excommunicated. This opinion dominated until well into the twelfth century. The *Glossa Ordinaria,* completed in the early twelfth century, echoed Hrabanus regarding Exodus 22:18: "*Malefici* are those who use the tricks of the art of magic and devilish illusions. They are the heretics, who should be excommunicated from the community of the faithful, who truly live, so that the witchcraft of their error will die with them."[24] Again we may notice that the witches are men associated with the devil and heresy, who are not to be killed but excommunicated.

Scholars have recently noticed a growing literalness in thirteenth-century interpretations of the Old Testament Law. Perhaps Catharistic rejections of the Old Testament provoked a new respect for its authority among the orthodox.[25] But a literal interpretation takes it for granted that one understands the literal meaning. Nicholas of Lyra, for example, tried vigorously to correct the Vulgate translation of the text by noting that the Hebrew referred to women. In his *Postillae,* surely one of the most popular biblical commentaries of the later Middle Ages, Lyra suggested substituting *sortilegam* for *maleficos,* a change of more than gender and number, moving the offense away from the actual harm done by black magic toward the spiritual offense of divination, of casting sorts as a way of predicting or deciding the future.[26]

Corrections such as this one did not easily change the received text of the Vulgate, as we know. Even Jacob Sprenger and Heinrich Institoris, the authors of the famous *Malleus Maleficarum* of 1486 or 1487, did not quibble with the received text, though they were bent on seeing witchcraft as mainly a female crime. In fact, they did not cite this text at all, perhaps because they regarded it as obvious that the punishment for stubborn heresy or relapsing into heresy was death.[27] Our text had little to offer in support of their view that witchcraft was essentially heresy.

Scholars are not yet sure which text of the Vulgate Luther used, but it may well have been the 1509 edition, which referred to *maleficos.* Aware of Lyra's criticisms and skilled in Hebrew, Luther revised the

Vulgate in 1529 to read *maleficas*.[28] In this way he surely contributed to the more concentrated attack on female witchcraft over the next 150 years.[29] In 1523 he published a translation of Exodus in which our text reads: "Die zewberynnen solltu nicht leben lassen," a formulation that remained unchanged, except for orthography, in his last edition of the Old Testament in 1545.[30] In this translation, as in *Gemeinde,* Luther succeeded in finding a word that did not seem to overcommit him to any one interpretation of the text, a word that did not imply that the offense of witchcraft was mainly the harm done (as seemed to be the case with *maleficos*) or that the offense was mainly spiritual (as seemed true with *sortilega*). It did imply, of course, that ancient Hebrew culture and sixteenth-century German culture were basically comparable, and that no new word was necessary to communicate the peculiar horror of witchcraft.

It was a dangerous comparison, for witchcraft had come to be something almost radically different from the various magical offenses punished in the Old Testament. By the fifteenth century witches were thought to be godless creatures who explicitly rejected their baptism, spat on the cross, abused the Eucharist, had sexual intercourse with the devil, sacrificed babies at a witches' sabbath—where the witches enjoyed promiscuous and incestuous sexual relations with each other as well—and wrought a variety of evils that interfered mainly with the sex lives of their neighbors (causing sterility and impotence), with their neighbors' cattle (especially causing milk cows to go dry), and with their neighbors' fields (causing frosts and hail that ruined the crops). It is worth noting that none of these crimes, apostasies, and horrors were mentioned in the Old Testament. By sanctioning the translation of *mekhashepha* with *Zauberinnen,* Luther contributed to the dangerous relevance that the Bible sometimes enjoys. He was, however, hardly unique in that.

This is not to say that everyone joined Luther in agreeing that Exodus 22:18 was mainly about witches of the modern variety. Andreas Osiander continued to follow the *Glossa Ordinaria* when he explained that force could be used against heretics because it was better that one should tie a millstone around the neck and drown anyone who should mislead "the simple Christians; therefore God commanded 'Thou shalt not suffer magicians to live' [Du solt die zauberer nit leben lassen]; and one should kill the false teachers who led men from God."[31] I should like to illustrate the variety of sixteenth-century responses to this text with three highly divergent interpretations.

My first example comes from Thomas Müntzer, whose rejection of Luther's message stemmed at least in part from his sense that the last judgment was at hand and that true Christians had to learn to share in God's judgment of others as well as of themselves.[32] The learned leaders of the church (both Lutheran and Catholic) "say shamefully that God does not reveal his judgments to anyone"; they are neutral hypocrites, "talking through their beards, these great authorities say 'No one can know who is chosen or damned!' Oh sure, they have such a strong faith, which is so powerfully certain that it has absolutely no understanding except in protecting the godless."[33] Grasping the nettle, Müntzer held that true Christians had to use force against the pollution of evil; the harvest had arrived, and it was time to uproot the tares from the wheat: "Then the beautiful red wheat will get sturdy roots and grow properly."[34] It seems like an odd harvest that comes when the wheat is still establishing its roots, but horticultural problems need not detain us. Müntzer's point was clear even if he did not convincingly deploy the parable of the tares.[35] In his famous Sermon to the Princes Müntzer pursued the theme of excluding or even exterminating the godless as he expounded the second chapter of Daniel. Rulers of Saxony, "if you want to be true governors, you must begin government at the roots, and as Christ commanded, drive his enemies from the elect, for you are the means to this end. Beloved, don't give us any empty deceptions, as if the power of God should do it without your using the sword. . . . Therefore don't let the evildoers live any longer, who turn us away from God, Deuteronomy 13 [verse 6], for a godless person has no right to live if he hinders the pious. God says in Exodus 22 [verse 18] 'Thou shalt not suffer the evildoers to live' [Du sollt die ubeltheter nicht leben lassen]."[36]

Müntzer applied our witchcraft text to his purposes, claiming a general meaning of all evildoing rather than just sorcery. It is clear, I think, that he was not thinking of the Hebrew text but of the Latin *maleficos,* for which *ubeltheter* seemed a literal equivalent. Of course, in aiming for a literal understanding of the text, Müntzer gave his translation an extraordinary extension to all evildoers.

Another effort at translating Exodus 22:18 resulted not in extension but restriction. When Johann Weyer, the physician to the duke of

Jülich-Cleves, undertook in 1563 to defend those whom he thought unjustly accused of witchcraft, he reinterpreted the crime of witchcraft as well. Emphasizing the variety of magical crimes punished in the Old Testament, Weyer objected to the corresponding translations into Latin on the basis of what the best rabbinical studies revealed. After consulting the orientalist Andreas Maes, Weyer explained the seven most common Hebrew words relating to magic.[37] *Mekhashepha,* he noted, refers to women who use evil acts to harm cattle, crops, and men. The Greek translators of the Septuagint translated the decree of Exodus 22 as "Thou shalt not allow *poisoners* to live," understanding *mekhashepha* as *pharmakous.* Certain Hebrew scholars of great learning held that the root *chasaph* referred properly to tricks or illusions. Maes himself thought that the word referred broadly to every magical act, noting in addition that the Syrians used the same word for performance of a religious rite.[38] This might imply that the ancient Hebrews had once used the term in that sense as well. Because of the richness of the Hebrew magical language, Weyer pointed out that German readers were almost necessarily misled by the word *Zauberer* for the magician (who deceives), for the witch (who imagines that she harms others), and for the poisoner (who really does harm others). Implicitly attacking Luther's translation, Weyer asserted: "I am not ashamed to proclaim publicly that all of the German writers whom I have so far chanced to read in the vernacular have stumbled badly in this sort of argument . . . even if they appear to have adduced the evidence of Sacred Scripture."[39] But what did Weyer himself think Exodus 22 referred to? Without explicitly arguing with Maes, for whom *mekhashepha* referred to every magical act, Weyer returned to the question later when he considered the appropriate punishments for magic and witchcraft, holding that the Septuagint had cleared up the whole matter. The witches of Exodus 22:18 were poisoners. This involved both a trust in the Seventy Translators and a medical materialism (in which *pharmaka* were understood as purely physical) that not all of Weyer's contemporaries could accept.[40] But Weyer could rely as well on the opinion of Josephus, who had glossed the prohibition of *pharmakous* this way: "Let no one of the Israelites possess a deadly poison prepared for other harmful uses. If any be found to possess such a poison, let him be punished by death."[41]

Germans were therefore wrong to translate *pharmakeia* as *Zauberei,* and the Italians were closer when they rendered it *avvelenamento,* or "poisoning." Recalling his earlier citations of Maes, who had noted the wider magical use of *mekhashepha* and *pharmakeia,* Weyer dropped back almost in puzzlement and noted, in a delaying maneuver, that in any case such words could not be extended to acts that were unknown in Moses' day.[42] The witches accused of attending sabbaths seemed to have nothing in common with Moses' magicians. Returning to the offensive, Weyer noted that even if the *mekhashephim* were guilty of offenses ranging from poisoning to other outrages, these were all distinct from the hallucinations of the *lamiae*—the old, poor women accused of witchcraft. "If you are unwilling to have this word refer to poisoners, you have my permission, if you prefer, to apply it to the magicians of whom I have spoken—men of bad omen certainly deserving of punishment in accordance with the laws."[43] Similarly, Germans needed to straighten out their use of *Zauberer,* which had fallen into vague and arbitrary usage.

In addition to dealing with problems of literal interpretation and translation, Weyer also called attention to the questionable assumption that whatever Moses had punished with death should be so punished in the modern age. How grotesque it would be if we executed a man for false testimony or a bride who was found to be not a virgin or a man who killed a thief breaking into his house by day.[44] And so Weyer, despite his apparent concession to philological fidelity, opposed the death penalty even for infamous magicians unless they truly poisoned someone.[45] Repeatedly Weyer revealed that his understanding of witchcraft as a capital crime was held captive by a narrow reading of the Septuagint's *pharmakous.* Although he appeared to allow a wider, more magical interpretation, he never meant to allow the execution of any persons other than physically dangerous poisoners. Weyer rehearsed the arguments for religious toleration from Chrysostom to Erasmus, implying that the offenses of witchcraft properly understood were religious and therefore not a matter for capital punishment.[46] Ironically, this meant, in effect, that after a great deal of philological erudition, Weyer agreed with the *Glossa Ordinaria* that witches were mainly heretics, concluding boldly that this meant that they ought not be executed.

I have dealt with Weyer at some length because he was the first to deal so extensively with the biblical and philological problems of witchcraft. His own bias toward exculpating the witches lured him into a primary reliance on the text of the Septuagint, just as Müntzer's bias led him to rely on the Vulgate.

A last example is from Dietrich or Dirck Philips, the Mennonite, who in circa 1560 composed the treatise *Van de Ghemeynte Godts,* which carefully set forth the marks of the Anabaptist church:[47] God gave magistrates the sword not to punish spiritual offenses but to maintain outward order. God's commandment that Moses should kill false prophets (as cited by Osiander, for example) had now been superseded by the new dispensation of Christ. Christians were not bound by the decrees of the Old Testament. If magistrates really tried to punish according to the Law of Moses, "they would be obliged to put to death not only the false prophets but also all image worshipers, and those who served idols, and who counsel other people to commit sacrilege (Exodus 22:18), and all adulterers, and all who blaspheme the name of the Lord, and who swear falsely by that name."[48] Here we have yet another view of what Exodus 22:18 really meant. For Philips the text referred not to evildoers, as it had to Müntzer, and not to poisoners, as it had to Weyer. Nor did it refer to *Zauberinnen,* as it did in Luther's translation. All of these translations might have implied a foul offense so horrible that the Law of Moses could rightly be employed to crush the perpetrator. As we can see, it was important for Philips's purpose to clothe the crime of witchcraft in the religious garments of idolatry and sacrilege. Aiming at a *reductio ad absurdum,* he had to make *mekhashepha* a religious offense of a fairly common variety so that he could illustrate the primitive harshness of the Mosaic code. Once again a religious position influenced the reading and translation of this peculiarly knotty text.

What can the social historian learn from these opinions? Perhaps that the solid entities he studies are often no more solid than the words men use to shape their mental world; but more, that biblical exegesis can actually exert a force on social realities. There is no space here to sketch out the conflicts among understandings of marriage and family in the sixteenth century, but I think that one could show that the dramatic transformation of divorce, on which the modern companionate marriage finally rests, depended on a notable shift in the understanding of adultery. When Martin Bucer urged a more lenient position on divorce, it was largely because he had come to understand the biblical idea of marriage as a compact—a trust that could be broken in many ways, and not just by physical infidelity.[49] We have hardly begun the task of understanding the social context in which these ideas took root, and it will be some time before we can connect faith and practice as effectively as Edmund Morgan did almost fifty years ago for the Puritan family.[50] But surely social historians need to be aware of the often biblical origins of the changes in social reality in the sixteenth century. I am also sure that it is important to notice how little of my original formulation could be put into sixteenth-century German terms. When I said that witchcraft reflected tensions in the community and the family, I did not realize that sixteenth-century Germans would not have understood, for they had no clear notion of community, family, or witchcraft as we conventionally use the terms. I would be prepared to go further and say that lacking the terms, they lacked these cultural artifacts—and that in their language we might get further by looking at changes in household (*Haus*) and congregation (*Gemeinde*) in order to understand the fear of hidden evildoing, of pollution, that witchcraft seems to have become.

Biblical scholars may wish to ask themselves why learned men managed with such consistency to misunderstand the texts that now seem plain to us. It sometimes seems that only those brave spirits such as Dirck Philips or Johann Weyer, for whom Scripture (or at least the Old Testament) was no longer exactly relevant, could see with any measure of historical understanding what Scripture may have originally meant. Of course their indifference was not perfect, and probably ours cannot be so, either. And yet they challenge us to reconsider our own exegetical task, forcing us to wonder again how we may hope to understand those ideas, movements, or men to whom we are already committed. Is it not still true that when our *fides* seeks *intellectum,* we run the risk of discovering no more than our own face reflected in the darkened glass?

GUY BEDOUELLE
Translated by John L. Farthing

The Consultations of the Universities and Scholars Concerning the "Great Matter" of King Henry VIII

The purpose of this essay is to show that while a certain reading of a biblical text could, in theory, play a decisive role in shaping political developments, in reality biblical exegesis must be considered as only one of many variables in a complex set of factors, in which politics has its own role to play. The relation between politics and biblical interpretation will be explored in connection with a famous example that is not often approached from the perspective of the history of exegesis—the series of investigations that were made by universities and scholars in the sequence of events leading up to Henry VIII's "divorce" from Catherine of Aragon. We shall see that in trying to make sense of a world as complex as that of late-medieval Christianity, the history of exegesis must take into account a rather discouraging array of parameters.

THE QUESTION IN ITS HISTORICAL CONTEXT

"The king's great matter," to use the euphemism that was current at the time, reached its provisional denouement on May 23, 1533, when Thomas Cranmer, archbishop of Canterbury, announced his judgment that the marriage between Henry VIII and Catherine of Aragon had been null and void from the very beginning (*ab initio*). Prior to Cranmer's declaration, however, the king's great matter had gone on for six years, since the preliminary investigations had been entrusted to Wolsey in May 1527. It was not until 1529 that the universities of

Europe were consulted and the theologians, more or less spontaneously, began to speak out. The British Library has many of these scholarly treatises, which give some idea of the extensiveness of the legal debates sparked by a question of scriptural interpretation.

I cannot give a detailed account of the political background of the king's great matter, and I will mention only a few points that are essential to an understanding of the political context within which it took place. At the time of Henry's "divorce" the Tudors were a new dynasty in England, and Henry wished to strengthen the dynasty through a male heir. Peace among the nations of Europe was quite fragile and was often solidified through a policy of matrimonial alliances. In the midst of the religious turmoil and conflict in Germany, Henry's *Assertio septem sacramentorum* provided a clear refutation of Luther and thereby won for the king the title of *Defensor fidei,* conferred by the pope himself. (This went a long way toward satisfying Henry's longing for assurances of his own legitimacy.) Emperor Charles V, nephew of Queen Catherine, seized Rome in May 1527, and the pope, Clement VII, seemed to have lost his independence. The Ladies' Peace of August 1529 reconciled the emperor and the French king, Francis I, bringing about the total collapse of Wolsey's foreign policy, and Wolsey was replaced as chancellor by Thomas More. There were still those in England who sympathized with Luther; they were especially active at Cambridge, and the "new faith" seems to have penetrated into several families that were close to the throne, such as the Boleyns, who had become Henry's protégés because of his love for Mary and then for Anne Boleyn.

In the summer of 1529 Henry VIII raised with the Curia the problem of the annulment of his marriage to Catherine of Aragon, which had been concluded on 11 June 1509.[1] It was on this occasion that certain "scruples" of the king-theologian (as he now viewed himself) were mentioned for the first time. The sentimental and dynastic concerns underlying these proceedings are well known; from the point of view of canon law, however, the situation in which these concerns came to expression was exceedingly complex.

In November 1501 Catherine of Aragon (1485–1536) had been married to the heir apparent to the English throne, Arthur (1486–1502), who was fourteen years old at the time. Arthur died on 2 April

1502. According to Catherine's subsequent testimony, the marriage had never been consummated. The "Catholic kings" of Spain at once negotiated a remarriage of their daughter with the new heir apparent, the future King Henry VIII. A papal dispensation was requested because of the affinity created by the earlier marriage (which made Henry and Catherine brother-in-law and sister-in-law to one another). This dispensation, granted by a papal bull, lies at the center of the dispute.

Canon Law

The concept of consanguinity was not so narrow in the Middle Ages as it has become in modern usage. Understood in a very broad sense, it included affinity as an effect of sexual intercourse. This union (*copula*), whether or not it took place within the bonds of a legitimate marriage,[2] was viewed as making the partners in sexual intercourse "one and the same flesh" (*una caro,* Matthew 19:5–6) in such a way that the bloodlines were mingled and the kinship of each was communicated to the other by way of affinity. Some theologians, however, were already affirming what was to become the dominant view, that only marriage establishes affinity.

Catherine of Aragon always claimed—and this under oath—that her marriage with Arthur had never been consummated. There was no basis, therefore, even in canon law, for Henry's request for a dispensation from this affinity. But Wolsey, who was a shrewd lawyer, saw at that point that the marriage involved a formal defect. In that case it would have been necessary to seek a different kind of dispensation, which was called a dispensation from an impediment to *publica honestas,* i.e., to maintain the good name of the married couple. The dispensation granted by Julius II did not take this into consideration; it dealt only with the case of a consummated union (*forsan consommatum*). There may have been a formal defect, then, which could have resulted in the invalidity of the marriage between Henry and Catherine.

Henry chose to fight the battle in a different arena, one in which theology and exegesis had a part to play. He was involving himself in debates over an exceedingly complicated set of issues. History shows that the opinion of the majority, along with the weight of canon law, rejected Henry's claims. It is at this point that we must turn to a consideration of the history of exegesis.

Leviticus 18 versus Deuteronomy 25

Henry VIII's basic plan was to cast doubt on the validity of his marriage on the basis of the prohibition set forth in Leviticus: "You shall not uncover the nakedness of your brother's wife, for it is your brother's nakedness" (18:16), and "it is a defilement for a man to marry his brother's wife: he has uncovered the nakedness of his brother, and they shall die childless" (20:21). Apparently Henry applied this last warning to his own case, because his children by Catherine, with the sole exception of the princess Mary, had all died in infancy.

By invoking these texts, Henry was implicitly posing a number of theological questions. To what extent was a regulation of the Old Testament still in force in the era inaugurated by the gospel? On the supposition that this regulation was still in force as part of the law of the church, was it to be regarded as belonging to the realm of positive divine law, representing precepts of the natural law that are in principle irrevocable, or did it belong to the realm of ecclesiastical law, capable of being modified by the authority of the visible church? If it were regarded as a part of divine law, how could the pope provide a dispensation from it?[3]

Complicating the situation even further was the fact that Holy Scripture itself seemed to foresee an exception to the Levitical policy by way of the law called the "Deuteronomic levirate" (25:5 et seq.): "If two brothers are living together, and it comes to pass that one of them dies childless, the wife of the deceased shall not marry a man from a different family; the brother of her husband [*levir*] shall go in to her and fulfill the office of a brother-in-law [*levirate*] by taking her as his wife." This seemed to apply precisely to the case of Henry taking Arthur's place and providing for him a posterity.

Was the law of the levirate still in force? What exactly did the text mean in the Hebrew? There were so many disputed questions. It is worth noting here that in the Gospels (Matthew 22:24, et seq.) Jesus himself accepts (albeit theoretically and for polemical purposes) the hypothesis of the possibility of successive levirates. In the interpretation of these texts, or rather in their application to Christians, the doctrinal tradition and the theologians of the day were far from unanimous. Henry sought to have his view prevail in a series of consultations with the universities and scholars.

THE DECISIONS OF THE UNIVERSITIES

The idea of a consultation of the scholars of the day—the theologians and canon lawyers—in "all the universities of Christendom"[4] was put forward in rather vague terms beginning in July 1527. According to Ralph Morice, who was later to become Cranmer's secretary and confidant, it was Cranmer himself (at the time a fellow of Jesus College, Cambridge) who suggested in August 1529 that a consultation of theologians should be organized for the purpose of enlightening the king's conscience and avoiding recourse to the church's jurisdiction. It was a bold proposal. Moreover, Cranmer had not reached the point of recommending that Henry appeal to the universities of Europe the decision of the ecclesiastical court that had been charged with ruling on the question.[5] Such recourse to the universities was not without precedent.[6]

Thomas Cranmer himself took part in a disputation which set six Oxford theologians against six from Cambridge. He interviewed the king and began to study the case with an eye toward putting together a dossier. But the consultation of the English and Continental universities was organized, beginning in September 1529, by representatives of the king. It is an undisputed historical fact that the king's agents passed around generous amounts of his money in order to ensure an outcome that would be in keeping with their sovereign's wishes.[7]

Cambridge and Oxford

The first two responses to the king's inquiry came first from Cambridge and then from Oxford, where the royal agents had invested quite a bit of energy and money. At Cambridge the decision was announced on 9 March 1530 by a carefully selected commission of theologians retained by the king's representatives. The commission "scrutinized the scriptural texts with the utmost diligence" and held a public disputation. Their verdict was that "up to the present time (*hodie*) it has been forbidden to marry the wife of one's deceased and childless brother, *that marriage having been consummated,* on the grounds of both divine and natural law."

Henry received almost the same response from Oxford. Since Catherine was insisting that she had been a virgin at the time of her second marriage, this response was somewhat ambiguous. The *determinatio,* dated 8 April 1530, was published after a number of incidents in the city and in the university itself in which the king attempted to put pressure on the scholars by means of numerous letters. The same formula that appears in the Oxford document was retained by the scholars at Cambridge. By the same token, the documents that emerged from the Oxford consultation describe a procedure to be followed that is quite similar to that employed at Cambridge, but no basic issues were raised, and no discussion of the relevant texts in Scripture and canon law is reflected in the documentary evidence.

The French and Italian Universities

In the sixteenth century the University of Paris, and most especially the faculty of theology at the Sorbonne, was accorded an essential role in the determination of doctrine. That is why Henry VIII arranged for a debate to be held at the Sorbonne beginning 21 October 1528. The king's position prevailed, but only by a plurality,[8] and the lack of an absolute majority for one side or the other set the stage for a continuation of the dispute.

We should note that the deliberations of the faculty of theology at the University of Paris took place at just the time when negotiations to secure the release of the children of Francis I, who were being detained by the emperor, had entered their final stage. The stormy, impassioned conferences began with a plenary session held on 8 June 1530. Noël Beda, who seems to have switched sides momentarily, and Pedro de Garay, unofficial spokesman for the Spanish court, defended the thesis that the papal dispensation was valid.

After scrutinizing both Scripture and tradition, the *censura* of the faculty, dated 2 July 1530, declared that the pope could not grant a dispensation in any case. No reference was made to the matter of the consummation of Catherine's marriage to Arthur. This poorly argued decision gave Henry a greater degree of satisfaction than did the *determinationes* of the universities in his own country (especially in light of the massive prestige of the Sorbonne throughout Christendom).

The decisions of the other French universities more or less followed the pattern set by the University of Paris: The Universities of Orléans and Toulouse (which described the question as *difficilis*), the theological faculty at Bourges (which placed its emphasis on the text from Leviticus 18), and the faculty of law at the University of Angers followed the same interpretation of the biblical and traditional resources that seemed to have a bearing on the case. Only the theological faculty at Angers—announcing its verdict on the same day as its rival faculty—declared on 7 May 1530 that even if the first marriage were consummated, marrying one's widowed sister-in-law was contrary to neither divine nor natural law, and the pope could, for just cause, grant a dispensation. This exception, which is not often noticed, may best be understood as the result of local factors such as the rivalry between the faculties of law and theology at the University of Angers.

In Italy the results were again, from the king's point of view, to some extent disappointing: The faculties of Bologne and Padua, in terms that were quite similar, referred to the Deuteronomic exception but concluded that the pope, "in spite of his immense powers," could not offer a dispensation in the case of the royal marriage. They did not take into account, however, all the considerations that had some bearing on this case. From the standpoint of the history of exegesis, one must acknowledge that the crucial exegetical issues were simply avoided: none of the "determinations" proposed a precise analysis of the biblical texts that were under discussion. This conclusion is somewhat mitigated, however, by the fact that for purposes of propaganda the text of the university decisions was published along with a treatise that was more exegetical and theological in nature.

The text of this treatise was the work of John Stokesley, the future bishop of London; Edward Fox, Wolsey's secretary; and a Franciscan from Italy, Nicolas de Burgo.[9] It was then reviewed by Cranmer, and it is beyond dispute that it was Cranmer who gave to the document its definitive form. The treatise accompanied the Latin and English editions of the *Determinations,* which were published by the royal printer, Thomas Berthelet.[10] Neither the English decisions nor the unfavorable verdict of the theological faculty of Angers can be found in this work.

Carefully avoiding possible objections—not citing the text from Deuteronomy, not even mentioning the matter of the consummation of the first marriage as a possible impediment—the treatise for the most part makes its appeal to Holy Scripture, but interestingly enough quite often deals with the question of the proper way of reading the Bible.[11] Bypassing the official ecclesiastical teaching office, the document appeals to the private conscience of the Christian reading the Holy Scripture.[12] Here we also find a warning against those who misuse the keys of divine knowledge, and we are reminded of the curse pronounced on the Pharisees (Matthew 23:13). In order to make the point perfectly clear, chapter 7 affirms that the pontifical ministry is to preserve the Word of God: the pope does not have the power to modify the content of the divine will.[13] In this text one finds no justification for a special teaching authority entrusted to the universities, in contrast to the position that had been advanced by the theologians—especially at the Sorbonne—who, in the years following the councils of Constance and Basel, had claimed such a position in the church for themselves. Commenting on their determinations, Cranmer rejected this claim; instead he affirmed the principle of a reading of Scripture independent of all interpretation provided by the hierarchy of the church, following the example set by Luther some ten years earlier.

THE OPINIONS OF THE THEOLOGIANS

Henry VIII received advice from less than ten faculties of European universities—a rather small number in view of the number of universities that were in existence at the time. Several other universities, upon request, offered their opinions as well, but these contributions to the debate were widely disseminated only when the king found them favorable to his cause.[14] In contrast, the theologians expressed themselves freely when speaking as individuals. About fifty works were published on the subject at various places in Europe (not to mention others which circulated in manuscript form). On the basis of these publications one may say that a lively public debate arose among the canon lawyers and the theologians. This significant debate shows, at least, that the exegetical and canonical questions raised in the king's "great matter" were of considerable interest in their own right, even though they were initially raised in connection with political and sentimental concerns that often overshadowed the theological debate.

An example of the scholarly interest in this affair is the consultation requested by Erasmus in a letter to his friend, the jurist Boniface Amerbach, in January 1531.[15]

The Reformers and the Sola Scriptura

William Tyndale took a position that seems paradoxical, at least until it is explained in light of the circumstances in which he arrived at it. In a work published in Germany[16] Tyndale attacks the prelates—and especially the bishop of Rome—quite violently; the opening words on the first page compare them to the scribes and Pharisees "who made the meaning of Scripture obscure through their traditions and misleading interpretations." The pope is portrayed as the grand destroyer of Scripture; in that connection Tyndale makes use of materials from the sixteenth chapter of Matthew's Gospel.

But when he turns to the question of the divorce, Tyndale's position becomes more objective: he argues that the text from Leviticus 18 must be understood as referring to a brother who is *still living,* and thus it has no application to the king's situation. A marriage between a brother-in-law and a sister-in-law does not violate natural law; for a just reason (e.g., to guarantee the peace and unity of the realm) a dispensation from the impediment may be granted without a problem.

It seems, in fact, that Tyndale's approach to these matters was determined by the fact that he was dealing with a divorce proposed and organized by Cardinal Wolsey, whose activities he consistently rejected.[17] A similar independence of judgment may be noted among the German theologians at a time when they had all the reason in the world to oppose Henry VIII, the author of the anti-Lutheran *Assertio septem sacramentorum.*

Intervening between Henry VIII and German reformers was the zealous Simon Grynaeus (1494–1541), a humanist at first close to Luther and then to Zwingli, who occupied the chair in Greek at the University of Basel from 1529 onward. After a visit to England he returned to Basel in January 1531 with the assignment to gather as quickly as possible the Protestant theologians' opinions on the king's great matter; he brought with him the Latin edition of the collected *Determinationes* of the universities.

The first opinion to reach Grynaeus, in August 1531, was that of Zwingli, whose position was supported by Oecolampadius (who earlier on had himself proposed a solution opposed to the one now advocated by Zwingli). In the view of the reformers of Zurich and Basel, the prohibition expressed in Leviticus 18:16 made it clear that marriage with one's sister-in-law was condemned by both natural and divine law.[18] Along with other theologians from Strasburg (such as Capito and Hedio), Martin Bucer—true to form—embraced a position that was more complex, changeable, and subtle. Almost all of his letters on this subject have been lost, but it is possible to reconstruct them from Grynaeus's responses. Informed of Zwingli's position and, later on, that of the Wittenberg theologians, Bucer wavered between an appeal to the conscience of the king (who might have rendered his marriage legitimate) and the rigor of the Lutheran view of the matter.

In Wittenberg in mid-September Luther and Melanchthon refused to affirm that the regulations of Leviticus and Deuteronomy were still binding on the Christian conscience: they would have had such a force only if they had been incorporated into the positive law. "Melanchthon's recollection is the dry dissertation of a humanist who is interested in both exegesis and the law; Luther's response has the ring of a manifesto in favor of the sanctity of marriage, for which Catherine of Aragon is called to witness."[19] For Melanchthon, the only possible solution would be a bigamy that was not contrary to natural law and which the pope could authorize quite exceptionally. This view—conjured up by Bucer and even, with a bit of humor, by Erasmus himself—was the advice offered ten years later to Philip of Hesse. Like Oecolampadius, Grynaeus was scandalized by what he called "a novel and unheard-of precedent in the Christian church, new and unknown . . . since it has not been put forward from the time of the church's beginnings."[20] After much beating around the bush, many solemn declarations concerning "the Word of God, which is at stake in this case as much as the conscience of the King and Queen," and many appeals to the king to "examine the Scriptures and pray to God,"[21] Bucer finally gave his own definitive response to the issues raised by the king's great matter. Bucer's position was closer to that of Luther than to Zwingli—who, moreover, was killed at just the same time in the Battle of Kappel (11 October 1531).

In a statement issued on 30 December 1531, Bucer in effect retracts his former position and answers a wide range of questions raised by this case. Interpreting the texts from Leviticus, he acknowledges the validity of the dispensation granted by Julius II "in the name of the church," and takes a stand in favor of the legitimacy of the royal marriage, which he regards as indissoluble by virtue of the fact that it had in the past received both the approval of God and the consent of the church.[22]

In his study of Grynaeus's investigations, J. V. Pollet outlines the ways in which the Reformers, while wishing to deal with the matter on the basis of Scripture (which they held to be, in principle, the "mother of truth and unanimity and agreement" [mater veritatis et unanimitatis ac concordiae], as Bucer expressed it),[23] were quite divided in the ways in which they approached the use of Scripture for resolving this particular case. For Zwingli, the Old Testament provided all that was needed for a resolution of the case, whereas for Luther the solution must come from the teachings of the Gospels, and especially of Saint Paul.[24] As far as Bucer is concerned, we should note that his conception of the *sola scriptura* was flexible enough to permit him to take into account many other considerations when dealing with a case as difficult as that of the king's "great matter." He was concerned about the consciences of the interested parties, and he also took into account the question of the public interest. For example, it was ultimately from a political/practical perspective that Bucer was willing to affirm that kings and princes ought to have certain powers. Holy Scripture was more a source of inspiration than a norm to be followed in a literal way. Let us also note the importance Bucer attached to the consent of the papal church, from which he had by this time distanced himself somewhat.

The Catholic Writers

Many Catholic theologians, humanist and nonhumanist, spoke out on the king's case,[25] but I will consider only two who figure significantly in the history of biblical exegesis.

The appraisal offered by Felix de Prato—like Luther, an Augustinian Hermit—is interesting insofar as it is the work of a specialist in Hebrew. The son of a rabbi, after his conversion to Christianity Felix published, along with Bomberg, a *Psalterium ex hebraeo* (Venice, 1515), and later he sponsored a critical edition of the Hebrew Bible. His great knowledge of the sacred language seemed to ensure that he would be able to resolve the obscurities of the Old Testament texts invoked by Henry VIII.

In reality, however, although he occasionally cites the Targum and compares the various Latin translations, Felix de Prato in this consultation makes little use of his considerable knowledge of the Hebrew, although he repeatedly declares his intention to base his reasoning solely on the Holy Scripture, while "leaving aside the arguments of the jurists."[26] After considering the arguments advanced against the dispensation, Felix de Prato starts by affirming clearly the freedom gained vis-à-vis the Old Testament in matters relating to marriage. In support of this freedom he invokes the words of Saint Paul in 1 Corinthians 7:6. In Felix's view, the Sovereign Pontiff, by virtue of the authority that Christ has conferred upon him, has the power to grant dispensations in a case such as that of Henry VIII.

Seeking a full understanding (*sano intellectu*) of the prohibition in Leviticus, he reasons that this rule concerns either a brother who is still living or one who is deceased but did not die childless. Only a marriage to the wife of a brother who meets one of these conditions falls within the scope of the prohibition. In fact, it may not be said—speaking in the strict sense—that the widow of a man who died childless had been one body or one flesh with him.[27] The prohibition in Deuteronomy no longer has a binding force in the scheme of things inaugurated by the New Testament, since it is not explicitly reiterated by the church. In any case, for an urgent reason the pope may grant a dispensation.

Felix de Prato's real interest centers in his desire to disentangle the regulations of the Jewish Law from the newness of the covenant established in Christ. He seeks to accomplish this by subjecting the texts cited by the king to a Pauline critique, especially in light of Paul's teachings about marriage in his First Epistle to the Corinthians. In addition, there is no doubt that for Felix the liberating power in relation to the Law which Christ claimed for himself is now put into effect by the pope.

Curiously enough, the conclusions of Cardinal Cajetan (1469–1534), even if they lead to the same result, appear to be closer to the letter of the Old Testament and to place greater emphasis on the Old Law than did the conclusions of the rabbi's son. It is well known that this famous Thomistic theologian, after having served as master-general of the Dominicans and then as legate to Germany (as such becoming Luther's great adversary in October of 1518), devoted himself to the study of Holy Scripture and for that purpose availed himself of the services of Jews who taught him about the Hebrew traditions.

In March 1530 Pope Clement VII sought from him a report on the question of Henry's divorce, and Cajetan completed the report in one week. "Cajetan found himself forced to turn Henry's own weapon—the Old Testament—against him, and he did so with a destructive force. His investigation showed that if the Mosaic Law were still in force, it would obligate Henry to take Catherine as his wife."[28]

Cajetan examines very carefully the biblical texts central to the debate. He shows that the same term, *levir,* is used in both cases and that one may not set Leviticus against Deuteronomy, as had been done in the argumentation surrounding the king's case. But as an expert theologian trained in scholasticism, Cajetan shows how "the obvious difference between the two texts is that while the law of Leviticus is generic, that of Deuteronomy is specific."[29] By this twofold legislation God has clearly determined what ought to be done in the case of a marriage between a man and his sister-in-law. "The question whether the laws of the Old Testament are applicable to believers who live under the New Testament, or whether they no longer have binding force, is of little importance in the case under discussion."[30]

In other words, Cajetan chose to situate himself within the framework set forth by King Henry VIII. Because Henry had scruples concerning the divine law, he was obligated to accept it in its full meaning and to follow it in all its implications: He should understand that from the moment of his marriage to Catherine he fell under the case described in the regulations concerning a levirate marriage in Deuteronomy 25.

Cajetan then studies the circumstances that could still render this law of the levirate legitimate and binding. In the particular case of the king, Cajetan argues that it does not meet the set of circumstances explicitly envisioned by the Scripture (i.e., Henry's purpose was not simply to ensure a posterity for his brother), but Cajetan goes on to show that this regulation is set in a broader perspective by its relation to "the common good." In this case the common good was peace between the kingdoms of England and Spain, as the bull of Julius II formally indicates. "The ecclesiastical dispensation was necessary only because of an impediment arising from human laws and for the purpose of attesting to the honorable character that this marriage took on in promoting the common good, which is peace."[31]

Pushing to its logical extreme his argument from the Old Testament, Cajetan applies to the pope the prescription of Deuteronomy 17:8–11: "In ambiguous and difficult cases the High Priest must determine the Law of the Lord."[32] In this manner Julius II had determined that "the end of the common good of peace was compatible with the divine law."

Just as much as Felix de Prato tried to keep his distance from the Old Law, Cajetan wanted to take into consideration the entirety of the Old Testament, as the king himself had suggested. But he could have chosen, as so many other authors on this subject did, to show how certain Old Testament laws had been annulled or at least had only a diminished power to bind the Christian conscience. For Cajetan, on the contrary, the law of the Old Testament continued to be applicable insofar as it was a positive expression of natural law and insofar as its content was moral.

It does not seem necessary to read into this a manifestation of Cajetan's preference for the literal sense of Scripture;[33] what we see instead is an indication of his remarkable independence in the matter of scriptural interpretation, for which he was severely criticized when treating the New Testament. Let us note, finally, that in a letter to King Henry VIII in January 1536—several weeks prior to the definitive judgment of Clement VII to the effect that Henry's marriage to Catherine was indeed valid—Cajetan had reaffirmed his original position, although he did make a slight modification in the argumentation by which he supported it. In addition, he refuted the objection that John the Baptist (in Matthew 14:4 and Mark 6:18) seemed to condemn the institution of the levirate by showing that the case of Herod does not qualify as an instance of the levirate. But this letter falls outside the period that we have chosen to consider here.

CONCLUSIONS

The Catholic writers were concerned with a sound interpretation of Scripture. This we have established with regard to Felix de Prato and Cajetan. One could make the same case with regard to the writings of John Fisher and Francisco de Vitoria, who were also proponents of the view that the royal marriage was valid. To be sure, they mingled canonical considerations with arguments from authority and from reason, but in this respect they are no different from the Reformers.

This leads us to our first conclusion: In such a controversial case, the results to which various authors came in 1530–31 cannot be classified according to confessional criteria (i.e., on the one hand, a reading based on the principle of *sola scriptura* and, on the other, an interpretation which would take account of tradition and canon law). It is true that ways of approaching the biblical text varied according to the theological presuppositions of the interpreters, but the complexity of the results to which different authors came on this subject presents a variety of viewpoints that cannot be fully explained by reference to the differences between standard Protestant and Catholic attitudes toward the relation between Scripture and tradition. From the uses made of Scripture on both sides of the line dividing Catholic from Protestant exegetes, one might get the impression that Scripture is a *nasus cereus*—flexible, malleable, capable of being twisted and changed into almost any shape. To use an expression borrowed from the debates of the sixteenth century, one may say that the case of Henry VIII does not provide a demonstration of the *claritas scripturae.* Indeed, from the hermeneutical point of view, the cleavage that seems to be pivotal transcends purely confessional allegiances; it is a difference of opinion regarding the position of the Old Testament in relation to the New, so that the crucial question is whether the Law has become totally obsolete or whether, on the contrary, it is still binding to some extent upon the Christian. Also at stake is the interpretative and magisterial role of the church.

Our second conclusion is directed more broadly toward the history of exegesis in the sixteenth century. The consideration of the biblical dossier of Henry VIII by the universities and theologians makes it clear that the interpretation of Scripture must be viewed in a broad context. We must take account, first of all, of theological categories—scholastic categories for most of the queen's defenders—but these must be understood in their organic relation to canon law. It is true that the case of Henry VIII stands on the borderline between the history of exegesis and the history of canon law. It serves, then, as a reminder that in the fields of church discipline, sacraments (especially marriage), and even ecclesiology, history of exegesis and history of canon law cannot be understood in isolation from one another.

I should add, finally, that there is a political dimension to a debate such as the one we have considered here. The case of Henry VIII arose at a time when the doctrine of the theologians was not really well established; the understanding of the bonds of affinity was at a certain stage, but it was still in the process of evolving. It was possible, therefore, to show a certain flexibility in one's position without attacking the tradition itself. To what extent was Henry VIII sincere in his scruples as a theologian? We should note once again that his case was not entirely clear as far as the church's teaching was concerned, even though, from an intuitive or commonsense perspective it was perhaps inevitable that the outcome would not be favorable to him.

How can we account for the ambiguous attitude of the English and French universities, which clearly wanted to please the king (but without compromising themselves)? Without casting doubt on their sincerity, we may say that these theologians tended to arrive at conclusions which one would have been able to predict on the basis of their national identity or political allegiances in the complex politics of sixteenth-century Europe.[34] Does this imply that we should adopt a thoroughgoing relativism with regard to the interpretation of any given text? For the present, we close with a question: In the King's great matter," did biblical exegesis become the servant of politics?

SCOTT H. HENDRIX

The Use of Scripture in Establishing Protestantism:

The Case of Urbanus Rhegius

Urbanus Rhegius's career as a Reformer falls naturally into two parts: the time he spent in south Germany as a Protestant preacher in Augsburg from 1524 to 1530, and his time in north Germany as superintendent of the church in the Duchy of Lüneburg from 1530 until his death in 1541.[1] Rhegius was lured to Lüneburg by Duke Ernest the "Confessor," who intended for him to organize the newly reformed church in his territory according to Protestant teaching and practice. Although he had seen controversy enough in Augsburg, which was a maelstrom of religious currents during the 1520s,[2] Rhegius scarcely anticipated the difficulties that awaited him in Lower Saxony. His skill in the interpretation of Scripture would prove to be a trusted resource in the rocky vineyard of north Germany. This same skill would also illustrate the extent to which Scripture became a tool in the hands of Reformers like Rhegius who were charged with establishing Protestantism.

Rhegius's exegetical skills were acquired and honed during his south German years. His most important acquisition was training in biblical languages, a skill he had in common with other scholars influenced by humanism. Rhegius may have learned Greek at the University of Freiburg (1508–12) or subsequently at Ingolstadt (1512–18); his earliest works demonstrate familiarity with the language. The origin of his enthusiasm for Hebrew is uncertain. Maximilian Liebmann speculates that John Eck may have sparked Rhegius's interest in both languages. Liebmann points out that the earliest manuscripts of Rhegius that we possess—two course announcements from the year

1512—contain the name of Rhegius (at that time Rieger) written with Hebrew letters.[3] Rhegius could have been exposed to the language in Freiburg, where Eck studied Hebrew with the Carthusian prior Gregor Reisch (d. 1525), or in Ingolstadt, where Reuchlin lectured on the grammar of Kimchi and named Eck as one of his students.[4] Rhegius might also have learned Hebrew from Matthäus Adrianus (fl. 1501–21), who taught the language in Heidelberg from 1513 to 1516 and had Johannes Oecolampadius and Wolfgang Capito as his students.[5] Wherever he learned it, Rhegius demonstrated special fondness for Hebrew[6] and referred to medieval Jewish grammarians like Abraham Ibn Ezra and David Kimchi along with Christian scholars like Sebastian Münster.

In later years Rhegius frequently used Hebrew in his explanations of Old Testament passages,[7] and he preached what he practiced. Advising a young pastor near Hannover in 1540 how to study Scripture, Rhegius first stressed that biblical languages should be learned with diligence. Without knowledge of Hebrew, exegetes were forced to look at the Old Testament with "foreign eyes." How perilous that could be for the prospective theologian had now become obvious, especially to those who had trusted the translations of Jerome for so many years but now did not always follow his rendering, even though they still commended his effort.[8] Rhegius recommended that the pastor not only read daily a chapter or two of the Old Testament in Hebrew, but that he also compare the Hebrew text with the Greek version. This comparison, claimed Rhegius, would help him in a marvelous way to learn the true sense of Scripture and to attain the gift of the Holy Spirit.[9]

The same disciplined pattern of study in both the Old and the New Testaments very likely accounts for Rhegius's impressive familiarity with Scripture. He could quote passages from all parts of the Bible as freely and easily as Luther could, and he did not have the ritual of monastic worship or an academic chair in exegesis to imprint the verses on his mind. In Ingolstadt Rhegius did lecture on Lefèvre's introduction to the *Politics* of Aristotle, but his academic training gives no evidence of an unusual concentration on Scripture. Besides the acquaintance he made through the study of Greek and Hebrew, Rhegius acquired his ready knowledge of the Bible on the job, as cathedral preacher in Augsburg and as chaplain at Hall in Tirol. After his conversion to Protestantism Rhegius supplemented his preaching in Augsburg with weekday exegetical lectures on Paul's Epistles.[10] His intensive study of Paul also generated two popular writings, first published in 1523, that exhibit his knowledge of Scripture and his readiness to use it. *A Brief Explanation of Some Common Points of Scripture* was an exposition of forty-eight theological loci found in Scripture, and *The Twelve Articles of Our Christian Faith* was an interpretation of the Apostles' Creed which showed how a proper understanding of the creed was based on Scripture.[11]

The regular study and exposition of Scripture remained part of Rhegius's schedule after he assumed his duties in north Germany. We can safely make such an assertion without adopting the effusive flattery of his translator and admirer, Johannes Freder (Irenaeus), who declared him worthy to be called bishop not just of Lüneburg but of all Germany.[12] As a close reader and translator of his works, Freder expressed general admiration for Rhegius's devotion and learning, but he singled out for special praise Rhegius's knowledge of languages (Latin, Greek, Hebrew) and his most popular exegetical work, the massive collection and interpretation of messianic passages from the Old Testament, the *Dialogus von der schönen predigt.*[13]

In north Germany Rhegius was challenged by three major tasks: (1) to break Catholic resistance to the Reformation in the territory of Lüneburg and in cities like Lüneburg and Hannover; (2) to protect Protestants from the threat of Anabaptist influence and the taint of Anabaptist excesses at Münster; and (3) to educate pastors for the new Protestant parishes in Lower Saxony. The nature of these tasks determined the kind of works that Rhegius produced during the 1530s and directly affected the way he used Scripture in these writings.

The first two tasks—the assertion of Protestant principles against Catholic and Anabaptist views—elicited a number of polemical works from his pen. Typical of these is his refutation of "a monstrous, astounding formula of absolution" allegedly written by nuns in the cloisters of Lüneburg and then used by two seventy-year-old confessors who could neither recite it nor understand it.[14] Rhegius decided to publish the absolution in order to warn simple people against the blasphemy of Christ that was still rampant under the papacy.[15] His method of refutation was straightforward. He dealt with the absolution one phrase at a time and refuted each phrase by listing passages of

Scripture which proved the phrase false. For example, against the attribution of forgiveness to the merit of Mary, Rhegius listed seven passages of Scripture, discussed one (Romans 3) in detail, and concluded that if the nuns thought that the merit of Mary added power to the merit of Christ, then all the passages cited would be false.[16] Rhegius also used Scripture to expose the social forces at work behind the resistance of cloistered women to the Reformation. Citing 1 Corinthians 1:26 ("not many were wise. . . . not many were powerful, not many were of noble birth"), Rhegius made fun of their status as noblewomen and ridiculed their claim to have died to the world. After visiting some of the cloisters, Rhegius quipped that the nuns lived as much apart from the world as kidneys lived apart from the body.[17]

The third task, training Protestant clergy and educating the laity who suddenly found themselves Protestant, consumed Rhegius's remaining energy.[18] There was no theological faculty in Lower Saxony until the University of Helmstedt was founded in 1576. Those Protestant preachers who did not study at Wittenberg learned the new theology from writings of the Reformers or heard it from their superintendents and colleagues in the church. Besides his advice to pastors to study Scripture on their own, Rhegius went about his pedagogical task in two ways.

First, he published works that were specifically designed to ensure the proper education and certification of Protestant pastors. The most popular of these was a homiletical handbook entitled *How to Preach on the Chief Points of Christian Doctrine Carefully and without Giving Offense.*[19] It was addressed to younger ministers of the Word in Lüneburg and was prompted by the poor sermons Rhegius himself had heard from misguided and brash young Protestant pulpiteers. In order to help dispel the laity's confusion over sensitive issues such as repentance, good works, predestination, and illumination by the Spirit, Rhegius cited key passages of Scripture that could serve the preachers as guidelines for a correct and balanced proclamation. Rhegius also wanted to make sure that new preachers would be much better prepared to use Scripture. Soon after the *Formulae caute,* Rhegius outlined an examination to be given to all candidates for ordination in the Duchy.[20] The structure of the exam was based on carefully selected passages, beginning with the familiar exhortations about church leaders in 1 and 2 Timothy and moving to a biblical argument for dividing all of Scripture into the categories of law and gospel.[21] This distinction was not sufficient, however. Ordinands had to be prepared to recite copiously passages from Scripture that correctly explained temporal and external punishments, the divinity of Christ, and all the articles of the Apostles' Creed. Furthermore, candidates were expected to show exactly which parts of Scripture were law and which were gospel and where in Scripture Christ was promised and where he was explicitly shown to be the Messiah.[22] When candidates appeared for the examination, they had to be loaded with Scripture.

As a second method of educating clergy, Rhegius himself demonstrated what he required. In Celle Rhegius revived his custom of exegeting Scripture on weekdays, showing a marked preference for the Old Testament, at least according to the sermons and lectures that he selected for publication. When he assisted with the Reformation in the cities of Lüneburg and Hannover, he instructed his fellow preachers in the exegesis of Scripture by modeling the discipline for them. In Lüneburg Rhegius lectured on Romans and then formulated theses based on the lectures to be defended by the preachers in debates with one another.[23] In Hannover in 1535 Rhegius lectured on the prophet Obadiah in order to show evangelical preachers how to understand and expound the prophets.[24] Although he did not hold a university chair in exegesis, his teaching activity resembled a modern extension or continuing education program, in which Rhegius became the professor of theology and exegesis for students who were already in the field.

Owing to his strong interest in the education of clergy and laity, Rhegius's reforming work has been described as predominantly pastoral and his use of Scripture judged typical of the edifying nature of much Reformation exegesis.[25] Certainly his love of proof texts and the copious citations in his polemical works make his use of Scripture appear unremarkable. Nevertheless, Rhegius developed a concept of interpretation which he applied consistently and quite visibly in his exegetical works. This concept was based on two principles: one can be labeled "apostolic," and the other "catechetical." These principles were stated and explained in the form of advice to preachers and fit, therefore, into the polemical and pedagogical purposes of his work.[26]

The apostolic principle of interpretation requires the preacher to use the Old Testament as the apostles did in order to find support for the gospel in the law and the prophets. This apostolic custom, according to Rhegius, is demonstrated in the Epistles of the New Testament and in the Book of Acts. These parts of the New Testament show us the right interpretation and use of the Old Testament, since the New is the light of and key to the Old.[27] If, however, the light seems dim and the Old Testament remains obscure, preachers should use the following syllogism in order to remind them of the method: (1) all the prophets were seeking the salvation and reconciliation of humanity with its creator; (2) no righteousness or salvation was promised apart from Jesus Christ; (3) ergo, all the prophets foretold the coming of Christ.[28] The syllogism itself was based on selected New Testament passages, especially 1 Peter 1:10–12, which identifies the prophets as foretellers of grace and predictors of the sufferings and glory of Christ.

A christological interpretation of the Old Testament is hardly distinctive, but Rhegius gave it an unusual twist. He did not stress the use of the New Testament to interpret the Old, but the use of the Old to confirm the New. The main reason for reading the Old Testament as the apostles did was not to understand it better but to strengthen faith.[29]

Rhegius went about the task of confirming the New Testament and strengthening faith with astounding energy. The most amazing product of this energy is the enormous collection of Old Testament passages which Rhegius identified as prophecies of Christ. The *Dialogus,* as he called it, was allegedly based on conversations between Rhegius and his wife Anna and first was written as a dialogue between them in 1532. Feeling sad one Easter Day, Anna said she wished she could hear the comforting sermon which Jesus must have preached to the two disciples on the road to Emmaus, when, "beginning with Moses and all the prophets, he interpreted to them in all the Scriptures the things concerning himself" (Luke 24:27).[30] Anna wanted to hear that sermon so that she could be joyful in the Lord and have her faith strengthened.

That desire was only too welcome to Urbanus Rhegius, who confirmed her feeling that people did not know Christ as they ought, even though they heard many sermons about him.[31] Therefore one should hear the best sermon of all, the sermon that Christ preached about himself. Urbanus warned his wife that the sermon would be long because Luke says that Christ used "all the Scriptures." But Anna offered no protest, and Urbanus rolled off six hundred pages of Old

Testament prophecies of Christ, beginning with the first promise of grace in Genesis 3. At the end, sounding skeptical and exhausted, Anna objected that the road from Jerusalem to Emmaus was surely not long enough for Christ to have preached all that; but Rhegius reminded her, the length notwithstanding, how marvelously the sermon strengthened faith. The prophets were the oldest teachers on earth, he said, and the gospel was the oldest teaching.[32]

Rhegius apparently believed that the more Scripture that was cited, the stronger faith would become. In his view there was no difference between the message of the prophets and the message of the evangelists. The sum of the prophets' teaching was repentance and faith in Christ, exactly as it is stated in Acts 20:21. The prophets preached repentance by scolding those who broke the law, and they preached faith by announcing the promise of grace.[33] Since Moses and David were also prophets, a large portion of the Old Testament was included under gospel. The difference that mattered was not the gap between the Old and New Testaments but the difference between the two ways in which Christ was proclaimed: through dark promises and figures as if seen from a distance, and through clear promises expressed in unambiguous language.[34]

Rhegius's *Dialogus* was designed to save readers of the Old Testament the work of making this distinction for themselves. It exposed the teaching about Christ in every possible Old Testament passage and formed a repository of texts stripped of their ambiguity and ready to use. This repository would also equip the preacher to engage more effectively in controversy. Rhegius argued that many preachers knew the gospel but did not read the law and the prophets. Only that preacher who was equipped with the apostolic principle of interpretation and thus had his arsenal filled with Old Testament ammunition was qualified to preside over the church.[35]

Rhegius illustrated the use of this principle in the lectures on Obadiah that he delivered in Hannover in 1535. The prophet provided him with ammunition to use against both "papists" and Anabaptists. In his lectures Rhegius does not ignore the historical sense, but he does identify the enemies of Israel—the Edomites—with contemporary persecutors of the gospel, and the Israelite kingdom with the Catholic church.[36] Two phrases in verse 17 allow him to elaborate. The holiness of Mount Zion, which is a figure of the true church, leads him to distinguish the evangelical understanding of the church's holiness from the perfectionism of Anabaptists and monasticism.[37] Furthermore, the possession of the house of Jacob, mentioned in the same verse, means that the church will possess people from all nations, an insight that refutes the blindness of the Jews and chiliastic interpretations. His twenty-year-old battle with the chiliasts, says Rhegius, has forced him to study this passage closely along with other prophecies, and he invokes his knowledge of Hebrew as an aid. If one can understand the idiosyncrasy of the Hebrew language, one can see that a spiritual possession, and not an earthly kingdom, was intended by Obadiah and by the Holy Spirit who spoke through him.[38] Obviously Rhegius's long polemical career enhanced his knowledge of Scripture and led him to rely on the apostolic principle of interpretation that he now recommends so highly to his evangelical coworkers.

Rhegius's second hermeneutical principle was the catechetical principle, which called for the preacher to use a doctrine from the catechism in order to explain the text of the sermon.[39] But the principle encompassed a larger understanding of catechism than documents produced for the instruction of the faithful. Rhegius maintained that Scripture should always be interpreted in accord with the received dogma of the church universal, and that preachers should be ready to cite opinions of the church fathers in support of their points.[40] Not just any opinion of a church father could be used, but only those which agreed with the consensus of the church that was required by the principle of catholicity. Rhegius described this use of dogma as the interpretation of Scripture in the "ecclesiastical sense" and argued that a proper understanding of Scripture was not to be found outside the *ecclesia catholica*.[41] Rhegius's Lutheran biographer, Gerhard Uhlhorn, was so nonplussed by this statement that he hastened to assure the reader that Rhegius did not abide by his own principle.[42] In fact, Rhegius abided by it very well, insofar as he understood both the early church and Scripture to support an evangelical interpretation of the faith. And the principle served him very well in the work he had to accomplish.

In the first place, he wanted to ensure that a consistent message was presented from Protestant pulpits. Rhegius recommended that all the pastors in one city study the Gospel text for the coming Sunday under the guidance of the superintendent, so that the "dogmas of our faith" would be explained in concert. If a difficult or controversial text had to be expounded, then testimonies from the church fathers should be used.[43] An example is the sermon on good and bad angels that Rhegius preached on the Day of Saint Michael and All Angels, September 29, 1535. In the sermon he cites Basil the Great in support of his assertion that the church has always believed in guardian angels. We should not, however, put our trust in them or invoke them, because Scripture teaches that we should hope in Christ alone. Since Rhegius, by his own admission, is afraid this prohibition will irritate people, he cites a long passage from Augustine on its behalf. Although he argues that the church has not rejected Augustine's words because they are grounded in Scripture,[44] he implies that Scripture alone is not enough to convince the people.

The second reason for interpreting biblical texts with the help of basic doctrines and the church fathers was to draw a practical lesson from the texts that people could apply easily to their lives. Rhegius suggested that the words of Jesus against killing in Matthew 5:21–26 be related to the Fifth Commandment, and that the stories of Jesus raising the dead be referred directly to the credal belief in the Resurrection.[45] Daily application of this catechetical principle would reveal many specific relationships between Scripture and articles of faith. Most important, preachers should inculcate the catechism in people, "for I have experienced over now these many years how greatly this labor profits the churches."[46]

Again, Rhegius practiced what he advised. According to his interpretation of Obadiah, verse 17, Edom's betrayal by its allies illustrates the First Commandment because in time of trouble Edom looked to human aid instead of to God, who alone is trustworthy.[47] Rhegius's exposition of Psalm 14 emphasizes the same idea. The fool who says in his heart "there is no God" speaks for all of us. Because of the corruption of original sin, we cannot believe that God cares about us and deserves our trust. And if we cannot keep the First Commandment, we will fail to observe the others as well.[48] In this commentary on Psalm 14 Rhegius recounts one situation in which catechetical interpretation had not had the desired effect. He once confronted a notorious drinker with the scriptural declaration that drunkards could not enter the kingdom of heaven. The man replied that Rhegius should go to church if he wanted to preach. Rhegius's comment on the incident is that the man misunderstood the meaning of "church"; he thought of the building instead of the people.[49]

The church order that Rhegius wrote for the city of Hannover reveals a third and more familiar purpose of the catechetical principle. Evangelical preachers should refer to the early church in order to refute the accusation that Protestants were teaching a new and different doctrine.[50] For example, when Rhegius rejected the merits of the saints as a basis for absolution (as we saw in the formula of the nuns), he argued unabashedly that this teaching not only stood in opposition to Holy Scripture but contradicted the Christian faith and the "ancient teachers" as well.[51] All Protestants tried to trace their roots to the early church; Rhegius was no exception. His extensive knowledge of the church fathers and his promptness to supplement texts of Scripture with evidence from the early church distinguish him, however, as a leader among Protestants who were eager to show they were truly catholic. This strong interest in the roots of Protestantism was for Uhlhorn the only mitigating aspect of Rhegius's adherence to the ecclesiastical sense of Scripture.[52] Uhlhorn should also have been comforted by Rhegius's appeals to the early church to support key Lutheran or Protestant teachings. Following one's own private understanding of Scripture instead of the church's interpretation had led, according to Rhegius, to the denial of the real presence of Christ in the Lord's Supper and to the application of the rock in Matthew 16:18 to Peter instead of to Christ.[53]

The apostolic and catechetical principles recommended by Rhegius suggest several conclusions about his own use of Scripture that can be applied to an appraisal of sixteenth-century exegesis.

First, in regard to Protestant exegesis of the Old Testament, the apostolic principle suggests that the central issue was not whether to interpret the Old Testament literally or figuratively, but how christological a legitimate interpretation of the Old Testament could be. By recommending that Protestant preachers follow the model of the apostles and, according to Luke 24, even of Christ himself, Rhegius stated and practiced an extreme form of christological exegesis of the Old Testament. Rhegius was more apostolic than the apostles; not even Luke dared to reconstruct the sermon of Christ on the road to Emmaus! Although Rhegius used the original language and the historical sense as the basis of a text's true meaning, he was not interested mainly in the literal sense but in the meaning it contained about the person and work of Christ. Were Protestants distinctive because they attended to the literal or historical sense of the Old Testament more than exegetes before them, or did they use the Old Testament to confirm their own reading of the New Testament as did generations of their predecessors?

Second, the catechetical principle enunciated by Rhegius indicates that he did not adhere to the principle of *sola scriptura.* Stated more precisely, Rhegius realized that such a principle did not exist and that Scripture was being distorted by people who thought it did. Uhlhorn's amazement notwithstanding, Rhegius argued that no true understanding of Scripture could exist apart from the fundamental articles of the faith as these were forged during the earliest centuries of the church. He certainly believed that no teaching or practice which stood in manifest contradiction to Scripture could be condoned, but he also argued that no group could stand on its private interpretation of a text. Rhegius was facing a twofold challenge. On the one side, his non-Protestant opponents were also appealing to Scripture, while on the other side, some of his followers were claiming that they did not need to know Scripture at all but could be enlightened immediately by the Spirit.

Therefore, says Rhegius in the *Formulae caute,* he has to explain verse 13 from Isaiah 54, which was cited in John 6:45 and became one of Luther's favorite proof texts for the priesthood of believers: "And they shall all be taught by God."[54] According to Rhegius, Christ intended for these words to refer to the "common teaching of the gospel" by which every one of the predestined is enlightened and saved. Beyond this illumination, however, the gift of prophecy (1 Corinthians 14:3) is given only to the teachers of the church, whose task it is to interpret Holy Scripture for the benefit of the faithful.[55]

These teachers were, of course, the pastors of Protestant parishes, and we have seen how their interpretation should conform to the catholic consensus of the early church. Rhegius was concerned both about the catholicity of the emerging Protestant churches and about the disorder which could result from lay access to Scripture and the concept of a common priesthood. In effect, Rhegius was designing a Protestant magisterium: pastors trained to exegete Scripture in accord with the credal doctrines of the early church. This principle may have widened the gap between Protestant clergy and laity, but Rhegius was less concerned about this gap than he was about replacing Roman priests with pastors who could give proper evangelical instruction to the people.[56]

Third, Rhegius's principles of interpretation illustrate how the task of establishing Protestantism shaped both its exegesis and its teaching. In this regard Rhegius's model was Philip Melanchthon, whose influence was not mediated through exegetical principles or personal impact, although Rhegius supported Melanchthon in the negotiations at Augsburg.[57] Instead, Melanchthon's influence was mediated through his *Unterricht der Visitatoren,* which Rhegius knew and used in Lüneburg.[58] As we know from his *Dialogus,* Rhegius was generally fascinated by the twenty-fourth chapter of Luke's Gospel, especially the story of Jesus' appearance on the road to Emmaus. But he was also specifically taken with a verse that Melanchthon had used to support the necessity of teaching repentance as the way to faith. According to Luke 24:47, "repentance *and* forgiveness of sins should be preached in his name to all nations."[59] This verse, supplemented by passages like Acts 20:21, became the foundation of Rhegius's own call for the preaching of both repentance and faith.[60] It also supported the division of doctrine into law and gospel in his outline for an ordination exam: According to Luke 24:47, the teaching of the gospel is twofold, repentance and the forgiveness of sins, and all of Scripture is subsumed under these two headings.[61]

Much more is involved here than Rhegius's support of Melanchthon against Agricola in the first antinomian controversy.[62] Melanchthon's work was a model for the clarification of Protestant teaching and practice, which Rhegius also had to provide for his preachers and parishes in Lüneburg. Thorny issues such as the place of repentance and the law in the Christian life had to be faced. In his own "instruction," the *Formulae caute,* Rhegius discusses elaborately such controversial issues as predestination and good works (the stress on good works is especially noticeable). The directions for examining ordinands seriously admonish pastors to preach faith and good works in such a way that neither is impugned. The preaching of good works, says Rhegius, should season the sermon with a little theological salt.[63] The concentration on these issues and the use of Scripture passages like Luke 24 to explicate them were determined by the situation

Rhegius faced in educating the first generation of Protestant clergy and laity.

For the shape of Lutheranism, however, there was a further implication. The basis and scope of Lutheran teaching was broadened beyond Luther to include the practical concerns and theological perspective of superintendents like Rhegius. Rhegius by no means rejected Luther; on the contrary, among Protestant leaders there was no more ardent admirer of Luther.[64] Even he was aware, however, that Protestant claims had to avoid too much dependence on Luther in order to establish their validity. In practical ways Rhegius demonstrated that Luther was not the only true exegete. Part of his advice to younger preachers was to study Melanchthon's commentaries on Romans and Colossians and Bucer's commentary on Romans in addition to Luther on Galatians.[65] Also, Rhegius knew and used Luther's translations of Old Testament books, but he sometimes preferred to rely on his own knowledge of Hebrew and deviate from Luther's interpretations.

This independence befit Rhegius's own apostolic and catechetical principles, according to which the interpretation of any one exegete had to be placed in the broader context of the faith of the church. The rule also applied to Luther, and Rhegius's willingness to learn from the early church and from other reformers may have contributed to the critical stance against Luther which later marked the University of Helmstedt.[66] Be that as it may, at the end of the Hannover church order Rhegius argued that Protestant doctrine did not depend on the exegesis or preaching of any individual teacher such as Luther. Instead he appealed to a passage which undergirded both his principles and, as far as he could see, did not need to be put into context. Protestants believed their doctrine, he asserted, regardless of who taught it, for the sake of him who said in the first place: "Repent and believe in the gospel" (Mark 1:15).[67]

KALMAN P. BLAND

Issues in Sixteenth-Century Jewish Exegesis

In the sixteenth century Judaism underwent the kinds of experiences and absorbed the varieties of new knowledge that usually compel religious communities to reassess their sacred scriptures. The literary expression of this reassessment gave voice to the communal need for reconciling the ever-changing circumstances of life with traditions inherited from the past. The more profound the change, the more pressing becomes the necessity to invent interpretations that either maintain the old or integrate it with the new. The unsettling effects of cultural and social dislocation must be neutralized, and biblical exegesis was the literary battlefield on which this particular struggle was waged. Sixteenth-century Jewish exegesis is a sensitive, reliable indicator of the historical ferment that excited Jewish scholars into producing a diverse and lively hermeneutical literature.

I

In the years immediately following the traumatic expulsion from Spain in 1492, an anonymous Jewish mystic, probably writing in Italy, composed a biblical commentary that resounded with the messianic and apocalyptic tenor of his era. He declared that "according to the words of the sages the Torah has seventy aspects, and there are seventy aspects to each and every verse; in truth, therefore, the aspects are infinite. In each generation one of these aspects is revealed, and so in our generation the aspect which the Torah reveals to us concerns matters of redemption. Each and every verse can be understood and explained in reference to redemption."[1]

Writing in Istanbul at approximately the same time, Rabbi Isaac Karo (1440–1518), who left his native Toledo several years before the Spanish expulsion to settle in Portugal, only to escape from there to Turkey in 1497, introduced his nonapocalyptic comments to Genesis 1 by explaining that

every science has a subject around which the entirety of that science revolves. For example, the science of medicine has for its subject the organs and the humors; physics has for its subject the existent which changes insofar as it is mutable; and metaphysics has for its subject that which exists inasmuch as it exists absolutely. So it is proper that our holy Torah have a subject around which it revolves, and one must know what that is. The answer: the [temporal] creation of the world.[2]

The differences in geographical location—Italy and Turkey—and in doctrinal affiliation—mystical and philosophic—that sharply distinguish these two texts permit a partial sampling of the multifaceted cultural heritage of Spanish Jewry as it interacted with the complex chain of historical events and historic processes triggered by the Iberian upheavals of 1492 and 1497.[3] Just as these texts become meaningful when read as diverse "responses" to an identical historical background, so too are the time and place of their composition illumined when these same texts are used to reconstruct sixteenth-century history.

If a sufficient number of Jewish biblical commentaries were combed for references to their historical background, and if these same texts were then explained by appeals to that background, a fascinating image of the sixteenth century would emerge: Renaissance humanism;[4] the Protestant Reformation;[5] the Catholic Restoration, or Counter-Reformation;[6] the Inquisition and the dilemmas and migrations of the *converos* and the *marranos;*[7] the development of the three main centers of sixteenth-century Judaism in Italy,[8] the Ottoman Empire,[9] and Eastern Europe;[10] and Jewish life and thought north of the Alps.[11] All of these would be seen through the refracting medium of sixteenth-century Jewish exegesis.

Knowledge of the sixteenth-century background in turn supplies the data to be used in accounting for the characteristics of the exegetical literature. Christian Kabbalah[12] and Hebraism,[13] and especially Renaissance humanism and rhetoric,[14] were powerful factors that stimulated and shaped the course of Jewish homiletics and biblical study. Pursuing these lines of historical research to reconstruct a more complete and satisfying picture of sixteenth-century human experience is unquestionably necessary, rewarding, and worthwhile.

It would be unfortunate, however, if the history of interpretation were to be systematically subordinated to the exclusive interests of social history or reduced to serving as handmaiden to the history of doctrine. The history of interpretation is, after all, the history of *interpretation.* Commentators practice the art of literary criticism; they somehow manage to discover or create the meaning and significance of scripture for their own time and place. The tasks undertaken by the history of interpretation, therefore, must include the identification and analysis of the presuppositions and methods by which an interpreter grafts into the tissue of a sacred, fixed, and authoritative Scripture the experience and thought of a generation of human beings.

II

Having already acknowledged that Rabbi Isaac Karo's commentary belongs to the postexpulsion era of Jewish life and therefore mirrors the social and intellectual history of his community, we are prepared to direct our attention to the art of Karo's interpretation. Neither his obvious dependence on the medieval tradition and on the corpus of traditional midrash nor what the following excerpt reveals about intellectual trends in sixteenth-century Turkish Jewry interests us here as much as the logic which generated Karo's treatment of Scripture and the format he used to present it.

What did he think needed to be said in order to make Scripture meaningful? Which linguistic or semantic aspects of Scripture did he feel obliged to address? What commanded his attention as being worthy of his audience's consideration? What was his understanding of the purpose of biblical study and of the Bible itself, and how did these views shape the form and content of his homilies? Answers to these questions require more data than a short excerpt containing Karo's pronouncements on a single topic. What follows, then, is the bulk of his homily on Genesis 28:12–22: Jacob's ladder dream, God's blessing, and Jacob's vow.

"Then he dreamed: A ladder was standing on the earth"—there are difficulties (*sefaqoth*) with this.

The first difficulty: What is the intention (*kawwanah*) behind the vision of the ladder?

The second difficulty: Inasmuch as it says "a ladder was standing on the earth," and immediately thereafter it says "I am God, the Lord of Abraham, your father," etc., it would seem that this constitutes the interpretation of the parable. What then is the relationship between the vision of the ladder, "the earth on which you are resting," and all the other things He said to him?

The third difficulty: He said—"This is nothing other than the House of God." Why did he use negative terminology? He should rather have said: "How awesome is this place, this is the House of God."

The fourth difficulty: What need was there to use the term *this* three times? He said: "How awesome is this place; this is nothing other than the House of God; and this is the gate of heaven." It would have been sufficient for him to say: "How awesome is this place, it is the House of God, and the gate of heaven," or, "How awesome is this place, this is the House of God, and the gate of Heaven."

The fifth difficulty: How is it that he introduced conditionality into his prophecy, for he said: "If God remains with me, . . ."?

The sixth difficulty: Concerning his statement, "from everything that You give to me, I will always set aside a tenth," it is not proper for one to say to a king, "Grant me a thousand florins, and I will give you a tithe."

The response concerning the intention of the ladder: It was made known to him that the power God gave to the angels when He created them does not suffice them. Rather, they must receive from moment to moment an influx from God, may He be blessed. Hence, it says: "The angels ascend" to receive the influx from God, may He be blessed, and "descend" together with their influx. It is not like a building, which after having been constructed, no longer needs a contractor.

The second [answer] concerning the intention of the ladder: An important topic was made known to him, namely, that no two angels belong to the same species. The human beings Reuben and Simon do not differ with respect to form, since they are all living and rational, but with respect to matter. Now, since angels are incorporeal, the only differentiation between them is the differential of species. Each angel is a species unto itself; individual angels do not belong to a common species. This is in accordance with what has been explained in metaphysics. Hence it says that these angels of God ascend and these descend, one being inferior in metaphysical rank to the other, another being superior to the other. Thus, they do not all belong to the same species so that they would all belong to the same hierarchical level.

The third [answer] concerning the intention of the ladder: To assert that truth is not in accordance with the heretics who claim that there is no immortality of the soul. Hence it says: "a ladder was standing on the earth," which is equivalent to man, and "its head," which is equivalent to the soul which reaches the Throne of Glory. This is not true for all men, but only when thoughts are good. Hence it says: "the angels of God," which are the good thoughts and commandments that elevate man's soul on high. But if his thoughts are evil, it descends.

The fourth [answer] concerning the intention of the ladder—and with this the second difficulty is also resolved, i.e., what is the relationship between the vision and the statement concerning "the earth upon which you are resting"—a profound topic was made known to him. There is a dispute among the philosophers with some asserting that the Holy One, blessed be He, causes a celestial sphere to move, while others say that the Holy One, blessed be He, does not cause a sphere to move. Now the truth is that He does not cause a sphere to move. This is the secret meaning (*sod*) of the fiftieth day of Pentecost, and the fiftieth year of the Jubilee.

There are forty-nine celestial spheres, each one having its own mover, with God transcending them all and without being a mover. Therefore, the fiftieth day is holy, and the fiftieth year is holy, inasmuch as there remains no sphere that the Holy One, blessed be He, should cause it to move. Hence it is written: "the angels of God ascend," insofar as they cause the heavens to move. But transcending all these movers is God. Therefore, He said: Even though I do not cause any sphere to move, I shall cause "the land upon which you are resting" to move on your behalf, to give it to you forever.

The fifth [answer] concerning the intention of the ladder: Because there are heretics who claim that eternal things have one originating cause and corruptible things have another, it says—"a ladder standing on the earth" which represents corruptible things, and "its head reached heaven" and "the angels of God," which represent eternal things, all of which have one and the same cause—"God was standing above it." Similarly, there is an opinion of the heretics that there are three originating causes: one is the cause of this corruptible world; another is the cause of the incorruptible heavens; and another is the cause of the incorporeal angels. For this reason it says: "a ladder was standing on the earth," which is corruptible, "and its head reached heaven," which is incorruptible, even though it is corporeal, "and the angels of God . . . ," which are incorporeal, all of which have one and the same originating cause—"God was standing above it." He is the cause of them all.

The connection between the vision of the ladder and what was said, i.e., "the land on which you are resting" implies that if your children believe in my unity and that I am the cause of all three worlds, then "the land upon which you are resting, I will give to you and to your descendants." For this reason, Jacob's children said to him: "Hear, oh Israel"—you are Israel our father—"the Lord, our God, the Lord is one" (Deuteronomy 6:5).

. . . The resolution of the fourth difficulty: He used the term *this* three times to correspond to the three Temples. "How awesome . . ." [corresponds] to the first Temple in which God's presence (*shekhina*) dwelled; "this is nothing . . ." [corresponds] to the second Temple in which God's presence did not dwell—for which reason he used negative terminology, "this is nothing," i.e., it lacked God's presence; and "this is the gate of heaven" [corresponds] to the third Temple when God's presence will return to Jerusalem. For this reason, the term *heaven* is used to indicate that it will be the work of heaven, and not of human construction as were the first [two Temples].[15]

Karo presumed that his audience understood the literal, exoteric meaning of the passage, and therefore he supplied no word-by-word or phrase-by-phrase running commentary to translate or paraphrase the biblical text. Because isolated words or phrases did not concern him, he did not consider grammatical or Masoretic questions of morphology, vocalization, and punctuation.[16] He did nothing to simplify the biblical narrative.

To the contrary, Karo's procedures were aimed at unveiling the complexity of Scripture. The structural components and organization of the homily suggest that Karo was intent upon bringing into relief the latent problematics of what a superficial reader might mistakenly consider to be a straightforward, univocal episode in Jacob's biography. The homily begins with questions and ends with resolutions. The questions are presented in an uninterrupted series of trenchant, perhaps audacious, challenges to the syntactical formulations and theological implications of biblical language. The tension created by a battery of questions that remain unanswered until the entire list is given is then relaxed through two mechanisms: multiple answers to a single question, and the convergence of diverse themes on a single biblical locus.

There is no hint that the list of questions is meant to be exhaustive, comprehensive, or final; the various resolutions are not offered as mutually exclusive, alternative explanations, but rather as complementary, interlocking, mutually reinforcing layers of meaning. The initial, relentless questioning followed by a plenitude of answers signal Karo's view that Scripture is vastly complex, and that it invites, or demands, vigorous, open-ended, agonistic, intellectual investigation.

Since Karo believed that Scripture is meant to be cross-examined and that the study of Scripture calls for a process of active intellectual inquiry, as opposed to the more passive reception of mere information, it is revealing to discover precisely what it is about the text that triggered his questions. The first "difficulty" arises out of the presupposition that prophetic imagery, no matter how spectacular, is no mere imaginative fabrication deficient in didactic purpose.[17] The verbally unarticulated, esoteric dimension of Jacob's ladder turns out to be a rather full lesson in metaphysics, in theology, and in the philosophizing rationale of ritual law. Revelation and religious experience—for Jacob and for Karo's audience—are taken to be opportunities for instruction in the metaphysical and religious sciences. If one expects to find in Scripture philosophic lessons to be learned, then the function of the interpreter is to spell these out for an audience that depends on the script of biblical narrative to relive Jacob's enlightenment.

The second, third, and fourth "difficulties" are generated by aesthetic presuppositions about what constitutes a reasonable, economical, or proper mode of verbal expression. Unlike the fifth and sixth "difficulties," which object to the implications of Jacob's language with respect to his understanding of prophecy and to his manners in royal etiquette, the third and fourth "difficulties" are triggered by the style of Jacob's language. Jacob appears to have trespassed against rules that disallow redundancy and frown upon negative formulations.

As the second "difficulty" shows, even God himself is held accountable for the elements of correct style. What engenders Karo's second "difficulty" is the sense that God's blessing is inconsistent with the didactic allusions implicit in the ladder vision, and that it therefore fails to conform to the syntactic and thematic integrity of the passage as a whole. Such blatant deviations from the aesthetic norms considered by Karo to govern intelligent speech trigger the need to explain why God and Jacob chose to couch their thoughts in the language recorded by Scripture.

Karo's procedure for resolving these breaches in style is premised on the view that God and Jacob can be presumed to subscribe to the canons of correct style, but they deliberately and purposefully depart from them in order to communicate special messages. Subtle allusions to philosophic doctrines or eschatological expectations fully warrant the temporary abrogation of rules governing ordinary discourse. Scripture is perfect in form and content because it is cunning. All objections to its literacy turn out to be only apparent objections. Only the careful reader who notices the apparent difficulties has discovered the evidence pointing to the true depths of scriptural teaching. The alert reader is led to appreciate and absorb the subtlety and magisterial sophistication of the Bible's pedagogic cunning. For Karo, there is nothing casual or adventitious in Scripture, no passage bereft of philosophical, theological, and moral instruction. His method for studying Scripture, therefore, roots itself in the systematic scrutiny of biblical language in search of veiled steps on the road to enlightenment.

These conclusions, derived from his homily on Jacob's ladder, are fully consonant with Karo's explicit remarks in the preface to his commentary. He reports that the essential motivation in composing his commentary was

> to cleave unto God's presence (*shekhina*), for our sacred Torah provides us with perfection in this world, as well as in the world-to-come. . . . The Torah was the creative instrument of the Holy One, blessed be He. Moreover, it is one of the seven things created prior to the creation of the world. . . . Our sacred Torah perfects the soul . . . [when our soul is filled with Torah], we acquire immortality. In our cleaving [unto Torah], we cleave unto God, our Lord, God is one. . . . Furthermore, the perfection of our Torah is great and mighty, for contained within it are included all the sciences.[18]

Assured in advance that Scripture is replete with science, the commentator is altogether justified in finding learned allusions to practical and theoretical wisdom. Because the Bible is perfect, studying it in the manner dictated by its perfection assimilates the soul to God. The art of Karo's treatment of Scripture was intended to serve the ultimate purposes of forging a connective link to God and endowing the soul with immortality. Karo understood this perfection to require an articulation of the implicit questions embedded in biblical style and a formulation of a plenitude of answers that recapitulate the convergence of all truth in the complexity of sacred Scripture. Prodded by the never-ending source of true learning, biblical study once again became the religious activity par excellence.[19]

III

Karo's enthusiasm for the sciences was not shared by all of his sixteenth-century Jewish contemporaries. Indeed, the debate over the status of philosophy and science was one of the central issues animating sixteenth-century Jewish thought.[20] Commentators and humanists like Ovadiah Sforno, together with some Talmudists and mystics, filled their works with erudite references to the philosophic literature which inspired them, while other Talmudists and mystics like Meir Ibn Gabbai fulminated against the defiling incursions of "pagan" knowledge into Judaism.[21]

In contrast to his controversial attitude toward philosophy and science, Karo's notion of the intimate connection between God and his Torah was universally espoused by mystics and philosophers alike, even though the philosophic understanding of that "extradeical" connection so drastically differed from the "intradeical," theosophical doctrines of the mystics.[22] Karo's presuppositions about the cunning of biblical style were also typical of sixteenth-century Jewish thought. Mystics, philosophers, and Talmudists operated with the same presuppositions that triggered Karo's "difficulties" and generated his technique for reading Scripture. This approach to Scripture did not strike them as fruitless pettifoggery, because they all shared a similar aspiration for finding God in the microscopic scrutiny of biblical language. Furthermore, their reading habits were conditioned by a common set of hermeneutical principles that informed the rabbinic mode of analyzing sacred texts. By the sixteenth century this rabbinic mode was firmly established and, in fact, had reached new heights.

Karo's homiletic method shows traces of what recent scholarship has identified as an innovative trend in Jewish intellectual circles. Originating in Salonika after the Spanish expulsion, this trend spread to the remarkable and influential Galilean village of Safed, and from there it was carried to Italian and East European Jewry. The Jewish sage and mystic active in Salonika and credited with developing this influential new method was Rabbi Yoseph Taitazak. Summarily characterized, this trend represents a fascinating synthesis of principles and habits of mind derived from Talmudic dialectics, both halakhic and aggadic, and the medieval philosophic literature devoted to logic and rhetoric whose Jewish and non-Jewish sources were well known to the scholars of Salonika.[23]

One of the Taitazak's disciples, Rabbi Moses Alsheikh,[24] brought this technique with him when he immigrated to Safed, where he settled and spent the remainder of his life as teacher and preacher in the center of that epoch-making community of mystics and saints.[25] Alsheikh polished Taitazak's technique and stamped it with the definitive form which so profoundly shaped the subsequent history of Jewish homiletics.[26]

IV

A radically abridged excerpt from Alsheikh's customarily involved and lengthy treatment of Scripture will have to suffice for conveying a reliable impression of this characteristic sixteenth-century way of reading Scripture. Our example is taken from his treatment of 1 Samuel 15, a text describing Saul's war against the Amalekites and his confrontation with Samuel following his failure to fulfill the prophetic conditions of the royal mission. Alsheikh begins his protocol for the Sabbath afternoon sermon by listing, again uninterruptedly, twenty-six questions, difficulties, or objections relating to the apparent stylistic peculiarities of the text and to their substantive implications for understanding the narrative as a whole, as well as the behavior of its actors.

The following excerpt contains the portions of Alsheikh's discussion that focus on Saul's decision to spare the king of the Amalekites and some of the Amalekite flocks. Scripture characteristically avoids explicit explanations for, or explicit statements of, the inner thoughts and conscious motivations of its characters.[27] Alsheikh is therefore responding, as many exegetes had done before him, to an apparent gap in the scriptural narrative. First, the questions:

. . . 9. He says, "Praised be you unto God" (verse 13). For the sake of what was this benediction made?

. . . 10. How did this relate to his statement, "I have fulfilled . . ." (verse 13)?

11. The logical possibilities are inescapable: If it seemed to him that he had

fulfilled [his charge], why did he feel compelled to say so explicitly? If it did not seem so, why did he lie with his opening words?

... 13. What is the force of this answer: "... they brought them from the Amalekites" (verse 15)? Did not Samuel know that they brought them from the Amalekites? This was, after all, the essence of his complaint—Why did they bring them from the Amalekites, rather than killing them in their place?

... 19. Concerning his reply—"I have obeyed the voice of the Lord" (verse 20), how could his heart have found it agreeable to say so? Did he not sense the tangible evidence? Agag and the flocks stood before his eyes. Furthermore, he made things all the more severe when he said, "I have gone on the path that God sent me, and I have brought Agag, king of the Amalekites, [back alive] ... and the people took ..." (verses 20–21). How can it be that he went on the path God sent him seeing as he brought Agag back alive, and the "people took" without his denigrating them?

... 22. Concerning his statement—"I have sinned, for I have trespassed against the word of God, as well as your words" (verse 24), are not his words identical to the words of God?[28]

Alsheikh prefaces his answers to each of these questions by advancing two assumptions. The first is based on the splitting of verse 3 into two parts: The phrase "Go and smite Amalek and utterly destroy (*ḥerem*) all that they have, do not spare them" was understood by Saul, according to Alsheikh, to be the direct, verbatim command issued by God: "Kill both man and woman, infant and suckling, ox and sheep, camel and ass" was understood by Saul to be Samuel's own addition to the divine charge. Alsheikh justifies Saul's parsing of the command by appealing to the ambiguity inherent in the word *ḥerem*. "It is possible to construe it to mean either physical destruction and annihilation or consecrating something for God by setting it aside. Samuel took the former interpretation, as indicated by his statement 'Kill ... ox and sheep, camel and ass,' whereas Saul applied it to two categories of property, some of the flocks he totally destroyed, others he consecrated unto God."[29]

Alsheikh's second assumption about Saul's thought processes direct the reader's

attention to what was subsequently recorded. It reads "from the Amalekites (*me-ʿAmaleqi*) they brought," not "from the Amalekite" (*me-ʿAmeleq*). The explanation: He [Saul] interpreted the statement of God, may He be blessed, to be referring to the nation called Amalek. The king, however, is called either the king of Amalek or the Amalekite (*ʿAmaleqi*), using the singular form, as if to imply that the king of Amalek is not to be subsumed under the general category of the Amalekites.[30]

Armed with these two ingenious considerations, Alsheikh then proceeds to answer each of the initial questions. His reply to the questions is couched in the form of an expansive reconstruction of Saul's speech and Samuel's retort:

Before Samuel could speak to him, he opened the conversation by saying "Praised be you unto the Lord," i.e., because of the way you construed what God, may He be blessed, said—"Put to *ḥerem* all that they have," taking it to mean to put them all to death, you are to be praised unto God. You were stringent in your pious zeal for God's glory against his enemies. As for me, I did not destroy beyond the minimum limit required. I merely fulfilled the word of God. . . .

Then Samuel replied: "What then is the sound of the sheep and the sound of the cattle" (verse 14)?

He [Saul] gave him two explanations. The first, "From *the* Amalekite (*me-ʿAmaleqi*) they brought them," he is the king who is not to be subsumed under the general category of the Amalekites. This is in accordance with what we have written that the Amalekites are one thing and the king of Amalek another thing. He is called "*the* Amalekite," using a singular form. This is the meaning of "from the Amalekite they brought them." Now just as the king is not subsumed under the general category of Amalekites, so too the command of *ḥerem* does not pertain to the cattle of *the* Amalekite. Furthermore, [Saul continued], if the cattle did belong to someone other than the king, there is another explanation; namely, the people of the sheep in order to sacrifice them unto God. . . . All in all, we followed the two different significations attached to the word *ḥerem*.[31]

Here again we are less interested in charting the commentator's obvious debt to the store of pre-sixteenth-century Jewish exegesis than we are in appreciating the art of his literary criticism. Although Alsheikh avoided the philosophic allegorizing favored by Karo, both shared a common propensity for rendering the simple into the complex. Both structured their homilies with an initial, relentless questioning and followed it with a series of answers that heighten the syntactic, thematic, and linguistic unity of the passage as a whole. Both were devoted to the process of rigorous intellectual inquiry into the subtle dimensions of biblical style. Both were keenly attuned to the nuances of language, and both appeared to delight in discovering implications and ramifications easily overlooked by the casual reader.

The presuppositions which triggered Alsheikh's questions and resolutions stem from an a priori notion that biblical characters conduct themselves as dialecticians who govern their affairs in the cold light of deliberate thinking and logical procedures. Biblical characters—and the commentators who study them—operate like lawyers or textual critics who scrutinize and evaluate contracts, documents, or testimony with a relentless devotion to the telling detail. Scripture is therefore to be read with the expectation that it faithfully records the subtle deliberations of its speakers. The commentator inducts his audience into the marvelous intricacies of biblical logic by exposing and imitating the dialectical precision of biblical discourse. Alsheikh's audience was not startled by the discovery that biblical style imitated Talmudic modes of textual and logical criticism; they were accustomed to, and admired, the challenges and nuances of rabbinic dialectics. It was Alsheikh's achievement, under the influence of Rabbi Yoseph Taitazak, to perfect a technique that allowed the Bible to be seen as an extension of, or better, as the paradigmatic model for, Talmudic literature.[32]

Alsheikh's thirteenth question was triggered by the transference of a rabbinic procedure to 1 Samuel 15:15. Saul is charged with making an obvious, unnecessary, superfluous assertion. This is a familiar strategy in Amoraic discussions of Tannaitic literature, where a stringent economy of expression is considered to be a prized virtue of intelligent style. Talmudic rhetoric demands that every word or phrase bear a specific and distinct meaning. When the reader discovers an obvious or superfluous statement, he is alerted to the need for discovering the rationale that would justify the apparent waste of words. Verse 15 became salient to Alsheikh because of its superficial excessiveness. In his attempt to explain Saul's apparent disregard for the canons governing rational discourse, Alsheikh was forced to find some way of defending Saul himself and, simultaneously, unpacking the apparent simplicity and difficulty of the biblical narrative.

To perform this kind of *explication de texte,* the commentator must combine considerable learning with intuition and critical acumen. His art requires him to possess a highly developed capacity for empathetic intimacy, for he must be able to identify with the entire range of characters—saint and sinner, hero and enemy—that populate biblical literature. For Alsheikh and his audience, Scripture conformed to a style that tantalized its readers intentionally. Receptiveness and the ability to conjure up satisfying, appropriate responses required a well-disciplined imagination.

Imagination was controlled, and creatively stimulated, by the commentator's overriding concern for the larger context and the precise analysis of individual words and phrases in their sequential appearance within the context that endows particular words with their meaning. Alsheikh's hypothesis and reconstructions were grounded at every turn in the precise and exacting language employed by Samuel and Saul. Alsheikh's method, like Karo's, was based on the view that nothing in Scripture is adventitious, casual, or superfluous. Scripture lacks mere embellishment or rhetorical flourish; its speakers disdain such niceties.

Both commentators assumed that their audiences knew the simple, exoteric meaning. In their own ways, each of them sought to make the Bible more familiar and realistic by showing how it embodied the ideals of their respective communities. Karo demonstrated the Bible's high density of philosophic, scientific, and religious enlightenment and guidance. Alsheikh unraveled the keen machinations that motivate and serve human behavior. For both, the Bible was weighed as a book composed of cognitive language comprising sentences, paragraphs, and extended passages that referred to life as it was lived by actual human beings or to thoughts entertained by and about the world of ordinary, albeit enlightened, human experience.

V

To appreciate more fully this conception of the Bible and its systematically related set of hermeneutical techniques, and to complete this survey of sixteenth-century Jewish exegesis, it is necessary to describe, however briefly, a widespread and radically different approach to the art of interpretation that was employed by some contemporaries of Karo and Alsheikh. For all their ingenious allegorizing or rhetorical dialectics, Karo and Alsheikh allowed biblical language to remain intact. The text of the Bible was the given; only its deeper meaning required explanation. Its apparent simplicity needed to be penetrated, but the script being analyzed did not require alteration. The message of the Bible was rational, and the unit of inquiry was the unity of rational discourse—intelligible words, sentences, sections, and chapters.

In this other method scriptural language was not to be taken for granted but instead deciphered. Both its text and its meaning were subjected to a radical transformation. The Bible could not be read until it was first decoded. Surface meanings and their implications, however profound, were to be eclipsed—transcended by the numinous power emanating from the very substance of the text itself. Scripture became a sacred cryptograph whose language was not to be read as a series of concealed references to the ordinary world of human experience, but instead rearranged to reveal a network of occult symbols pulsing with the dynamics of divinity itself.[33] This phase of sixteenth-century exegesis, so radically different from the school represented by Karo or Alsheikh, may best be described as the transcognitive trend in Jewish hermeneutics.

A convenient review of the methods and theory comprising this mystically inspired, transcognitive trend is to be found in sections 27–30 of Rabbi Moses Cordovero's systematic treatise entitled *Pardes Rimmonim* (Paradise of pomegranates). Cordovero, a contemporary of Alsheikh in Safed, is correctly numbered among the most important and influential kabbalists of the Jewish mystical tradition.[34] His orderly and comprehensive treatment of pre-Lurianic Kabbalah provides a reliable source of information for this brief glimpse into the transcognitive trend in Jewish exegesis that atomizes the biblical text.

Section 27 discusses the mystical significance embedded in the shape of the letters of the Hebrew alphabet; 28 treats the mystical significance of the Hebrew vowels; and 29 reviews the mystical significance of the Masoretic system of tropes and punctuation. Section 30 is subdivided into four sections dealing with the various techniques of permutation (*Ẓeruf*), in which the letters of the biblical text are rearranged; substitution (*Temurah*), in which the actual letters of the text are converted into other letters according to diverse systems for encoding the alphabet; *gematria,* in which the actual letters or their substitutes are converted into numerical values that lead to hidden equivalences in accordance with a broad choice of methods; and *notariqon,* in which the actual letters of words or phrases are lifted out of position in order to create new words or acronyms.[35]

In his introduction to section 30 Cordovero explains that

knowledge of the secrets (*sodoth*) of our sacred Torah is acquired by means of permutations, numerical equivalences, substitution alphabets, initial letters of words, final letters, and medial letters, beginnings of verses and endings of verses, skipping of letters, and rearrangements.

These matters are sublime and recondite, their theosophical references (*sodam*) are indeed sublime. We lack the capacity to grasp them due to the magnitude of their hiddenness, for they vary by means of these methods infinitely, without end. For this reason it is written: "Its measure is greater than the earth" (Job 11:9).[36]

Cordovero spells out the theory underlying these methods in the remarks that precede the section dealing with letters. He polemicizes against the view that considers the letters of the Bible to resemble the ordinary, conventional signs arbitrarily chosen to represent oral speech or mathematical entities. The Torah, according to Cordovero, is categorically unlike a text written by a physician, for the medical text itself is not a therapeutic tool but is intended solely to convey the science of medicine. Once the student has mastered the content of the medical text, he can, unlike the text of the Torah, dispense with it. Cordovero disagrees with those who believe that the true intention of Scripture is the revealing of its inner meaning, its guidance to the perfection of the soul, so that one who fails to learn its teachings derives no benefit at all from studying it. Cordovero insists that even a mechanical reading of Scripture without understanding its hidden truths is valuable as long as the one reciting the text is aware that such hidden truths are indeed to be found by those wise enough to comprehend them.

Cordovero defends his point of view about the sacred status of the Bible itself by citing a key text from the Zohar:

Rabbi Simeon said: If a man looks upon the Torah as merely a book presenting narratives and everyday matters, alas for him! Such a torah, one treating with everyday concerns, and indeed a more excellent one, we too, even we could compile. More than that, in the possession of the rulers of the world there are books of even greater merit, and these we could emulate if we wished to compile some such torah. But the Torah, in all of its words, holds supernal truths and sublime secrets.[37]

Cordovero "concludes from this passage that the Torah may be seen in four different ways, and that within each and every one of these four ways there are thousands upon thousands upon countless thousands of aspects."[38]

The first way, or lowest category, of reading Scripture corresponds to perceiving the Torah's "garment," or its narrative. Sheer recitation of Torah accompanied by an awareness that it alludes to theosophical truths even without knowledge of the exact mysteries is praiseworthy. The second way, and next level up, corresponds to perceiving the Torah's "body." This entails an understanding of the simple meaning (*peshat*), i.e., the laws, the midrashic interpretations, the reasons for the commandments, the comments of the legal codifiers, and the six orders of the Mishnah.

The third way, and next level up, corresponds to perceiving the Torah's "soul." This is the category of those who occupy themselves with the Kabbalah, the mystical tradition and secrets discussed in the Zohar. It includes those who contribute their own additions to the realm of theosophical speculation.

The fourth way, and the highest possible category, corresponds to the "soul-within-the-soul" of Torah. This way of reading Scripture includes insight into the spirituality of the letters, their existence, their combinations with one another, and their occult interrelationships. "He who penetrates to the true depth in this matter can create worlds."[39]

Intelligibility is no longer the norm that determines the content of Scripture or the semantic unit to be addressed by the exegete. The Kabbalah would concur with Karo and Alsheikh, himself a devotee of mystical learning, that the Bible is no mere literature. It would also agree that the Bible has an exoteric, superficial meaning and an esoteric, interior meaning that pulsates in the deep structure of the text itself. Mystics and philosophers would also agree that the ultimate reference of biblical language points to God. But where philosophers understand biblical allusions to mean statements about God, and therefore to be in the form of rational assertions subject to the canons of intelligible discourse, the transcognitive mystics interpret biblical allusions as constituting the hierarchical unfolding of God himself, and therefore transcend the limitations of ordinary language. The products of transcognitive manipulations of the text are often unintelligible combinations of letters and ciphers. The ineffability of the divine ultimately requires a language that mysteriously turns back on itself, canceling itself out in order to express what defies utterance.

With this approach to the interpretation of Scripture, premised on the ontological identity of God and Torah and therefore requiring a set of techniques capable of effacing the lower levels of rational discourse that have their ultimate source in the translogical, neoplatonically colored realm of pure, undifferentiated being, sixteenth-century exegesis shades off into meditation techniques for inducing mystical ecstasy or theurgic techniques for magical praxis.[40] Dreams and wakened states of experience require different canons of interpretation.[41] It has been the purpose of this essay to show how sixteenth-century Jewish exegesis applied this hermeneutical truism to the reading of Scripture, and thereby created the artful diversity of its exegetical writings.

RICHARD A. MULLER

The Hermeneutic of Promise and Fulfillment in Calvin's Exegesis of the Old Testament Prophecies of the Kingdom

In his study of Calvin's New Testament commentaries, T. H. L. Parker observes that Calvin was well acquainted with the several patterns of interpretation available to him in the early sixteenth century: the double-literal pattern of Nicholas of Lyra, the literal-prophetic model of Faber Stapulensis, the emphasis of Erasmus—not without a sense of allegory—on the mastery of philological tools, and the doctrinal mode of exposition followed by Bucer, Bullinger, and Melanchthon.[1] To this catena of exegetical models we may add the exegesis of Luther and Oecolampadius: both wrote extensively on the prophets, and Oecolampadius in particular was esteemed by Calvin as an exegete.[2] Parker argues the distinction between Calvin's method and the other extant models: Calvin stressed the mind of the historical writers of Scripture and not, as Faber did, the *mens Spiritus sancti;*[3] Calvin was separated "decisively from Erasmus" by his concern for the historical in Scripture, and from Lyra and all those who retained some elements of allegory by his attention to the "simple," grammatical sense of the text. Nor did Calvin adopt the dogmatic method of exposition followed by Bucer, Bullinger, and Melanchthon.[4] Parker's conclusions stand in agreement with those of Clavier,[5] Kraus,[6] Visher,[7] and Girardin.[8]

Of this group of scholars, Kraus provides the clearest summary of Calvin's exegetical method and the most convenient point of departure for our present inquiry. He elaborates eight exegetical principles: (1) clarity and brevity, (2) seeking to determine the intention of the author, (3) interest in the original historical context of the passage, (4) establishment of the simple grammatical meaning, (5) understanding the passage in its context, (6) exposition beyond the biblical wording according to the author's intention, (7) attention to figures of speech, and (8) recognition of "the scope of Christ" as the center from which all of Scripture derives meaning.[9] Kraus notes one other characteristic, though not as an exegetical principle: "Contemporary applications to the life of the church arose out of kerygmatic analogies which made a direct impression on the exegete and were not brought in as 'interpretations' or 'speculations.'"[10]

With the significant exception of an essay by Henri Strohl on the exegetical methods of the Reformers, in which similarities between Calvin's method and late medieval exegesis are argued,[11] Kraus's view appears to express a general consensus. There are, however, a series of pressing reasons to dissent, along with Strohl, from the consensus. With the exception of "clarity and brevity" which distinguishes Calvin from prolix interpreters of Holy Writ in all ages, not a single principle noted here separates Calvin definitively from the medieval exegete. Lubac,[12] Smalley,[13] and Preus[14] have documented the interest of medieval exegetes in such matters as the intentions of the Scriptures' authors, the original historical context of the passage, the simple grammatical meaning (theologia symbolica non est argumentativa!), the literary context of the passage, and the figures of speech utilized in the text.[15] The remaining two characteristics—exposition "beyond the biblical wording" and recognition of the "scope of Christ"—together with Calvin's recourse to kerygmatic analogies place us within the world of the medieval exegete and cause the greatest problem for the interpretation of Calvin as a harbinger of critical exegesis. Kraus comments that Calvin, "for all his significant and effective approaches, was yet bound by a mindset that was oriented to the unity and inner harmony of scripture."[16] Most of the principles cited by Kraus and the others come, moreover, either from Calvin's famous letter to Grynaeus at the beginning of the commentary on Romans or from the *Institutes,* so that the principles themselves, as enunciated, do not emerge from Calvin's encounter with the text and do not necessarily represent his working hermeneutic. Finally, I submit that any discussion of Calvin's exegetical principles that tends to distinguish the "critical" principles with which Calvin adumbrates modern exegesis from the few embarrassing "precritical" principles remaining in Calvin's method has missed the crucial historical question of how all of Calvin's exegetical and hermeneutical principles came to belong to one fairly consistent whole.

THE HERMENEUTIC OF PROMISE AND FULFILLMENT

The Old Testament prophecies of the kingdom provide an ideal subject for an analysis of Calvin's hermeneutic because, unlike texts drawn from the New Testament, or comments on exegesis drawn from a dogmatic source like the *Institutes,* they both manifest the working hermeneutic of the exegete and press, more pointedly than any other class of texts, the problems of literal meaning, future referent, and ultimate intended implication of a text. Calvin's exegesis of passages which refer to an impending "day of the Lord" on which the righteous will be vindicated and the wicked punished is particularly instructive: Calvin seldom refers these texts directly to the eschaton. Frequently he argues that "the day of the Lord" or "that day" are references to a time of judgment chosen by God within the ancient history of Israel.[17] Nor does Calvin single out these phrases as technical terms.[18] More important, in instances where the prophecy as a whole demands an eschatological reading, Calvin has recourse to a pattern of promise and fulfillment. Commenting on Amos 9:11, "In that day I will raise up the tabernacle of David that is fallen," Calvin argues that the text, as a word of consolation and hope, refers to the Messiah. Specifically the text refers to the reunion of the dispersed Israel: all the "scattered members" will be united "under one head," which is to say under the Messiah in whom all the promises of God are fulfilled.[19]

The ultimate reference to the end time is not lost to Calvin, but he sees it as an indirect or mediated reference. The reference of Amos 9:11 to the restitution of Israel and to the "restoration of royal dignity . . . to the throne of David" indicates primarily the First Coming of Christ.[20] The promises of the Old Testament find their fulfillment in the New Testament and in the establishment of Christ's kingdom. Yet it is precisely in this establishment of the kingdom that the indirect or mediated reference to the eschaton occurs: the text of Amos notes the triumph of the kingdom, whereas the kingdom, both in the First Coming of Christ and in its present continuation, lies under siege. The "already" and the "not yet" of the fulfillment work to extend the meaning of the prophecy over the entire length of Christ's kingdom toward the final consummation, when the result of his First Coming will be fully manifest.[21]

Calvin's reading of Daniel follows a similar pattern. The prevalent view of Daniel in Calvin's time was an antipapal, or presentist, reading which identified the empires of Daniel's prophecies with empires and kingdoms of the West after the time of Christ and interpreted the "little horn" of Daniel 7:8 as Antichrist, and usually as the papacy. Bullinger,[22] Oecolampadius,[23] and Luther[24] held variants of this position. The other option of the day was to consider the penultimate events described by Daniel—the "little horn" and the "fifth monarchy"—to be still in the future: thus the radical Reformation.[25] Calvin, as distinct from these positions, understood all the events of Daniel's prophecy as fulfilled either prior to the time of Christ or shortly thereafter as results of Christ's coming—any other view would distort the text.[26] The controlling factor in the interpretation, here as in the interpretation of references to the "day of the Lord," is the structure of promise and fulfillment.

HISTORICAL SITUATION AND KERYGMATIC ANALOGY

The strict promise/fulfillment model, in which the Old Testament is fulfilled in the New Testament, coupled with the idea of an extended meaning of the text which encompasses the entire kingdom of God, provided Calvin with a structure of interpretation within which both a grammatical-historical reading of the text and a strong drive toward contemporary application can function. This structure is particularly apparent in Calvin's commentary on the book of Joel. In his preface to the prophecy Calvin notes several tentative dates for the book, with the comment that all are conjecture and that the exact date is "obscure and uncertain."[27] It is evident, however, that Joel's mission is to Judah and that the ten tribes of Israel do not figure in his message. The threat of invasion is directed entirely against Judah, and it is clear that the enemy is Assyria. The prophecy, according to Calvin, points to the divine use of Assyria as an instrument of chastisement and then to the subsequent destruction of the Assyrians themselves. In its main outlines the fulfillment of Joel's prophecies occurs within the bounds of the Old Testament. Judah can seek her hope beyond the Assyrian threat.[28]

Joel 2:30–32 provides Calvin with an ideal opportunity to show the relation of the text, historically interpreted, to the New Testament fulfillment of Old Testament prophecy and, with the fulfillment as a logical pivot, to the present-day life of the church. Joel's prophecy of terrible portents prior to the day of the Lord seems to contradict his previous prophecy of the deliverance of Israel. Calvin notes that there is no real contradiction: God promises "tokens of kindness" but "mingles" them with "exercises for patience" lest the faithful look to the promises as an excuse for "self-indulgence" and fail to "seek higher things."[29] "We now understand the prophet's design," concludes Calvin, "he intends not to threaten the faithful but rather to warn them, lest they should deceive themselves with empty dreams, or expect what is never to be, that is, to enjoy a happy rest in this world."[30] Earlier (verse 28), Calvin had argued a direct prophetic reference to Christ;[31] the present passage, he now argues, is similar to Christ's discourse in Matthew 28 concerning the destruction of the temple as a sign of the Second Coming. The disciples, like the Jews of old, expected an immediate triumph over the world and a dawn of "eternal beatitude." This, Christ announces, is not to be: history does not move toward a better age of the world but rather moves from evil to evil with hardly a sign of the grace of God. Only after much tribulation will the kingdom appear.[32]

Calvin has now established two pivotal points for his analysis of the text: first, the bearing of the original context upon the interpretation, and, second, the relation of the logic or dynamic in the text to the fulfillment in the New Testament. The promise points beyond all the temporal disasters of ancient Israel to her Messiah; but the Messiah himself, in the establishment of his kingdom, teaches of further earthly troubles in similar words of warning and hope.[33] To borrow Kraus's term, Calvin has seen a "kerygmatic analogy" between the words of the prophet and the prophetic words of Christ, and therefore between God's promise to ancient Israel concerning her hope in the Messiah and the Messiah's own promise to his church concerning its future hope in him.[34] Careful attention to the literal meaning and to the original context, far from being adumbrations of critical method which distance Calvin from the preceding exegetical tradition, now become manifest as tools for drawing out the meaning of the text for the present life of the kingdom—and in addition, the "kerygmatic analogy" appears as a crucial (ninth) element in the list of Calvin's exegetical principles. Furthermore, even though Calvin can maintain, strictly speaking, that he has delineated but one literal and grammatical meaning of the text, the exegetical interest presented in his remarks has not deviated very far from allegory and trope.

Calvin's correlation of historical situations by means of kerygmatic analogy can be reduced, moreover, to a distinct hermeneutical principle. Calvin enunciates it here (Joel 2:30–31) in terms of the tribulations following the vindication of God's people, but he makes very clear the point that this is a general principle and not just a statement regarding one text:

> . . . *the day of Jehovah, great and terrible.* It may be asked what day the Prophet refers to: for he has hitherto spoken of the first coming of Christ; and there seems to be some inconsistency in this place. I answer, that the Prophet includes the whole kingdom of Christ, from the beginning to the end; and this is well understood, and in other places we have commonly stated that the Prophets speak in this manner: for when the discourse is concerning Christ's kingdom, they sometimes refer to its commencement only, and sometimes they speak of its termination. But they often designate with one connection in discourse [*uno complexu designat*] the whole course of the kingdom of Christ [*totum cursum regni Christi*], from its beginning to its end; and such is the case here.[35]

As used here by Calvin, *complexus* is a technical term in rhetoric, indicating a connection in discourse as important to the meaning of a text as the grammatical *sensus.* Calvin surely knew the critique from Quintillian, "vitium non est in sensu, sed in complexu," and the distinction between finite and infinite issues—the infinite being universal or philosophical questions and the finite being "ex complexu rerum, personarum, temporum ceterorumque."[36] As Breen pointed out, Calvin was steeped in Quintillian and used the *Institutionis oratoriae* as a constant reference aid.[37] Calvin will not move from the grammatical and historical *sensus* to an allegorical *sensus,* but he will develop the *complexus* of ideas presented in a text to cover an extended meaning virtually identical in content to that covered by allegory or trope but more closely governed by the grammatical and historical *sensus* of the text. As Calvin argues in the dedicatory letter to his Daniel commentary, "the similarity of the times [*temporum similitudo*] adapts these [predictions] to us and fits them to our use."[38]

This "similarity of the times," or analogy of historical situations in *complexus,* enables Calvin to argue, in the context of the next several verses of his comment on Joel (3:1–3), against exegetical restriction of the reference of the prophecy to a single temporal fulfillment to the exclusion of a broader eschatological meaning:

But the Prophet says, *In those days, and at that time, when the Lord shall restore the captivity of Judah and Jerusalem.* This "time" the Jews limit to their return: they therefore think, that when liberty to return was granted them by Cyrus and Darius, what the prophet here teaches was then completed. Christian teachers interpret this prophecy of the coming of Christ. But both distort the words of the Prophet into something other than what was demanded by the context of the passage [*quam postulet circumstantia loci*]. The Prophet doubtless speaks here of that redemption of which we have spoken: but nevertheless has at the same time included [*complexus simul fuerit*] the kingdom of Christ. And this, as we have seen elsewhere, is common. When therefore the prophets testify that God would be the redeemer of his people, and promise deliverance from the Babylonian exile, they lead the faithful as by a continuous treatment or uninterrupted course to the kingdom of Christ. For what else was that restoration than a prelude to that true and real redemption which was truly exhibited in the person of Christ?[39]

Similarly, in his comment on Isaiah 65:17, "For lo, I will create a new heavens and a new earth," Calvin first notes the hyperbole of the text in its grammatical and historical *sensus:* the implication is not a new physical creation, because the prophet speaks specifically of the "restoration of the church after the return from Babylon." Yet the hyperbole is not unwarranted, because the text ultimately refers to the "blessing" of Christ and to his "whole reign" from the First to the Second Coming.[40] The comment on Isaiah 26:19, "Thy dead men shall live," argues both against a "Jewish" reading, which restricts the meaning of the text to the First Coming of the Messiah, and against Christian interpretations that refer the text exclusively to the Second Coming.[41] The dead men who live are believers not only in view of the final Resurrection but in view of the spiritual character of their lives as contrasted with the lives of the reprobate.[42] As in the commentaries on Joel and Daniel, Calvin sees the key to a broadened interpretation of the promise not so much in *sensus* as in *complexus,* in the historical course of the kingdom and in the kerygmatic analogy between the past and the present of God's people: The prophet addresses the "lamentable state" of God's ancient people with a word of hope, just as now believers "obtain life in the midst of afflictions" from this same text and look toward full consolation in the last day.[43]

Always avoiding the language of allegory, Calvin sometimes speaks of the extended meaning of a text beyond its original context as a synecdoche, a figure of speech—like *complexus,* a technical term borrowed from rhetoric—indicating inclusive or extended implication and usually the signification of a larger whole by the naming of a part. For example, when Malachi speaks of the purification of the "sons of Levi," he speaks directly to his time of the restoration of true worship, but insofar as the sons of Levi are the "first fruit" of God's redeeming work, the part ought to be taken for the whole: "the promise belongs to the whole church."[44] By finding a synecdoche in the text, Calvin can argue literally and grammatically, in terms of rhetorical structure, that the text refers both to an immediate fulfillment in the reforms of Ezra and Nehemiah and to the coming of Christ "into his temple," and beyond that, to the reforming of the church in Calvin's own time.[45] On Malachi 3:5, "And I will come near to you in judgment," Calvin writes, "as there are like blasphemies prevailing in the world at this day, this passage may be accommodated to our circumstances."[46]

The pattern of Old Testament fulfillment, New Testament fulfillment, and present fulfillment evident in Malachi appears on a more elaborate scale in Calvin's commentary on Zechariah 3:1–5. He begins by analyzing the meaning of the prophet's address to the exiles of Judah only recently returned to the land. They are despondent over the appearance of the temple and the priesthood in comparison to the glory of Jerusalem before the exile: "The Prophet then bids the faithful to be of good cheer, though the appearance of the priesthood was vile and mean, because God would not overlook its contemptible state; but the time of restoration had not yet come; when it came, the ancient dignity of the priesthood would again appear."[47] Though thus rooted in the postexilic period, the reference of the prophecy extends also to the priesthood of Christ: "And though this vision was given to the Prophet for the use of his own times, yet it doubtless also pertains to us; for that shadow-priesthood [*sacerdotium illud umbratile*] was an image of the priesthood of Christ, and Joshua, who was then returned from exile, bore the character [*personam*] of Christ the Son of God."[48] The way in which the prophecy relates "to us" rests here on the "similarity of the times" and the suitability of the prophetic word as an example for the present:

> We ought first to contemplate the zeal and godly concern of the Prophet, which he had for the glory and honor of the priesthood. . . . And this example is exhibited to us for imitation, so that we ought to desire the increase of those favors of God by which the priesthood of Christ is signified [*insignitur*], until it arrives at the most perfect state. But we see that many are against such a wish; since today there are those who profess enthusiasm for sincere piety, but are satisfied with a mere shadow [*umbra aliqua*]; or at least it would abundantly satisfy them to see the church purified only in part. . . . But the prophet calls us [*nos propheta vocat*] to do something very different.[49]

Here Calvin has clearly moved out of the merely rhetorical categories into the realm of typology. Significantly, the signs or shadows do not merely point forward, along the line of historical promise and fulfillment from the Old Testament to Christ, but also backward from the promise in the present to Christ, and, resting on him, to a future fulfillment. This dynamic, moreover, raises the *exemplum* to a level of direct relation or address: The prophet, writes Calvin, "calls us." The idea of direct address appears throughout the next several verses.[50]

PROMISE, FULFILLMENT, AND THE CHRISTOLOGICAL CENTER

Kraus, it must be admitted, has come very close in places to a full sense of Calvin's mode of interpretation. On two occasions he cites Calvin's exegetical and hermeneutical caveat prefaced to the comment on Psalm 72:1.[51] Kraus notes this comment as an example of "the scope of Christ" as exegetical principle: The Old Testament "looks to the future for the fulfillment of promises and prophesies" in such a way that Christ, as fulfillment, focuses and unifies the whole of Scripture.[52] And Kraus sees this sense of unity as something lost, hopefully not irretrievably, to the modern exegete.[53] He also cites the passage as an example of Calvin's emphasis on the real, simple, or grammatical meaning of the text and quotes the observation, "We must always beware of giving the Jews occasion of making an outcry, as if it were our purpose, sophistically, to apply to Christ those things which do not directly refer to him."[54] The question that Kraus fails to ask is how these seemingly divergent exegetical tendencies relate to one another in the interpretation of the psalm.

Calvin's complaint against excessively christological interpretation ought probably to be seen against the background of the famous psalm commentary of Faber Stapulensis where, in the name of a single, literal meaning, Christ is taken to be the sole reference of the text, and David disappears entirely as a focus of meaning.[55] Calvin's caveat is not an objection to a christological promise-fulfillment hermeneutic but a demand that the historical figure of David be allowed its rightful place in the scheme of promise and fulfillment and that the literal meaning of the text be lodged in the promise as first given to the historical David. Literal meaning—exacting analysis of original context—becomes the pivot upon which the larger, still literal, meaning of the text may be built. David himself recognized, according to Calvin, that "the terms upon which he and his posterity possessed the kingdom" pointed directly to Christ, and that "the temporal well-being of the people" was a "type or shadow" of the everlasting spiritual kingdom to be established in Christ.[56] "What is here spoken of everlasting dominion cannot be limited to one man, or to a few, nor even to twenty ages; but there is pointed out the succession which had its end and its complete accomplishment in Christ."[57]

Thus the text "and he chose David his servant" (Psalm 78:70) refers literally to David, the "peasant," who was "taken from his mean shepherd's cot, and exalted to the dignity of a king."[58] In David the kingdom is clearly seen to rest on grace alone. Even so, by extension the passage refers to the fulfillment of the kingdom in Christ, whose origins were also "lowly and contemptible."[59] Calvin's hermeneutic of promise and fulfillment might thus equally well be called a hermeneutic of multiple fulfillment: The text applies to David himself, who fulfills the will and promise of God, albeit in a limited way; but it also applies, quite frequently, to David's immediate heirs, especially to Solomon; and finally it points to Christ, who is the highest fulfillment of the prophecy.[60] The literal meaning of the text is the historical succession of the promise as it moves toward its highest fulfillment: Calvin's interest in the "scope" of Scripture therefore breathes the same air as his emphasis on the literal sense of the text.[61]

The pattern of fulfillment, moreover, constantly refers to the literal reading of the text—the pattern of the kingdom presented in the original form of the promise. Thus in the commentary on Psalm 2 we learn that even as David's ancient kingdom was a pledge of the eternal kingdom, so do the declarations of David concerning his own condition function literally (Calvin specifically denies any allegory at this point) as predictions of Christ.[62] David's complaint in the psalm over the grand conspiracy of nations against his kingdom refers both to the wars of ancient Israel and to the enmity of all nations against Christ's kingdom.[63] Not only the fulfillment of the psalm in Christ but the literal applicability of David's complaint to the kingdom of Christ is manifest in the apostles' use of the psalm in prayer as a description of their own situation (Acts 4:25–27).[64] Since the highest fulfillment of the kingdom in Christ so mirrors the trials of the first fulfillment in David,

> a twofold consolation may be drawn from this passage: First, as often as the world rages, in order to disturb and put an end to the prosperity of Christ's kingdom, we have only to remember that, in all this, there is just a fulfillment of what was long ago predicted. . . . The other consolation . . . is . . . when we see Christ well nigh overwhelmed with the number and strength of his enemies, let us remember that they are making war against God over whom they shall not prevail, and therefore their attempts . . . will come to nought.[65]

According to this hermeneutic, the fulfillment of Old Testament prophecy does not occur in a rigidly prescribed pattern of events.[66] Christ provides in his first advent the logical as well as historical terminus of the meaning of prophecy: His Second Coming does not add new substance to his earthly work. Old Testament references to the "last day," the "day of the Lord," and the "restoration of Israel" can, in the preexilic prophets, refer to the return of Israel from Babylon, to the coming of Christ and the new age inaugurated by him and, by extension, to the life of the present-day church. In the prophets of the restored Israel—Haggai, Zechariah, Malachi—where prophecy of a future kingdom can no longer indicate the historical reestablishment of Israel, the text is referred to Christ and his kingdom and, through Christ, points to the age of the church and the Second Coming.[67] This general paradigm applies also to a preexilic prophet like Hosea, who prophesied to Ephraim rather than to Judah: The loss of the entire northern kingdom directs promises of restoration to the kingdom of the Messiah without an intervening ancient fulfillment.

This paradigm, we might add, applies equally well to the analysis of Calvin's New Testament commentaries: Since the New Testament records the establishment of the messianic kingdom, of which the present age of the church is a part, it points more directly to the present and to the end time than does the Old Testament. The letter of the New Testament does not function so obviously in terms of promise and fulfillment, because it is the fulfillment and, in its literal *sensus,* the rule for interpreting the direction of Old Testament prophecy.

SOME COMPARISONS

The pattern of interpretation that we have loosely termed a hermeneutic of promise and fulfillment appears in the Old Testament commentaries of Calvin's major Protestant predecessors, with minor variations. Luther, like Calvin, roots the relation of the text of Joel to Christ by reason of the prophecy of the day of Pentecost (2:28), but he virtually exhausts the meaning of the text in the fulfillment, manifesting little interest in the original, historical context of the prophecy.[68] Nor does he view the terrifying portents as a problem for resolution, either logical or historical. The revelation of the gospel is itself "a day awesome and great," and the primary reference of the text, therefore, is to Christ.[69] The deliverance of which Joel speaks lacks, for Luther, the ultimate eschatological dimension found there by Calvin, insofar as Luther concentrates on the promised "kingdom of faith" created in the hearts of believers through the Word of God.[70] In the absence of any strong historical interest, the text yields itself more directly to allegory and trope than in Calvin's exegesis, but the underlying exegetical purpose is much the same—the meaning of the text for church and believer. Steinmetz's analysis of the interpretive dynamic of Luther's early lectures on Psalms applies here also: "The advent of Christ by grace is the point in time at which the literal-prophetic sense becomes the tropological sense."[71] The absence of historical emphasis also moves away from the kind of "kerygmatic analogy" we have seen in Calvin.

The commentaries of Oecolampadius are of particular importance, not only because they were valued by Calvin, but also because they were reissued in Geneva, under the editorship of Capito and Bullinger, in 1558, when Calvin was lecturing on the minor prophets, only a year prior to the appearance of Calvin's own lectures in print.[72] Oecolampadius tends less toward tropes than Luther, but he evidences no greater interest in the historical circumstances surrounding the text than does the Wittenberg Reformer. An avowed purpose of Oecolampadius's effort was the establishment of the literal meaning of the text over and against earlier allegorical readings; to this end he availed himself of the great rabbinic Bible printed by Bomberg in Venice in 1517–18.[73] But here, too, the hermeneutic of promise and fulfillment tends to crowd out the historical, with the result that Oecolampadius lodges the meaning of the text strictly in the fulfillment. In commenting on Joel 2:28–31, Oecolampadius recognizes no referent of the prophecy prior to the time of Christ.[74] The tumult and tribulation noted in the text refer to the destruction of Jerusalem—and are well documented, portents and all, in Josephus.[75] The seeming dialectic of promise and threat refers to the salvation of those who accepted Christ and the condemnation of those Jews who rejected their Messiah. Similarly, the comment on Isaiah 65:17 points directly to the coming reign of Christ, and not to an Old Testament restoration of Israel.[76]

A consistently greater historical interest, and therefore a more obvious similarity to Calvin's patterns of interpretation, appears in Melanchthon's commentaries on the prophets. Unfortunately, Melanchthon's preference for theological statements of the "argument" of biblical books or for *enarrationes* upon entire chapters rather than verse-by-verse comment renders extensive comparison impossible. In the case of Zechariah 3, where Calvin establishes a lengthy analogy of historical situations, Melanchthon simply points to Christ as the *summus sacerdos* typified by the high priest Joshua.[77] The central issue addressed by all the prophets, according to Melanchthon, is the call to repentance together with the repetition of the promise.[78] More than either Luther or Oecolampadius, Melanchthon argues the necessity of examining the history in the writings of the prophets and the consideration "in partibus historiae" of the church in all times. The history contains examples for the present which inspire fear of God and confirm our faith and hope.[79] Consideration of doctrine springs immediately from the dangers, the causes for punishment, and the redemptive moments recorded in the history.[80]

CONCLUSIONS

For all its deep interest in literal meaning and historical context, Calvin's exegetical method stands in an intellectual and theological continuity with earlier Reformation models and, through them, with some of the basic interests of medieval exegesis. The underlying structure of promise and fulfillment that gave a certain rigor of interpretation to the fourfold exegesis and to the double-literal and literal-prophetic models remained prominent in Calvin's thought, nor did he shun the typological thinking underlying the hermeneutic of promise and fulfillment. Where Calvin follows and develops the earlier Reformation models, he tends to look more closely at the primary literal meaning of the text as a means to overcome rampant allegory. His sense of history and of historical example may be viewed as a development of Melanchthon's emphases. None of the exegetes—Luther, Oecolampadius, Melanchthon, and Calvin—wanted to lose the flexibility of reference available to the allegorical method: The text must be allowed to speak to the church. Calvin's explicit use of rhetorical categories like synecdoche or *complexus* may in this context be seen as a shifting of the mode of analysis out of an allegorical or literal-spiritual mode (which postulated more than one *sensus* of a given text) to a rhetorical mode in which one *sensus* could nevertheless point toward multiple referents.

These considerations bring us back, at a slightly more sophisticated level, to our opening caveat: The wedge driven between Calvin and earlier exegesis and the bridge built between Calvin and modern "critical" method cannot be affirmed at the expense of the unity of Calvin's hermeneutic. Against Kraus, Parker, and the others who tend to read Calvin's exegesis as an adumbration of modern critical method but admire the theological content, the contemporary relevance of Calvin's conclusions, and, above all, the christocentric character of the promise/fulfillment motif, we note the interconnection of these various elements of Calvin's method and the use which Calvin's historical and grammatical interests serve. On the other hand, against Strohl, we must recognize that Calvin's method is not a return to medievalism after several decades of advance into the new age: Some elements of Calvin's method appear medieval because neither he nor his predecessors had moved exceptionally far from the late medieval models. Against both—Kraus, on the one side, and Strohl, on the other—we recognize the continuity in development of exegetical method from the late Middle Ages into the sixteenth century. Calvin's exegesis does represent a more textually, grammatically, and historically oriented hermeneutic, but it remains within the bounds of a hermeneutical approach in which the final implication of any text is determined by the broader context of promise, fulfillment, and the ongoing history of God's people.

R. GERALD HOBBS

Hebraica Veritas and *Traditio Apostolica*

Saint Paul and the Interpretation of the Psalms in the Sixteenth Century

I

The publication of Johannes Reuchlin's *De rudimentis Hebraicis* in 1506 marked a significant moment in the history of biblical exegesis.[1] The Swabian nobleman was not the first Christian to publish a Hebrew grammar for Latin readers: that honor, at least for northern Europe, belongs to the Alsatian Franciscan Konrad Pellican.[2] Nor was Reuchlin to contribute greatly to the corpus of exegetical literature; his sole venture into this field seems to have been his little primer on the seven penitential Psalms.[3] Yet it was Reuchlin's combined dictionary and grammar that gave access to the mysteries of the sacred tongue for that crucial first generation of humanist exegetes, in particular those north of the Alps. And although his work was superseded over the next two decades by the more comprehensive volumes of Sanctes Pagnini, Sebastian Münster, and others,[4] the publication of the *De rudimentis Hebraicis* is as appropriate a moment as any from which to date the new era of Christian Hebraist exegesis of the Bible.

In his preface to the third book Reuchlin evinces some awareness of the controversy his project will arouse. To those who would discount his efforts because he came to Hebrew only in mid-life, he reminds the reader that both Saint Jerome and Nicholas of Lyra had done the same. In a more serious vein, he anticipates the accusation that his studies may ultimately bring disrespect upon the memory of the sainted Fathers whose interpretations of Scripture are thereby called into question. What if, he asks, one does discover that both Jerome and

Lyra—the patron saints of Christian Hebraica—on occasion misunderstood the Scripture? Jerome himself demonstrated numerous errors made by the translators of the Septuagint, and was in turn reproached for like faults by Lyra. The latter's work drew vigorous criticism from Paul, bishop of Burgos. Indeed, Jerome went so far as to comment unfavorably upon the grammatical skills of the apostle Paul himself! "In these matters relating to the method of interpretation and the art of grammar as well as the truth of the idiom, why may I not set forth what I have gleaned from the most learned Hebrews—those very people to whom Jerome himself testifies that he had recourse whenever he was troubled by a question in the Old Testament. For though I venerate Saint Jerome as an angel and reverence Lyra as my teacher, I worship the truth as God."[5]

Within this sparkling defense of the freedom of academic inquiry one finds the anticipation of conflicts that would mark biblical interpretation in the sixteenth century. The truth venerated as the written words of Scripture would confront the truth of centuries-old traditions in the life of the church. The right of the individual interpreter would be set against the authoritative teaching of the community. Within the sphere of the Old Testament, assertion of the supremacy of the Hebrew original would encounter the vigorous defense of the Septuagint text tradition and thereby of the Vulgate. The consequences of this choice would pit advocates of interpretations drawn from rabbinic sources against defenders of the ancient traditions of patristic exegesis.[6]

A particular facet of that debate is the subject of this study: the problem created for exegetes of the Old Testament by the use made of these Scriptures by New Testament writers. If the evangelist Matthew, for example, in quoting from the Hebrew Scriptures, gives a textual reading or a sense that differs from that of the Hebrew original, how does a Christian resolve this discrepancy between inspired authorities?

The problem was not discovered in the sixteenth century, of course. Patristic interpreters had also noted the difficulty. In the preface quoted above, Reuchlin refers to Jerome's remarks on Paul's use of a portion of Psalm 14 in the Epistle to the Romans,[7] and he cites Jerome's disparagement of the apostle's ability to express himself well in Greek.[8] Nonetheless, the same Father speaks for the general tenor of patristic exegesis when he begins his commentary on Psalm 2: "It is audacious to want to interpret this psalm after Saint Peter has done so; indeed to think anything else concerning it save what Peter has said in the Acts of the Apostles."[9]

What was generally the stance of Jerome was even more true for Augustine, for whom the apostolic witness was invariably compelling. Thus these two fathers communicated to medieval exegesis a primacy of honor for the apostolic tradition that was faithfully reflected in the Gloss, and generations of interpreters followed their lead.

At the same time, Hebrew was held in high esteem throughout the Christian Middle Ages.[10] Saint Augustine himself, despite his preference for the Greek text of the Bible, shared the belief in the historic primacy of Hebrew, "the primitive language of the human race."[11] Many early medieval exegetes paid lip service to the *Hebraica veritas,* though most knew no Hebrew and drew their references to the Hebrew truth from the translations made by Jerome *iuxta Hebraicam veritatem.* It is one of the ironies of this history that Jerome's translations had themselves become the truth to which they were intended to point. In consequence a good part of what purports in medieval exegesis to be reference to the Hebrew turns out, upon closer examination, to be simple repetition of comments made by the Fathers, and in particular Jerome. To this observation we must make honorable exception of those who, like Lyra, Andrew of Saint Victor, and Herbert of Bosham, found the means of seeking the truth at its source.[12] We shall not understand the question we have set regarding exegesis in the sixteenth century unless we are conscious of the strength of both of the traditions to which our exegetes were heir.

Hebrew Scriptures were frequently quoted in the New Testament as authors demonstrated the links between the Christ event and the faith of Israel. For the purposes of this study I have confined myself to the use of the Psalms. The various compilations of these quotations disagree to some extent in detail, which is hardly surprising given the variety of styles of quotation, paraphrase, and allusion within the New Testament itself. I depend here upon the chart of sixty-three instances given in the tables of the Aland Greek New Testament.[13] From amongst these a selection was made of six questions that could have suggested themselves on the basis of apparent discrepancies between the Hebrew and the form of the quotation of the Old Testament in the

New. While this list is by no means exhaustive, it does illustrate the range of the problem that presented itself to the sixteenth-century exegete.

Another limit involves the choice of exegetes. These come generally from the period 1500–1560, with a few additions from the latter part of the century to permit some comparison with post-Tridentine exegesis.[14] I have been careful to include a variety of regions as well as of differing camps in the Reformation controversies. The level of the exegetes' Hebrew competence varied considerably. Finally, the study looked both at scholarly commentary and at biblical translation, and in the case of the latter, both at the popular genre of *paraphrasis* and at translations intended for ecclesiastical use (and therefore governed by stricter canons). This attempt to discover what effect, if any, the scholarly debates were having at the level of popular piety was complemented by the inclusion of works directly intended to serve the latter: English and French metrical Psalms, and English liturgical and paraliturgical texts.[15] In all, some forty-eight sources were examined; they are identified and coded for easy reference in the Appendix.

The limitations of the study will be apparent. There is obviously an element of the arbitrary in the selection of subjects as well as of sources. Certainly there are absences to be regretted. I feel most keenly the weakness of the radical tradition, notably the absence of Miguel Servetus; and the latter half of the century deserves wider representation.[16] Furthermore, this study has confined itself to considering the impact of conflicting authorities upon Psalms commentaries and translations. A parallel study of the corresponding New Testament scholarship would doubtless find much of interest.[17]

II

The six questions to which we now turn in sequence are as follows:

1. Who authored the Psalter?
2. Is the Psalter one book or several?
3. How should the Psalms be numbered?
4. Must one accept the interpolation of a New Testament reading into the text of a psalm?
5. Which punctuation of the text is correct?
6. Should the Psalms be interpreted literally or allegorically?

Who Is the Author of the Psalms?

David's role in the composition of the Psalter has been a time-honored question for both Jewish and Christian interpreters, prompted not only by the scriptural references to David as liturgical musician but also by the presence of his name in the superscription of a number of psalms, particularly in the form *le-david.* To understand the problem as it presented itself to sixteenth-century exegetes, we must be aware that whatever the original sense of this formula (*le* followed by a proper name), it had been widely understood to indicate authorship. In the Masoretic text of the Hebrew, seventy-three psalms have the superscription *le-david,* while some twenty others use the same formula with a different proper name. This leaves almost one-third of the Psalter with no indication of "authorship." The situation was further complicated by the fact that the Septuagint text tradition differs significantly from the Hebrew on this point, having different superscriptions for a number of psalms as well as crediting to David psalms untitled in the Hebrew. The modern student finds here interesting evidence of the growth of the Psalter collection itself and of traditions of its interpretation in the first and second centuries B.C.E. For sixteenth-century interpreters, this factor introduced complications into the authorship question and became a potential source of conflict of authorities.

"David the sweet singer of Israel" (2 Sam. 23:1). Already in the canonical Hebrew Scriptures one can trace the elaboration of the Davidic legend.[18] A strong rabbinic tradition ascribed the entire Psalter to David. Another point of view allowed for other authors (thereby accounting for the presence of their names in the superscriptions) but made David the compiler of the whole.[19] This identification of the book with David is also evident in New Testament usage, where "David says" is a standard way of introducing a quotation from the Psalms.[20] Amongst Christian exegetes, Augustine and Jerome reflect opposing sides of the question, with the former conferring his magisterial authority upon the unique authorship of David.[21] Both points of view found their advocates among medieval Christians. Thus in the great glossed Bible of Sebastian Brant one reads in Nicholas of Lyra a commentary on the disagreement of Augustine and Jerome, with preference for the latter's point of view and multiple authorship. On the same page Paul of Burgos defends the honor of David and Augustine, and, as expected, Matthias Döring rebounds in defense of Lyra's position.[22]

Amongst our sixteenth-century interpreters only a handful explicitly assert Davidic authorship of the whole, while the contrary view is vigorously maintained likewise by a few.[23] While many employ titles which maintain the Davidic association—such as *Psalms of David* or the like—this is clearly a convention which does not preclude their assigning specific psalms to other authors; so, for example, the English Geneva Bible, which uses this title but adds in a marginal note that David was the author of "most" of them. The silence of others on the subject may echo the sentiments of Konrad Pellican, who left the question aside, "not wanting to give occasion for endless and useless questioning by the merely inquisitive" on a subject wherein contradictory and equally plausible conjectures could be advanced.[24]

The question of authorship comes to our attention on two occasions in the New Testament when David is named as author of a psalm which bears no superscription in Hebrew: at Acts 4:25–26 (Psalm 2) and Hebrews 4:7 (Psalm 95). In both instances some Septuagint and Vulgate text traditions gave the psalm a Davidic title.[25]

In the first instance (Psalm 2) we begin by noting that all our sources concur with the christological reading of the psalm given in Acts 4. Sebastian Münster even argues Jewish support for such a reading: "No Christian since the Apostles does not think this psalm, which makes such clear reference to the birth, passion and resurrection of the Christ, is to be expounded concerning him. The Jews generally say likewise, even if they consistently deny that it is to be understood of *our* Christ."[26]

Some of those who comment on the text leave aside the authorship question.[27] Others note the discrepancy in the text traditions with respect to the superscription.[28] In his text edition of 1516 Pellican preferred to omit the title even in the Septuagint, a judgment with which his Basel colleague Erasmus concurred in a lengthy commentary.[29] On the other hand, Bellarmine is unequivocal: given that revelation has settled the question in Acts 4 in favor of David, it is more likely that those Septuagint manuscripts that preserve the Davidic superscription are primitive, while the others, together with the Hebrew, are defective.[30] It is hardly surprising that Reignier Snoy, Richard of Le Mans, and François Vatable express their deference to the apostolic authority here, since all three credit the full Psalter to David. But they are joined by the remainder of our commentators, for whom the weight of the preaching of Saint Peter overrides any possible objection. As Luther puts it: "The authority of the primitive church compels us. . . . This understanding has been confirmed by heaven."[31]

The second instance (Psalm 95, at Hebrews 4) shows a similar pattern among our sources. Two particular matters merit comment. Richard of Le Mans extrapolates from this particular instance to the larger whole. The pronouncement of the Holy Spirit (at Hebrews 4) with respect to this untitled psalm is meant to settle the question of the authorship of the entire Psalter.[32]

For another group of exegetes, the matter is complicated by their awareness of a Jewish tradition that assigned Psalms 91–100 to Moses on the basis of a rule that where a psalm is untitled (as are all of these), it is to be ascribed to the author last named in a previous title.[33] Bucer reports the tradition twice, once in his preface (from Hilary), and again at Psalm 90, where it is attributed to Talmudic sources which he read in David Kimhi.[34] Münster and Pellican likewise knew this tradition. All three Rhinelanders omit any reference to authorship in their discussion of Psalm 95, despite the New Testament tradition. Their silence may have paved the way for Calvin, who is known to have read all three; he dares to leave the question open with the passing comment "whoever the author may be."[35] Was this an oversight on Calvin's part, or did he indeed dare to put in doubt the apostolic attribution to David? One piece of evidence from his Genevan circles favors the latter conclusion. In the first edition of the Psalms commentary attributed to François Vatable (1546), a note observes the Jewish tradition but adds that the apostle Paul in Hebrews assigned the psalm to David. This note disappears in the posthumous Geneva edition of 1556 issued by Robert Estienne. On the other hand, in his commentary on Hebrews Calvin several times refers to the psalm as David's.[36]

I offer a whimsical excursus into the popular religious literature of our century to conclude. In a collection of American gospel songs I recently encountered the following:

> I was reading today in King David's sweet psalm
> A portion that came to my soul as a balm;
> With mine eye I will guide thee till life here is past,
> And afterward take thee to heaven at last.[37]

We have here an apparent conflation of two passages. Psalm 32:8 and Psalm 73:24, though the text is principally from the latter. Psalm 73, however, is entitled "A psalm of Asaph." The old tradition still has life in it!

Is the Psalter One Book or Five?

This is a minor question treated amongst the prolegomena from patristic times on. Jerome, on the strength of the fivefold division of the book in Hebrew, speaks of five books.[38] Hilary of Poitiers, on the other hand, insists there can be but one book, inasmuch as both Christ in Luke 20:42 and Peter at Acts 1:20 made reference to "the book of the Psalms."

Amongst our sources, the titles given to the translations and commentaries vary considerably and are apparently unrelated to this question. The few exceptions would seem to be Antonio Brucioli, Pellican (in his 1532 *Commentaria*), Sebastian Castellio, and Bucer, each of whom recognizes the five books of the Hebrew.[39] Bucer added a note in 1532, however, which dismisses the question as insignificant, since the Jews also refer to the Psalms as one book in five parts.[40] Cardinal Cajetan and Vatable each note that at Luke 24:44 Christ uses a plural in reference to the Psalms. On the other hand, Bellarmine and Richard of Le Mans defend the apostolic tradition of a single book.

The Numbering of the Psalms

Anyone who has worked on older versions of the Psalms will be aware of the confusion engendered by the existence of two different systems of numbering the individual psalms. Sixteenth-century exegetes were divided between the two systems. Most Hebraists tended to favor that of the Masoretic text, although long years of familiarity with the church's use of the other system meant that there were frequent lapses when they cited by memory. A minority, however, remained formally attached, for a variety of reasons, to the more familiar system based upon the Septuagint.[41]

The issue comes to our attention thanks to a quotation of Psalm 2:7 set in the mouth of Saint Paul at Acts 13:33.[42] The received text of the

Acts passage, as in most modern Bibles, reads "in the second psalm" or "in the psalm," and a number of our sources therefore perceived no problem.[43] In the *Novum Instrumentum* of 1515, however, Erasmus had preferred the Western reading "in the first psalm," a reading attested, moreover, in a number of patristic sources. In his commentary on the Second Psalm Erasmus gives a lengthy discussion of the problem. On the basis of the textual evidence he argues that "second" is a pious emendation meant to rid the church of an apparent threat to apostolic authority. "It is the height of impious audacity to wish to remedy something in holy Scripture in this way just because we don't understand it or because it offends us! For this reason the orthodox Fathers . . . try by various means to defend Scripture, so that the apostolic authority will not clash with the original."[44]

Erasmus looks at the options presented by his patristic sources. He dismisses Hilary's argument that while the Septuagint preserved a recondite oral tradition, Saint Paul, who knew better, accommodated himself to the disorder of the Hebrew for the sake of his Jewish listeners. Instead he considers Jerome's two suggestions. On the presumption that the apostle cannot be mistaken, either the present first two psalms were at one time a single unit (for this some thematic and literary evidence can be cited), or in Paul's day the present First Psalm was a preface to the entire Psalter, so that our Second Psalm was the first in the numbered sequence. Erasmus prefers the latter hypothesis.

Amongst those exegetes who consider the question, the French catenist Augustin Marlorat presents both options. Calvin, the older Melanchthon, and the English Geneva Bible side with Erasmus's preference for the preface theory. The 1520 Pagnini, Bucer, and the Italian Benedictine Isidoro Chiari prefer the other hypothesis; and Bucer adduces in support evidence from rabbinic sources: "The Talmudists also mention, as Rabbi David Kimhi reports, that this psalm [2] was once a part of the previous one; and thus it finishes with the same expression "Blessed" as the other one begins. . . . How it came about that afterward the copyists made two psalms from one I shall not even attempt to explain, since it has no value for the teaching of godliness."[45]

Interestingly, no one suggests renumbering the psalms to coincide with what was, according to Erasmus, Paul's Bible. Bellarmine, on the other hand, while noting the problem raised by Erasmus, argues that the reading "in the Second Psalm" is preferable textually; in this he has the support of most modern text critics.

The Interpolation of a New Testament Passage into the Text of a Psalm

In arguing for the depravity of the human race in Romans 3, Paul brings a string of proof texts from Scripture: Psalms 14:1–3, 5:9, 140:3, 10:7; Isaiah 59:7–8; Psalm 36:1. The collection is artfully constructed, and some modern scholars have argued that Paul is making use of an already existing catena.[46] Our interest lies in the fact that at some point early in the Christian era this entire catena found its way back into some Greek copies of Psalm 14 and thence into several of the Latin versions.[47] Jerome, following Origen, included it in the Gallican Psalter with appropriate diacritical marks. But these soon disappeared in the course of copying, and the medieval Psalter contained the conflated psalm text—although Jerome's *Iuxta Hebraeum* did not, and his commentary drew attention to the interpolation.[48]

Here, too, our sixteenth-century sources handle the problem in a variety of ways. In his *Quincuplex Psalterium* Jacques Lefèvre d'Étaples restores the critical apparatus in his fifth column, the *conciliatus*.[49] Pellican, however, in the *Quadruplex Psalterium* of 1516 drops the offending passage from both the Greek and from Jerome's Gallican Psalter. This bold step—and the absence of the interpolation from other editions of the Septuagint—may explain why so many of our commentators and translators likewise omit it without a word of comment. Cajetan does observe the problem but argues that it is the result of some copyist's assumption that the Hebrew psalm text was defective, Saint Paul having the correct form.

More interesting are those who retain the interpolation. Lefèvre, Agostino Giustiniani, and Luther (*Operationes in Psalmos,* 1519) all do so on the ground that Paul's quotation in Romans 3 is proof of the presence of the unit in Psalm 14 in the Septuagint of his day.[50] Giustiniani, it is true, gives the unit only in the Latin, omitting it from his text of the Greek. In defense of its authenticity, however, he notes that it is to be found in the Syrian and Coptic, both of which he believes to be descended from the Septuagint. Le Mans and Bellarmine both retain the unit; although certainly not primitive, its presence in the psalm is inoffensive. Dietenberger, Snoy, and the Sixtine Vulgate retain it without comment.

Pellican, surprisingly, waffles. As we have seen, it is omitted in 1516, and he does so as well in 1527. In 1534, however, it is printed in parentheses, apparently in keeping with his desire in his Bible to accommodate himself to the traditional form of the text for pastoral reasons. A similar motivation must lie behind its retention in the Coverdale English Psalms, the version used in the Great Bible.[51] From there it passed into the Book of Common Prayer and is therefore used in Anglican liturgy to the present day. Baïf, on the other hand—despite its presence in the Sixtine Vulgate—did not include it in his metrical version.

The Punctuation of the Text

As this affected sentence, and therefore verse, divisions there is wide divergence amongst the versions. It becomes an issue for us in the use of Psalm 95:7–11 in Hebrews, chapters 3 and 4. There are two significant discrepancies between Masoretic and New Testament punctuation, and they govern the transitions between verses 7–8 and 9–10. The former is of particular interest here because the punctuation affects the interpretation of the passage: it occurs at Hebrews 3:7, 15, and 4:7.

The key clause is "today if you will hear his voice." In the Masoretic tradition this is clearly attached to the end of verse 7, so that one translates: ". . . we are the people of his pasture and the sheep of his hand today, if you will hear his voice." If, however, the punctuation is that of the Epistle to the Hebrews, the clause is attached instead to the following verse, so that one reads: "Today if you will hear his voice, harden not your hearts." The textual witness of the older Latin versions favored the New Testament form. Lefèvre follows this model in all five versions of the *Quincuplex Psalterium* including Jerome's *Iuxta Hebraeum;* the reader is also pointed to the interpretation of the passage by "Paul the Christopher." But Pellican the editor again shows his independence by punctuating the *Iuxta Hebraeum* in accordance with the Masoretic pattern.

Among our sources, three groups of roughly equal size can be distinguished. The first follow the Masoretic, despite the apostolic tradition. Not surprisingly Bucer is in this group, supporting his choice with quotations from David Kimhi and Abraham Ibn Ezra.[52] It is more unusual to find Zwingli here, since he as a rule favored the Septuagint over the Masoretic tradition.[53]

The second group retains the New Testament punctuation. Both Bugenhagen and Bellarmine justify this choice, the latter raging against modern heretics who impugn the apostolic authority. In this group one is struck by the presence of Giustiniani and the Zurich Latin Bible, for each purports to follow the Masoretic text.[54] Liturgical and paraliturgical texts fall into this group as well: Baïf, the Sternhold and Hopkins metrical Psalter, the Coverdale Psalms in the Great Bible, the Book of Common Prayer, and the 1534 English *Prymer.*[55]

The third group attempts to respect both traditions. Cajetan and Calvin both note the Masoretic but furnish a rationale for the New Testament version.[56] This compromise, with leanings toward the New Testament, is reflected in the French Bible of Pierre Robert Olivétan: "les ouailles qu'il conduict de sa main. Si vous ouyez aujourdhuy sa voiy, Nendurcissez point vostre coer."[57] The 1546 Vatable follows a similar pattern, with a note pointing out that "today" is "the time of the Gospel revelation." Estienne's 1556 reedition of Vatable, however, contains a lengthy note (apparently drawn from Bucer) which shifts the bias in favor of the Masoretic.

Some interpreters waver between groups. In addition to the changes within the Vatable editions just noted, one sees this again in Pellican. His 1527 Psalter follows his text edition of 1516, but in the 1534 Bible he retreats at least partway, using a Mesoretic versification for the Vulgate but essentially a New Testament punctuation. So, too, Luther, who follows the Masoretic in his 1524 German Psalter but returns to the New Testament form in the 1531 and subsequent editions. Finally, one notes that George Joye gives two versions. In the 1530 *Psalter of David* he follows Bucer (whom he is translating) and the Masoretic, but in the various Prymers wherein he placed the Bucer Psalms he uses the more familiar New Testament version.

Literal versus Allegorical Interpretation

It is not difficult to find examples of ways in which a New Testament quotation employs an other-than-literal sense of the Hebrew. Nor would most Christians in the sixteenth century have disagreed with Luther, who wrote, commenting upon the use of Deuteronomy 30:12–14 in the tenth chapter of Romans: "In Deuteronomy, chapter 30, Moses does not put down these words with this meaning in mind. But the apostle, out of the abundance of his understanding in the Spirit has brought to light their inner kernel of meaning."[58]

Our illustration comes from that same chapter of Romans, namely, Paul's use of Psalm 19:4 at Romans 10:18: "But I ask [writes Paul] have they not heard? Indeed they have; for 'their voice has gone out to all the earth and their words to the ends of the world' [RSV]."

Paul is speaking of the apostolic proclamation of the gospel, and early Christian interpreters followed him, taking this to be the plain meaning of the psalm. Thus, for example, Augustine considers the whole psalm to speak of Christ, while Gratian enshrines a quotation of Pope Leo I referring to this verse as "the apostolic trumpet."[59] Nicholas of Lyra is aware that the unalerted reader might take this psalm to be a hymn in praise of the glory of God in nature, and he flirts with this as the literal sense before deciding that revelation had given Paul the proper literal sense, that is, the publication of the Gospel by the apostles.

This issue of the proper literal sense—was this psalm written concerning creation and to be understood primarily thus, or is Paul correct in taking it as a prophecy of the apostolic preaching[60]—was complicated by an apparent difference between the reading of the Masoretic Hebrew and that of the Septuagint. The expression **ὁ φθογγος αὐτῶν**—rendered by Jerome as "sonus eorum," literally "their sound"—stands in the Septuagint where the Hebrew reads *qwm,* which, as pointed out by the Masoretes, would be rendered literally "their line." This was a potential difficulty for the sixteenth-century interpreter. A certain number of our sources, however, stand by the traditional "sonus" without hesitation.[61] Two paraphrases—those of Zwingli and Jan van Campen—adopt new expressions which clearly depend upon the Septuagint tradition, as does the metrical paraphrase of Thomas Sternhold.[62] But a distinct majority follows the Masoretic text with a variety of new renderings: "linea," "regula," "amussis," "filum," and their vernacular equivalents.[63] Several of these, it is true, then proceed to expound some harmonizing principle that will bring Masoretic and Pauline senses together. Thus Luther's: "And although the Hebrew has 'Into all the earth their rule [regula] has gone forth' whereas the apostle in Romans 10 says 'sound,' it comes back to the same thing. For the Gospel 'sound' is that 'rule' according to which the Church is built, etc."[64]

More innovative are those who propose a change in the reading of the Hebrew. Olivétan, Le Mans, and Bellarmine all suggest the possibility that the Hebrew once read *qwlm,* which would explain the Septuagint rendering and Jerome's as well. Le Mans, who excoriates those who would detract from the apostolic authority in this instance, credits the suggestion to Agostino Steucho of Gubbio, the Vatican librarian.[65]

Early in our period Lefèvre d'Étaples singled out this psalm for mention along with three others, as illustrations of his hermeneutical point. His remarks are so pertinent to the discussion at hand that I quote him extensively.

> In order that it might be more obvious how great is the difference between the proper and the improper sense, let me offer a few examples which will show this.
>
> The rabbis understand Psalm 19 to deal with the first giving of the law. Paul takes it not as the first but the second giving of the law when through the apostles and their blessed successors, it was promulgated to all nations. . . .
>
> It would be tedious to go through each psalm to show that what the rabbis contrive to be the literal sense is not this at all, but a fiction and a lie. . . . How can we rely on the interpretation of those whom God has stricken with blindness and terror, and not fear that when a blind man offers us guidance we will fall into the ditch together? It is impossible for us to believe this one to be the literal sense when it makes David a historian instead of a prophet. Instead let us call the literal sense that which is in accord with the Spirit and taught by the Spirit![66]

About one-half of our commentators are of Lefèvre's mind, at least with respect to this psalm. Furthermore, three of them join him in denouncing the alternative as "judaïzing" exegesis.[67] On the other hand, proponents of such an alternative generally employed a hermeneutical schema—by analogy, allegory, or the mystical—to permit the reconciliation of this natural interpretation with the Pauline.[68] Bucer is perhaps the most interesting—as he is the earliest—of these; his argument is picked up and followed by Pellican (in his Commentaries) and by Vatable. The creation sense is primary, and the psalm should be read thus; this accords with Saint Paul, who cited the text by analogy—*a minore ad maius*—from God's glory in creation to the greater splendor of the apostolic preaching. An allegorical treatment of the psalm, as Bucer considers the alternative, is therefore quite unnecessary, despite its popularity.[69]

Zwingli, and apparently Campensis, run against the stream: having preferred a Septuagint-based translation for the key word, they nonetheless favor a creation interpretation of the psalm! But the most unusual is Calvin. Like Bucer, he refuses the view that Saint Paul's use is allegorical. To his mind, "Paul's intention is not at all ambiguous. He meant to say that long centuries before, God had made clear to the Gentiles his glory. . . . From this then we conclude that those who have imagined that Paul abandoned the literal sense were quite thoroughly deceived."[70]

Thus Calvin—followed by Marlorat and Estienne in the 1556 Vatable—concludes our study of conflicting authorities by an unusual reversal, resolving the supposed discrepancy in favor of the natural sense of the Hebrew.

III

A balance sheet for a study such as this is not easy to draw up. It will have become apparent that we cannot, on the basis of this survey, provide any clear-cut final score, such as Hebrew Truth 4, Apostles 2, or whatever! Nonetheless, it is possible to offer certain further observations in the guise of a conclusion.

In the first place, one can see some evidence, even over so limited a period, of the emergence of streams of interpretation, each with certain characteristics and a definite style for dealing with these apparently conflicting authorities. The clearest illustration of this tendency is perhaps furnished by what happens in reeditions of works. The Veit Dietrich annotations to the Eobanus Hessus work interpret the work of the humanist in a distinctly Wittenberg tone.[71] We have noted on several occasions the strengthening Genevan, or to be more accurate, Swiss–South German, accents in the second posthumous edition of Vatable. A similar development can be observed in the reedition of Antonio Brucioli's Italian Bible in 1562. But it would be a mistake, especially in the earlier decades of our period, to suppose that these schools can be equated to a Catholic-Evangelical split—the coalitions were more complex and shifting. For example, Richard of Le Mans, of Psalm 19:4 attacks Lefèvre, Cajetan, and Pagnini (all Catholics) and claims as allies not only fellow Catholics Steucho and Jan van Campen but also Zwingli.[72]

Second, individual exegetes changed their positions. Thus Luther, Pellican, and George Joye all modified their stance in a conservative direction with respect to the punctuation of Psalm 95. At a number of points Bucer's Latin commentary of 1529 marks a significant change from his part in the 1526 *Psalter wol verteutscht,* and his 1532 revision sees many further shifts. These changes may have come about as a result of further reading or an increased knowledge of Hebrew. They also resulted, however, from a changing context or the needs of a particular audience; for example, from scholarly Latin commentary to vernacular translation or homiletical notes. Pellican explains in the preface to his 1532 commentaries on the Bible that he has preferred to use the Vulgate rather than a new translation out of pastoral concerns.

In the third place, I would agree with Guy Bedouelle that to read these conflicts as grammar against theology is an unhelpful over-simplification.[73] It is true that external theological authorities do appear as forces shaping exegetical decisions; for example, the decisions of Trent concerning the primacy of the Vulgate, or the Lutheran understanding of the Law in the interpretation of Psalm 19. But these forces sometimes have unpredictable consequences. A good example of the complexity of choices is furnished by the discernible Zurich tendency toward the Septuagint tradition. This turns out to be based upon Zwingli's view that in the Septuagint one comes closer than in the Masoretic text to the Hebrew Urtext. Thus what appears to be a theological bias in favor of the apostolic authority turns out to have important text-critical motivation.

Fourth, we must not overlook the significance of attitudes toward Jews and Judaism in the conflict. Simon Markish is fundamentally correct in his thesis that much so-called anti-Semitism in Erasmus is to be assigned to the formal rhetoric of religious polemic.[74] Yet the fact of the anti-Judaistic rhetoric and the fears, religious and other, remain. And when Christians turned to a concentrated study of the Hebrew, they perforce drew upon the only significant source for the explication of that material—the rich resources of medieval Jewish exegesis and philology. This consequence, as logical and inevitable as it seems to us, was far from pleasing even to some Hebraists.[75] What comes as a traditional descriptive term for literal exegesis—the Jewish sense—in a Melanchthon[76] can be an outpouring of hostility against the perilous encroachment of the Jews in Luther or Richard of Le Mans: "You destroy all credibility in your translation, when you prefer to abandon the apostle rather than your rabbis. . . . This is judaïzing.[77]

Finally, the role of the *usus ecclesiae,* in both liturgical and para-liturgical texts, requires much more exploration, as Fraenkel pointed out in 1976. On the one hand, one is struck forcefully by the evidence of liturgical conservatism. The role of ecclesiastical custom in the retention of the interpolation in Psalm 14 which Cassiodorus observed in the sixth century is still to be reckoned with in English liturgical texts today.[78] At the same time our samplings in the metrical psalms suggest considerable influence of the Hebrew tradition and a respect for the point of view enunciated by Joye in his preface to the 1530 Psalter: "the trowthe of the Psalms must be fetched more nigh the Hebrew verity."

DAVID C. STEINMETZ

Calvin and the Patristic Exegesis of Paul

T. H. L. Parker in his book *Calvin's New Testament Commentaries* observes that Calvin appears to have relied chiefly on the Fathers and certain of his contemporaries in the development of his own exegesis.[1] While Parker himself makes no attempt to explore the question of Calvin's use of patristic sources (apart from noting that Calvin especially favored Chrysostom, Augustine, Jerome, Origen, and Ambrose), he does suggest that the subject merits further independent study. Aside from the earlier monograph on Calvin and Augustine by Luchesius Smits[2] and the more recent essays by Walchenbach[3] and Meijering,[4] very little has been done to illuminate the relationship of Calvin to the exegetical tradition of the early church.

In the dedicatory letter to Simon Grynaeus (1539) which serves as a preface to his commentary on Romans, Calvin indicates that he has been particularly helped in his understanding of Paul by such Protestant commentators as Melanchthon, Bullinger, and Bucer, and by the "ancient commentators, whose godliness, learning, sanctity and age have secured them such great authority that we should not despise anything they have produced."[5] While he does not mention any ancient commentators by name in the preface, he does refer in the course of his exposition to Ambrose (though it is probably Ambrosiaster that he has before him), Augustine, Chrysostom, Eusebius, Jerome (very likely Pelagius in his guise as Pseudo-Jerome), Lactantius, and Origen. Of medieval commentators from Sedulius Scotus to Denis the Carthusian there is no mention, though Erasmus, omitted from the preface, is frequently cited in the text. Of course, Calvin may have known some of the more famous opinions of the Fathers through medieval glossators or through references to them in the writings of his contemporaries. It seems more likely, however, that whenever possible Calvin consulted the writings of the Fathers themselves. This is certainly the case with Chrysostom, and probably with Origen as well.[6]

The reliability of the Fathers as interpreters of Paul has been the subject of some debate among modern historians. Judgments have ranged from the almost rhapsodic evaluation of Chrysostom by M. J. Lagrange, who regarded Chrysostom's commentaries on Romans and Galatians as revelations not easily surpassed of the mind and soul of Paul, to the wry dictum of Adolf von Harnack that Marcion alone of the second-century theologians avoided the common fate of failing to understand Paul by misunderstanding him instead. Even historians who stood between the two extremes were inclined to concede that the early church, while remarkably sensitive to certain themes in Paul, was curiously dense about others. Not only the heretics but even the orthodox Fathers from time to time made heavy weather of Paul.

The more recent critical essays on patristic exegesis by Karl Hermann Schelkle[7] and Maurice Wiles[8] have given us a more satisfying and complete picture of Pauline studies in the early Christian era. The Fathers stressed what they regarded as the anti-Marcionite and anti-Gnostic features of Paul's theology. They emphasized, against Marcion, that the law was a schoolmaster to bring men and women to Christ (though they gave this genuinely Pauline theme more prominence than Paul himself had done), and they explained away Paul's apparent hostility to the law by drawing an un-Pauline distinction between the moral and ceremonial law. They interpreted Paul's teaching on grace in such a way as to strike a balance between divine sovereignty and free human response and to minimize those predestinarian elements in Paul that smacked of Gnostic or Manichean determinism.

The Fathers were also anti-Gnostic in their resolve to interpret "flesh," whenever possible, as a moral or theological category and to suppress any notion that Paul was hostile to the physical body as such. Christological passages were given a precision more appropriate to the theological debates of the third and fourth centuries than to the theological world of the first-century church, though one may argue that such precision, however anachronistic, was not necessarily a distortion of the thrust of Pauline thought. Only in their discussion of faith do the Fathers seem to have faltered and seriously misrepresented Paul. They tended, on the whole, to reduce faith to intellectual assent to the dogmatic truths summarized in the creeds, a reductionism, one must hasten to add, not found in the Pauline exegesis of the great third-century commentator Origen.

In short, the Fathers were concerned to present the teaching of Paul as a well-rounded and philosophically consistent system rather than as an occasionally fragmentary, pastoral response to a cluster of disparate and specific problems in the past. Paul was less a prophet to them than a teacher of orthodox theology and a guide to proper Christian practice. What such an exegesis lost in the way of religious vitality, it gained in the way of pedagogic utility.

In order to determine how much this vision of Paul influenced Calvin's Pauline exegesis, I propose to compare Calvin's exegesis of Romans 8:1–11 with patristic exegeses of the same passage. Although allusions to Pauline writings are widespread in the theological literature of the patristic age, the number of complete commentaries on Paul's letter to the Romans is relatively small.[9] Among the Greek commentators only Origen and Chrysostom have left substantial commentaries on Romans, and, in the case of Origen—apart from some Greek fragments unknown to Calvin—the complete commentary exists only in the Latin translation of Rufinus. It is therefore clearly a bowdlerized and amended version. Augustine, whose discussion of Pauline themes is scattered throughout the entire corpus of his writings, never completed his commentary on Romans, though he did make a start when he was a presbyter in Hippo Regius. Most of his comments were gathered together in one remarkable volume by Florus of Lyon in the ninth century, a book very popular in the twelfth century but probably unknown to Calvin in the sixteenth. Latin exegesis of Romans is represented by an interesting series of expositions of Paul written by Pelagius before his great controversy with Augustine and an anonymous commentary once ascribed to Ambrose and now believed to have been written by an anonymous author known as Ambrosiaster.[10]

My principal basis of comparison with Calvin will be two of the longer patristic commentaries on Romans 8: the homily on this passage that John Chrysostom[11] preached in Antioch sometime before 397 and the exegesis that Ambrosiaster[12] wrote, probably in Rome and certainly no later than 384. Both were composed at roughly the same time; namely, after the Council of Nicaea and before the great Latin controversy over grace and free will precipitated by the teaching of Pelagius. They reflect the theological situation in two of the principal theological centers of fourth-century Christianity, one Greek, the other Latin. They are less well known than the commentaries of Origen, Pelagius, and Augustine, and are without a doubt two of the most remarkable commentaries on Paul written in any language at any time.

Chrysostom and Ambrosiaster deal with four interrelated problems in the course of their exegeses of Romans 8:1–11: (1) What does Paul mean by the law, and how are the various kinds of law to be distinguished from one another? (2) What is the significance of the anthropological terms *soul, spirit, flesh,* and *body,* and how do they function in Paul's argument? (3) How should one understand the person and work of Jesus Christ, who came "in the likeness of sinful flesh," who "condemned sin in the flesh," and who works in believers by his Spirit? (4) What is the relationship of the gift of salvation to the moral obligations of the Christian, particularly now that the Christian stands under grace rather than under the law? These exegetical questions are perennial ones, and Chrysostom and Ambrosiaster tackled them with considerable verve and imagination.

AMBROSIASTER

The Meaning of Law

Ambrosiaster's understanding of the meaning of the word *law* is not altogether transparent to the reader. Some things, however, are clear. The Law of Moses, while it is spiritual in the sense of having been given by the Holy Spirit, is not the law of the Spirit of life because it does not remit sin or bring sinners—who stand under the sentence of death—back to life.[13] Indeed, the Law of Moses can simply be identified with the "law of death" in the sense that it condemns and slays sinners.[14] The Mosaic law, while undoubtedly given by God, serves to intensify the predicament of the non-Christian.

Ranged against the Mosaic law is the "law of the Spirit of life." *Law* is used here not in the sense of a legal code but rather in the sense of a general principle of universal applicability. It is through a law of just this sort that the Spirit, by remitting sin, delivers Christians from what Ambrosiaster calls "the second death." Because the Spirit does this work and is the final object toward which the Christian faith is directed, the principle of the Spirit's operation is called the "law" of the Spirit of life. Furthermore, because the Spirit only delivers from second death those persons who believe the gospel, the law of the Spirit is simultaneously a "law" of faith.[15]

The Mosaic law is a law of death, not because of any defect in its essential nature but because of the law of sin.[16] There is a principle at work in unbelievers persuading them to deny the fundamental tenets of the Christian faith and to embrace things that run contrary to the law of the Spirit (Ambrosiaster had particularly in mind the fascination of pagans with astrology).[17] The justified are made friends of the Mosaic law, not through the law itself (the law code as code being no match for the awesome power of sin) but through the activity of the Spirit.[18] The righteousness that was the aim of the Law of Moses is only attained in human life by the power of the Spirit through the remission of sins.

The Anthropological Terminology

The most striking feature of Ambrosiaster's discussion of the anthropological terminology of Paul is his perception that each of these terms—spirit, soul, body, and flesh—is a designation not for a faculty or portion of the human personality but for the whole person considered from some special angle or in some particular relationship. Ambrosiaster is full of little sayings that turn on the recognition of the holistic character of Pauline anthropology: e.g., the baptized person when given the Holy Spirit is called spirit;[19] the soul when it sins is called flesh;[20] the resurrection of the body is a synonym for the resurrection of the whole human being;[21] to talk about weak flesh is really to talk about human weakness;[22] even the whole world, that is, everything that is visible, can be identified as flesh.[23]

In all this terminology, however, it is the word *flesh* that is the most worrisome. Ambrosiaster is clearly concerned to avoid any Gnostic identification of flesh as physical reality with evil and hastens to affirm in the strongest possible language that the substance of the flesh (in the sense of physical matter) is not the enemy of God.[24] God is opposed to the prudence of the flesh, an anti-God state of mind that is implacably hostile to invisible realities as both morally inconvenient and logically improbable.[25] Indeed, so eager is Ambrosiaster to avoid the pitfalls of Manichaean dualism that he sounds at times almost like Martin Luther, especially in his discussion of the Pauline phrase "prudence of the flesh."

Prudence is that virtue of the mind which enables it to distinguish what is sensible from what is stupid.[26] Like any human virtue, prudence can be turned to unworthy objects and can evaluate the human situation from a distorted perspective. When prudence is rightly ordered, it is called wisdom or prudence of the spirit.[27] Prudence of the spirit gains peace for the human soul by pursuing invisible and spiritual objects.

Prudence of the flesh, however, leads to death because it regards the visible world and the realm governed by human reason as the only trustworthy reality.[28] People submissive to the prudence of the flesh deny the wonderful works of God in Isaac's miraculous birth, the virgin birth of Jesus, and the event of the Resurrection.[29] They are easily swayed by the predictions of astrologers, whose tables make creatures (namely, the stars) coequal with God.[30] The prudence of the flesh regards as self-evident the conviction that nothing can happen in the world that sinful reason regards as unlikely. What matters to the flesh is what can be seen, touched, cataloged, and statistically evaluated. The prudence of the flesh is not subject to the law of God because it repudiates the acts of God.[31] The visible world defines the limits of reality. Therefore there is no salvation for the worldly wise who, out of respect for the world and its ephemeral values, resist spiritual wisdom.[32]

Christology

When Paul claimed that Jesus came in the likeness of sinful flesh, he was not, so far as Ambrosiaster is concerned, suggesting a docetic Christology. The humanity of the Redeemer is true humanity. His flesh differs from ours only in the sense that it was sanctified in the womb of Mary and born without sin.[33] In short, while Jesus bears the same substance of flesh that we bear, he did not have the same birth.[34] A virgin womb was chosen for his birth so that his flesh might differ from ours in sanctity.[35] Physically we are one; morally we are distinct.

Ambrosiaster's doctrine of the atonement turns upon his understanding of the sinlessness of Jesus. Jesus was as innocent of sin as Adam was before the Fall.[36] Therefore the devil did not have the same legitimate claim to Jesus as it had to Adam and Adam's progeny. When, however, Satan lost patience with the sinless Jesus and set in motion the forces that crucified him, he acted unjustly and committed homicide against a completely innocent man.[37] By the act of homicide Satan lost the last shred of any legitimate claim to Adam's children.[38] On the contrary, his contempt for the question of guilt gave Jesus the right to act against him in justice, and not merely in sheer naked, sovereign power. The murder of a just man is central to Ambrosiaster's doctrine of the atonement.

Jesus condemned "sin in the flesh" in three ways: (1) he refused to sin himself; (2) he atoned for sin through the cross; and (3) as an effect of his death and Resurrection he remits the sins of the faithful.[39] If we follow the example of our Savior, we do not commit sins ourselves and we condemn sin wherever it appears.[40] In this way we imitate the action of Jesus, who broke the lordship of Satan over the souls in captivity. Satan has been so weakened through the atoning act of Christ that he can no longer hold in second death any souls sealed with the sign of the cross.[41]

Ambrosiaster feels it important at this point to introduce what sounds suspiciously like the later doctrine of the *filioque*. He regards this not as an alien imposition on the theology of Paul but rather as a logical conclusion from it. When Paul speaks of the Spirit of Christ, he is speaking of the Spirit of the Father as well as of the Son.[42] The Spirit who is active in the church is as much a Spirit of the Son as of the Father.

Ethics and Redemption

Ambrosiaster does not have a great deal to say on this subject. Still, the thrust of his argument is plain enough. Romans 8:1–11 is an admonition to good behavior.[43] Christians should not appear to be unworthy of the name by which they are called.[44] Christians are not saved by their morally responsible activity. Nevertheless, morally responsible action is a necessary response to the proclamation of salvation in Christ. The Spirit deserts human beings who devote themselves to the prudence of the flesh.[45] But the baptized, the friends of the law, the faithful who devote themselves to the prudence of the Spirit find salvation in Christ to be a secure status.[46] Christians are not in the flesh—i.e., they do not love the visible world and its tangible perquisites—but are in the Spirit—i.e., they risk their lives on a reality they cannot see, touch, or empirically verify.[47] As Ambrosiaster understands Paul, faith is both dangerous and exciting.

JOHN CHRYSOSTOM

The Meaning of Law

Chrysostom's homily begins with the fourteenth verse of chapter 7, and therefore Romans 8:1–11 cannot be treated in isolation from Chrysostom's comments on the verses immediately preceding it. Chrysostom believes that Paul is eager to clear the law of any suspicion that it is the root of the human predicament.[48] The law is spiritual in the sense that it is a teacher of virtue and hostile to vice.[49] It points unfailingly to what is right and attempts to lead us away from sin of every kind. If the law fails to achieve its objective, the fault cannot be lodged in the law itself but must be attributed to some other source.

Chrysostom distinguishes natural law from the Law of Moses. The knowledge of good and evil is an original and fundamental part of human nature.[50] The Law of Moses confirms the conclusions of natural law, accusing more intensely what natural law already recognizes as evil and heaping lavish praise on what natural law already confesses to be good.[51] However, while the Mosaic law confirms the conclusions of natural law, it is unable to abolish the agency of evil in the sinner.[52]

Sin overcomes even a mind that delights in the law.[53] When Paul talks of the law of sin, he is not referring to sin as a law code or even as a principle. Sin is a law in the sense that it compels strict obedience from everyone who complies with it.[54] In other words, sin exercises power and places its adherents in thralldom. The Spirit is the only law or power that can deliver sinners from the law and power of sin.[55] The law of the Spirit of life furnishes everyone who believes in Christ with a large measure of the Spirit. The Spirit frees believers from the Law of Moses. Freedom in the Spirit is not freedom from moral obligation but freedom to discharge it.[56] Chrysostom draws no antinomian conclusions from the Pauline doctrine of freedom.

The Anthropological Terminology

Chrysostom agrees with Ambrosiaster in interpreting the anthropological terminology of Paul holistically, particularly the word *flesh,* but he does so somewhat more cautiously than Ambrosiaster. Flesh is, of course, a metaphor for a life that is worldly and thoroughly self-indulgent.[57] As a physical reality, flesh is morally neutral and Paul has no intention of disparaging it.[58] But if the flesh, which does not have a reasoning power of its own, is allowed to transgress its proper bounds, it devotes itself to the pursuit of the things of this life and debases the mind that should have governed it.[59] Paul calls the whole person—body and soul—"flesh," giving the mind a name from its inferior part.[60] Similarly, while the "mind of the flesh" is always wicked, since it is unreservedly committed to worldly goals, Christ can through grace give the morally neutral flesh wings so that the redeemed person may be regarded as wholly spiritual.[61] At any rate, the clash between flesh and spirit in Pauline thought is not interpreted as a clash between material and immaterial realities. As Chrysostom understands Paul, the flesh can be spiritual and the soul carnal.

Christology

Chrysostom does not elaborate a doctrine of the atonement in his exegesis of Romans 8, but he does make some important christological and trinitarian observations. On the one hand, Chrysostom wants to stress the unity of the Trinity and takes the argument of Paul in 8:9–10, which juxtaposes "Spirit," "Spirit of God," "Spirit of Christ," and "Christ" as an occasion for remarking that where one Person of the Trinity is present, there the whole Trinity is present as well.[62] On the other hand, Chrysostom wants to emphasize the unique thing that marks off the Second Person of the Trinity from the other two;

namely, the assumption of real humanity. Therefore, like Ambrosiaster, Chrysostom interprets the phrase "in the likeness of sinful flesh" to mean that Christ shares a common nature with us, except that his humanity is undistorted by sin.[63] So far as the substance of the flesh is concerned, there is no difference between his humanity and ours.

Yet while Christ did not come "in sinful flesh" but only in its "likeness," he did identify himself fully with the weakness and frailty of our flesh. Christ assumed a flesh that was, to say the least, in grave difficulty, threatened on every hand by sin and death.[64] It was entirely appropriate that Christ should gain a marvelous victory over sin and death by means of the very flesh that had been defeated times without number.[65] As Chrysostom understands the thrust of the gospel, Christ condemns sin, and not the substance of poor human flesh.[66]

Ethics and Redemption

Romans 8:1–11 is addressed to the problem of sin after baptism.[67] Christians now have the power through the Spirit of not "walking after the flesh."[68] They are now able to achieve the righteousness, the end, the scope, the well-doing which the Mosaic law intended.[69] Indeed, Christ makes believers able to do more than the law commands.[70] The power of sin cannot be broken by weak human flesh. But the Spirit can achieve what the flesh cannot. While Chrysostom ends his homily with a stirring summons to ethical action, he is quite clear that it is the gift of grace, particularly the gift of the Spirit, that gives such exhortation any force or point.[71] You can do it not because you should but because the power of the Spirit at work in you is far greater than the power of sin.[72]

While there are differences between Ambrosiaster and Chrysostom in their treatment of Romans 8, those differences highlight a far more fundamental unity in both their approach to the text and their exegetical results. Although at times they treat Pauline themes anachronistically by speaking about matters more precisely than Paul himself had spoken, still the overwhelming impression they create is one of sound, relevant, imaginative exegesis that casts fresh light on the mind of Paul. They are remarkably shrewd in identifying the crucial problems in the Pauline text and reflect faithfully the unresolved tensions in

Paul's thought about the nature of the flesh and the role of the law. It is easy to understand why Calvin admired their exegesis, even if he did not follow them in all details.

JOHN CALVIN

There is a reciprocal relationship in Calvin's exegetical work between his struggle with the biblical text and his continuous revisions of his systematic position in the successive editions of the *Institutes of the Christian Religion.* Calvin intended the *Institutes* to be both an introduction to the Bible for the beginning student and a concise summary of its essential doctrine. At the same time he subjected the *Institutes* to continual correction and modification as his exegetical labors with particular texts led him to fresh or altered insights.

In the 1536 edition of the *Institutes* Calvin alludes to Romans 8:1–11 eight times.[73] If we keep to the categories emphasized by the Fathers—namely, law, anthropology, Christology, and ethics—we find very little evidence that Calvin was particularly concerned at that time with the exegetical traditions of the early church. While he cites Ambrose (not Ambrosiaster) to support his contention that the "prudence of the flesh" seeks to penetrate God's hidden judgments apart from his Word,[74] and agrees with the Fathers that 8:9–11 teaches the unity of the Trinity (since the Holy Spirit is the Spirit of both the Father and the Son),[75] he is not terribly interested in patristic themes. Calvin does not cite Romans 8 to support the holistic character of human nature or to highlight the ambiguity of the word *law.* He does not explain the puzzling phrase "likeness of sinful flesh" or react to the patristic notion that the death of Christ rendered Satan culpable. Calvin's interest lay elsewhere, in a Protestant polemic against such medieval Catholic commonplaces as the distinction between commands and counsels[76] and the sacramental obligation of the penitent to do works of satisfaction.[77] The death of Christ put a decisive end to all penitential works of satisfaction.[78]

In the final Latin edition of the *Institutes* (1559) the situation has noticeably altered. That is not to say that the thirty-three allusions to Romans 8:1–11 are altogether new. Calvin still scores polemical points against the Catholic church and even embellishes one or two older charges with further details. For example, the "prudence of the flesh," which was earlier condemned for its vain curiosity, is now excoriated for its empty speculations about the intercessory activity of departed saints.[79]

On the other hand, one catches repeated glimpses of the patristic exegesis of Paul. Like Ambrosiaster and Chrysostom, Calvin interprets the anthropological terminology of Paul holistically: the whole person is involved in sin,[80] the whole person is flesh,[81] and all the emotions of the flesh are implacably hostile to God.[82] In his Christology, however, Calvin goes beyond the Fathers. He agrees with them that Christ was truly human, though sinless (hence "in the likeness of sinful flesh"),[83] and that he expiated human sin in his flesh.[84] But Calvin also had a sixteenth-century agenda. He contends against Osiander that the sole purpose of the incarnation was redemption[85] and explains the relationship between Christ and the Holy Spirit in such a way as to exclude both Catholic and Lutheran understandings of real presence.[86] More than the Fathers, though not in contradiction to them, Calvin read Romans 8:1–11 as a celebration of the activity of the Spirit in regeneration, sanctification, assurance, and resurrection.[87]

The commentaries on Romans also give evidence of a development in Calvin's use of his patristic sources. John R. Walchenbach argues that although Calvin knew the writings of Chrysostom before 1536, he did not become intensely interested in Chrysostom as an exegete until the period 1539–46.[88] In any event, it is certainly true that no Fathers are cited by name in the 1540 commentary on Romans 8:1–11. While three opinions are cited anonymously, none, so far as I can determine, is a reference to a patristic author.

In the 1556 commentary Calvin cites Chrysostom once, though the position he attributes to Chrysostom was held by Ambrosiaster instead. Eight opinions mentioned by Calvin are those of Calvin's contemporaries and so can be set aside: Erasmus, who is cited by name on four technical points (verses 2, 3, 6); (2) the Libertines, who despise the law of God (verse 7); (3) the Sophists (read Scholastics), who defend the freedom of the human will (verse 7); (4) the "advocates of free will," who equate the Spirit in chapter 8 with the mind or superior part of the soul (verse 9); and (5) the "Papists"—probably Catholic controversialists like Latomus or Cochlaeus[89]—who deny the claim that Protestants are indwelt by the Holy Spirit, though Calvin does not make clear the grounds for this denial (verse 9). Calvin also alludes to

Pseudo-Oecumenius, an eighth-century Byzantine commentator who was first published in the West by Donatus of Verona.[90] The allusion to Oecumenius hangs on a small grammatical point that Calvin does not accept but is also not prepared to reject absolutely.

The three remaining anonymous attributions are to ancient authors: namely, Origen, Ambrosiaster, and Augustine. Together with the misplaced allusion to Chrysostom (though he is reflected elsewhere in Calvin's exegesis), Calvin believes he has taken into account the opinions of four of the most important early commentators. Interestingly enough, he rejects the opinions of all four. In fact, of the thirteen opinions he cites, he cheerfully dismisses twelve.

Origen

Some interpreters, according to Calvin, believe that when Paul spoke of the weakness of the law (verse 3), he was "depriving only ceremonies of the power to justify." Calvin may be alluding to a much more finely nuanced argument in Origen[91] (though the point is repeated by Lanfranc[92] and Haymo of Auxerre[93] as well) which plays spirit against letter and Old Testament against New. What cannot justify is law understood according to the letter. Origen cites two ceremonies of the old covenant to substantiate this point: Sabbath keeping and temple sacrifices.

Ambrosiaster

Other interpreters equate the law of sin and death with the Law of Moses (verse 2). This position, as we have seen, was held by Ambrosiaster,[94] though not by Chrysostom (or, for that matter, Augustine[95] or Pelagius,[96] either). Calvin finds this equation too harsh, even invidious. He tries an even more radical demythologizing of the "law" than the Fathers attempted. The law of the Spirit of life is simply an inept and inappropriate way to refer to the Holy Spirit.[97] The law of sin and death refers to the "dominion of the flesh and the tyranny of death which follows from it."[98] The law of God stands in the middle between two conflicting powers. It teaches righteousness but cannot confer it. Rather, as Calvin laments, it "binds us in bondage to sin and death by still stronger bonds."[99] While Calvin portrays his objection to the position of Ambrosiaster in severe language, it is difficult to see that there is a substantial difference between them on the main issue.

Augustine

Calvin also rejects the "opinion of those who explain *the law of sin* to mean the lust of the flesh, as if Paul had said that he had conquered it" (verse 2).[100] This objection appears to be directed against Augustine and the Augustinian tradition of biblical interpretation. To be sure, Augustine does not use the phrase *concupiscentia carnis* in his comment on 8:1–2, or the related terms *fomes peccati* and *consuetudo peccandi.*[101] Those terms are, of course, used by Peter Abelard,[102] Hervaeus of Bourg-Dieu,[103] William of Saint Thierry,[104] Pseudo-Bruno the Carthusian,[105] Hugh of Saint Cher,[106] and Thomas Aquinas[107] in their comments on these verses. Augustine speaks rather of *carnalia desideria* and of life *sub lege* and *sub gratia.* Fleshly desires remain in Christians even after baptism. Nevertheless, they are not a source of condemnation for Christians because Christians do not obey them. This victory over sin marks life under grace rather than the old life under the law. Life *sub lege* was life in subjection to the flesh. Concupiscence in believers, in other words, is not sinful unless it is freely consented to by an act of the human will. The Augustinian tradition is clear on that point, and it is a tradition that Calvin rejects.

Chrysostom

The one really puzzling note struck by Calvin in his discussion of Romans 8:1–11 is his ascription to Chrysostom of an opinion found in Ambrosiaster. It was Ambrosiaster who argued that "sin had been condemned on account of sin (*de peccato*), because it assailed Christ unjustly and contrary to what he deserved" (verse 3), not Chrysostom. Clearly Calvin made a mistake. He may have been misled by Bucer, who, while properly ascribing this exegetical comment to Ambrose (Ambrosiaster), nevertheless adds, "with whom Chrysostom agrees."[108] Or he may simply have suffered a lapse of memory. Walchenbach has already demonstrated that many of Calvin's references to Chrysostom in his commentary on 1 Corinthians were made from memory. They are inexact, sometimes prejudiced, and rarely up to the rigorous standards that govern modern research. Under the circumstances it is hardly astonishing that Calvin from time to time made an inexact ascription. On the whole, it would be far more astonishing if he had not.

Calvin's exegesis of Romans 8:1–11 can be summarized very quickly, particularly if we use the four categories—law, anthropology, Christology, and ethics—under which we discussed the Pauline exegesis of Ambrosiaster and Chrysostom.

Law

Unlike Chrysostom, Calvin does not find any reference in this passage to natural law. The only law (in the proper sense of the term) that Calvin finds in these verses is the Mosaic law. The law of the Spirit of life and the law of sin and death are loose and inexact expressions for the two powers that confront the Mosaic law: the Holy Spirit, on the one hand, and the dominion of sin and death, on the other.[109] The Mosaic law teaches a righteousness it cannot confer and thereby intensifies the human predicament.[110] The fault lies in human corruption, and not in the law itself. Indeed, Calvin lashes out against the Libertines, who argue that since everything in nature and history happens by the will of God (a point Calvin is not prepared to dispute), everything that happens is by that very fact morally good (an opinion Calvin categorizes as blasphemy).[111] That something happens is not in and of itself a sufficient moral sanction. The law of God is the standard according to which actions and events must be judged. The law is a reliable guide to the will of God, even if it is "impotent" (Calvin believes that no weaker term will do justice to Paul's argument) to effect the good it teaches.[112] Paul's discussion of the law therefore resolves itself very rapidly into a discussion of anthropology.

Anthropology

Calvin combines a very clear emphasis on the unity of human nature with a very strong suggestion that there are higher and lower faculties in the human personality. On the one hand, he defines flesh as "all the endowments of human nature, and everything that is in man, except the sanctification of the Spirit."[113] On the other hand, he talks about the body in deprecating terms as that "stolid mass" as yet unpurified by the Holy Spirit,[114] or he refers to the human spirit as that "part of the soul" which the Holy Spirit has purified from evil.[115] But it is the holistic language that predominates. Paul uses flesh and spirit to refer to the soul.[116] He neither blames the poor human body as the source of sin and death nor celebrates the human soul as a source of continual life.[117] When Paul uses the term *mortal bodies,* he is referring to everything in human nature subject to death.[118] While body and soul can be distinguished, and there are some senses in which the soul is superior to the body, the human predicament embraces the whole human person in its relationship to God. Flesh is not a faculty but the *totus homo* in opposition and rebellion against God. Calvin rejects the doctrine of free will. The "mind of the flesh" (Calvin prefers this translation to the "prudence" of the Vulgate or the "affection" of Erasmus) "includes all the feelings of the soul from the reason and understanding to the affections."[119] This mind is not only *not* subject to the law of God; it cannot be subject to the law of God (a declaration that puts an end to the arguments of the Sophists and their "non-Christian philosophy" of the freedom of the will).[120]

Christology

Calvin agrees with the main patristic point that the phrase "likeness of sinful flesh" means that there is no substantial difference between Christ's humanity and ours, except for his freedom from sin.[121] "Likeness" here refers to "sinful," and not to "flesh," as though Christ were a docetic apparition. Christ's flesh had the appearance of sinful flesh because it sustained the punishment due our sins and also because Christ learned sympathy with us by bearing our infirmities.[122] While Calvin rejects Ambrosiaster's interpretation of verse 3, that "sin had been condemned on account of sin (*de peccato*), because it assailed Christ unjustly and contrary to what he deserved," he does not doubt that Christ was unjustly condemned or that he was an innocent expiatory victim. He agrees with the point, which goes back to Origen, that *peccatum* is a sacrifice on which a curse has been laid.[123] He also spends some time repeating the axiom that the Spirit of the Father is the Spirit of the Son[124] and attempting to reconcile the Pauline perspective which "ascribes to the Father the glory of having raised up Christ" (verse 11) with the Johannine claim that "Christ certainly rose of himself and through his own power" (John 10:18).[125]

Ethics

Calvin observes that the children of God are spiritual not because they are perfect but because the beginnings of new life are stirring in them.[126] While they are always imperfect, they are always subjects of the mercy that pardons their sins and the power of the Spirit who regenerates them.[127] Free remission of sins is offered to believers who "join repentance to faith, and do not misuse the mercy of God by indulging the flesh."[128] Calvin regards this passage as an important consolation for the "trembling consciences" of the godly.[129] Christians are beyond "every danger of condemnation" if they struggle against the flesh.[130] Perfect consolation is not a reward for perfect obedience. Freedom from condemnation does not mean that there is nothing blameworthy in the Christian or that the Christian has "completely put off all the feelings of the flesh."[131] What it does mean is that divine mercy comforts the godly as though the struggle itself were already the final victory.

CONCLUSION

There is, of course, no time for a grand conclusion in an essay of this brevity, nor should we really attempt one. Nevertheless, one can make some modest observations.

1. It would be a mistake to judge Calvin's relationship to the Fathers solely on the basis of his explicit references to patristic literature. If, for example, one relied only on the index of the *Corpus Reformatorum* as a guide to Calvin's knowledge of the Fathers, one would conclude that Calvin referred in his commentaries on the New Testament to Chrysostom 105 times, to Augustine 101, to Jerome 38, to Ambrose 23, and to Ambrosiaster not at all. Careful examination of Romans 8:1–11 has shown that the relationship of Calvin to the Fathers is far more complicated and cannot be unraveled without paying careful attention to the anonymous attributions scattered throughout his commentaries. When Calvin referred to "some commentators" or "the opinion of

those who hold," he may very well have had in mind the exegetical comment of some unnamed Father. One also cannot exclude the possibility that when Calvin referred explicitly to an author, he may from time to time have suffered a lapse of memory.

2. Calvin's attitude toward the Fathers changed in the period between his earliest and latest works. Walchenbach noted this development in his study of Calvin on 1 Corinthians, and our examination of Romans 8 tends to confirm his conclusions. In the period between the 1540 commentary on Romans 8:1–11 (in which Calvin cites no Fathers) and the 1556 commentary (in which he cites four), Calvin accepted the Fathers as commentators whose views had to be taken into account as he wrote his own exegesis. He does not appear to have developed such respect for medieval exegetical literature, and there is some reason to believe that he did not know that literature in the same depth. But the Fathers clearly formed part of his working library as he attempted to understand the mind of Paul.

3. Calvin did not use the Fathers in the way that a medieval commentator used his ancient authorities. The Fathers were not cited by Calvin in his exegesis of Romans 8 because he agreed with them and needed their authority to strengthen his argument. Nor did he cite them because their teaching was binding on him and foreclosed in advance the range of his exegetical options. He did not attempt to harmonize the teaching of the Fathers or to reconcile differences between them, though he did feel obliged to reconcile what appears to be a disagreement between Paul and John. In every case, explicit and anonymous, in which Calvin has referred to patristic exegesis, he has quarreled with it.

One ought not make too much of this quarrel. After all, as we have already seen, there is a wide range of issues on which Calvin is in complete agreement with the Fathers. Disagreements over smaller points of exegesis ought not obscure that larger consensus on anthropological and christological issues. Still, it is true to say that Calvin treated the Fathers as partners in conversation rather than as authorities in the medieval sense of the term. They stimulated Calvin in his reflections on the text. They presented him with ideas and suggestions he did not find in the writings of his contemporaries. Nevertheless, they did not have the last word. Paul did. A commentary is useful only to the extent that it illuminates the mind of Paul. *Medicus non est qui non medetur.* But the text of Paul takes precedence over even the best of the commentators, ancient and modern.

Calvin, after all, was writing a commentary on Paul, not on Origen or Chrysostom or Augustine or Ambrosiaster. Calvin kept his pages as uncluttered as possible because it was Paul himself, not his commentators, that Calvin wanted to interpret. To cite too many of the Fathers too often, or in an unassimilated fashion, would conflict with Calvin's exegetical ideal of lucid brevity. But that Calvin did not clutter his pages with citations does not mean that the Fathers were not constant companions in his study. Calvin regarded the interpretation of Paul as a work carried on not only in association with his contemporaries but also in conversation with the greatest interpreters of Christian antiquity.

JOHN B. PAYNE

Erasmus on Romans 9:6–24

Paul's letter to the Romans, chapter 9:6–24, has posed problems for interpreters from the time of Origen to the present.[1] How is one to understand these passages, which seem to make election to salvation depend entirely upon the divine and not at all upon the human will, which announce the mercy and the power of God beyond human comprehension and measure? How is one to interpret the verses concerning the election of Jacob and Esau, God's having mercy upon whomever he wills and hardening the heart of whomever he wills, and the comparison of God to the potter who molds the clay as he wishes?

The Fathers, both Eastern and Western, with the exception of Augustine in his later anti-Pelagian period, struggled mightily over these passages to show that they should not be interpreted in a way that denies the responsibility of human free will. Their discussions furnished fuel for the heated debate concerning Romans 9 in the sixteenth century, a time in which the questions of predestination and the relation between the divine and the human wills were especially hot ones.

These passages and the patristic exegesis of them would figure prominently in the famous quarrel between Erasmus and Luther on free will. However, it is my intention not so much to rehearse that debate as to set forth the exegesis of Erasmus which preceded, accompanied, and followed that debate and to assess the hermeneutical factors which shaped his exegesis: his own basic disposition, his philological and historical sense, his authorities, and the religious situation.

My analysis of Erasmus's interpretation of Romans 9:6–24 rests on his paraphrase first published in 1517 and substantially revised in 1532. It takes into account also the annotations published first in 1516 and revised in editions up to 1535, though the annotations on Romans 9:6–24 offer little of theological substance in contrast to those on other chapters of Romans. My exposition draws also on the abundant material in the *De libero arbitrio* (1524) and the *Hyperaspistae II* (1527).

The major themes of Erasmus's exegesis of Romans 9 in his 1517 paraphrase are, on the one hand, the goodness and mercy of God, and on the other hand, the freedom and responsibility of man. In God there is goodness and leniency, no injustice and arbitrariness, and hardly any wrath. The words of 9:14–19, concerning God's having mercy on whom he wills and hardening whom he wills, Erasmus interprets as the words not of Paul himself but of an impious opponent, and this interpretation follows that of Origen and the Fathers after him.[2] God does not harden the minds of men but uses the stubbornness of those who refuse to believe to illustrate the magnitude of his kindness and the glory of his power. "Pharaoh might have been corrected if he had not resisted by his own obduracy. But the divine leniency provoked his impious mind even more."[3]

In connection with the simile of the potter and the clay in 9:21 Erasmus, like the Fathers, discourses on the mysterious wisdom and power of God.[4] Though God is all-powerful, God does not use his power for evil purposes. "God can do whatever he wishes. But at the same time, since he is the best, he does not desire anything but the best. And he ought not to be blamed if he uses our evils for a good purpose."[5] God's gentleness and clemency are further illustrated in 9:22–24: He tolerated the unbelieving and stubborn Jews for a long time and received into grace both Gentiles and Jews after they had repented and been corrected.[6]

God is gracious and good and is true to his promises, but his promises are not indiscriminate. As Erasmus says in his paraphrase of 9:6: "Their [i.e., the Jews'] impiety is not so strong that God fails to fulfill what he promised. . . . However, it was not promised indiscriminately but only to those who were truly descendants of those men," that is, of the patriarchs, who "through firmness of faith" show that they "truly fit the name of Israelite."[7] Only those who display the faith of Abraham deserve the happiness that was promised to his descendants. In his emphasis on faith as a merit which deserves the promise of God, Erasmus shows again the influence of Origen,[8] Ambrosiaster,[9] and probably also Pelagius, though he was not aware that the commentaries on the Pauline letters which came down through the Middle Ages in the name of Jerome were actually by Pelagius.[10]

The 1517 paraphrase of 9:16, "so it depends not upon man's will or exertion but upon God's mercy," is not content with disregarding the verse as the words of an impious opponent but seeks to explain, just as did Origen, that the verse does not exclude some participation of free will in salvation: "It is not by willing or by exertion that salvation is attained, but by the mercy of God. . . . And yet some part of it depends on our own will and effort, although this part is so minor that it seems like nothing at all in comparison with the free kindness of God."[11] Later, in 1532, Erasmus modified this interpretation.[12]

If the salvation of some of the Jews and Gentiles is owed mostly to divine grace but in part also to human free will, Erasmus emphasizes that the destruction of most of them is due entirely to their own ill will. Romans 9:19, "Thou sayest to me: Why then does he still find fault? For who resists his will?" Erasmus interprets again as the words of the impious opponent who wants to ascribe to God the cause of our sin. He says in reply: "No one resists the will of God, but the will of God is not the cause of your destruction. He did not harden the heart of Pharaoh in such a way that he himself caused Pharaoh's stubbornness."[13] Likewise, he wishes to make it clear in his comments on the simile of the potter and the clay in Romans 9:21 that man, not God, is responsible for sin. "God has not made you into a filthy vessel. You have defiled yourself, and you have devoted yourself to ignoble purposes." It is due to their own fault, their own stubbornness and obduracy—as Erasmus does not tire of repeating—that most men perish, though "God will still fulfill for those few who have believed what he has promised to all."[14]

As I have already indicated, Erasmus's exegesis of Romans 9 closely follows those of the Fathers—especially Origen but also Jerome,[15] Ambrosiaster, and Pelagius, who were all intent on stressing that however much Paul talks about grace in this chapter, he does not intend to deny free will. With the exception of the late Augustine, they all hold to the view that the divine election takes place *post praevisa merita.* In his paraphrase intended for a popular audience and thus written in a simple style, Erasmus avoids the use of the language of predestination and foreknowledge, namely, that God predestines to salvation those whom he foreknows are worthy of it and to damnation those whom he foreknows are unworthy, but he clearly interprets Paul as saying that salvation is granted only to those who deserve it by the merit of faith, while destruction comes to those who deserve it because of their obstinate disbelief.

In a letter to Marcus Laurinus on February 1, 1523,[16] written presumably to answer some Lutheran critics of his paraphrase, Erasmus indicates that he was following Origen and Jerome in ascribing a certain minimum to free will. He says he wrote his paraphrase before Luther published his dogma that whatever we do, whether good or evil, is of absolute necessity. He says he did not undertake to treat the question thoroughly but only to touch on it in passing, just as Paul did, "who disdains to reply there to the impious interrogator." And yet how much less did Erasmus attribute to free will than did the ancient and more modern scholastics. He writes that he saw two dangers which he sought to avoid, the Scylla of confidence in works, which he confesses to be "the greatest plague of religion," and the Charybdis, "the even more formidable evil by which now not a few are held who say, 'Whether we follow our own inclinations, or torment ourselves, or give in to our passions, nevertheless it comes about because God has once so established it.'" The Christian moralist explains the intention of his choice of language: "Thus I so measured my word, that I attributed a certain minimum to free will lest I open the window to such a dangerous indolence that each one would do whatever was pleasing to him since all effort toward a better life had been cast aside."

Erasmus would find himself compelled once more to wrestle with the difficulties of Romans 9 and the patristic interpretations of it as he tackled Lutheran dogma in *De libero arbitrio,* which he wrote the following year. In this treatise, after setting forth a series of biblical texts which he thinks support the freedom of the will, Erasmus turns his attention to certain texts which seem to oppose it. Here he proposes three sets of passages from Romans 9 and their corresponding parallels in the Old Testament: (1) Romans 9:17 and its basis in Exodus 9:12, 16, and 33:19 concerning the hardening of Pharaoh's heart; (2) Romans 9:11–13 and its referents in Genesis 25:23 and Malachi 1:2–3 concerning the election of Jacob and Esau; and (3) Romans 9:20–22, with its connection to Isaiah 45:9 and Jeremiah 18:6 concerning the simile of the potter and the clay.[17] As Zickendraht pointed out long ago,[18] and Godin[19] more recently, Erasmus's discussion of all three of these sets of passages is replete with specific borrowings from Origen, especially from his *Peri Archon,* book 3, chapter 1, even where he does not acknowledge his debt.

Concerning the first set of passages, which deal with the hardening of Pharaoh's heart, Erasmus expressly follows Origen with the sentiment that since God is not only just but also good, the hardening of Pharaoh's heart must be interpreted as figurative speech. The biblical text must be understood as teaching that an occasion was provided by God, but that the actual hardening was due to Pharaoh, who "by his own ill will was made more stubborn by things which should have led him to repentance."[20] In order to explain this figure of hardening, Erasmus makes use of four colorful comparisons drawn from Origen's *Peri Archon* in exactly the order that Origen recites them, though compared with Origen his discussion is much more compressed:[21] (1) the comparison of the divine goodness to the rain which at once occasions good fruit from cultivated but thorns and thistles from uncultivated land; (2) the comparison of the divine leniency—which, in tolerating the sinner, brings some to repentance while making others more stubborn in their ill will—to the same action of the sun, which both melts wax and hardens mud; (3) the simile of the indulgent father who says to his son, "I spoiled you," meaning that he is criticizing himself for not having at once punished the boy's faults, and thus having abetted his corruption;[22] and (4) the comparison of God to the experienced surgeon who prefers a wound to heal slowly so that the diseased matter might be brought out of the open wound and a permanent health ensue. This comparison is intended to illuminate passages from Isaiah 63:17: "O Lord, why hast thou made us err from thy ways and hardened our heart, so that we fear thee not?" and Jeremiah 20:7: "O Lord, thou has deceived me, and I was deceived, thou wert stronger than I, and thou hast provided," both of which are also found in Origen in a similar context. But Erasmus draws on Jerome as well as on Origen for his interpretation of the first passage: "God hardens when he does not at once punish the sinner, and has mercy as soon as he invites repentance by means of afflictions."[23] In the second case, God "is said to seduce when he does not at once recall from error, and this in Origen's opinion conduces meanwhile to a more perfect health."[24]

Though Erasmus follows closely these Origenistic comparisons which seek to explain God's impartial goodness and long-suffering leniency in dealing with sinners, he does not, of course, adopt Origen's speculative cosmology and eschatology, which permits the Greek Father to extend God's patient care and therapeutic cure into the many ages to come. He does not suggest, as does Origen, that God's providential care for Pharaoh continued beyond his life and drowning in the Red Sea.[25] Rather, utilizing Origen's less speculative comment in his commentary on Romans in which he notes that the Lord says, "But for this purpose I have raised you up," not "For this purpose I made you,"[26] Erasmus underlines the goodness of God's creation, the responsibility of the human will, Pharaoh's own guilt, and God's intentional use of Pharaoh's malice to bring about the salvation of his people.[27] He even goes so far as to say that God willed Pharaoh to perish, but only on the basis of his foreknowledge of Pharaoh's sin.[28]

Making use again of Origen's view, he interprets similarly the passages concerning Jacob and Esau. However, unlike Origen, he first points out that the passages in Genesis and Malachi do not properly pertain to eternal salvation, but rather to the temporal fortunes or misfortunes, in the first instance, of Jacob and Esau themselves, and in the second, of the kingdoms of Israel and Edom. But even as used tropologically by Paul, the words "Jacob I loved, but Esau I hated" are intended not so much to apply to the question of eternal salvation as to repress the arrogance of the Jews who thought that the grace of the gospel was especially owed to them.[29]

He draws also on Origen for the view that God's love (that is, his election of Jacob-Gentiles) and hatred (that is, his rejection of Esau-Jews) were based upon their deeds, which were deserving of love or hatred. And Erasmus points to Romans 11:20, which states that the Jews were broken off by their unbelief while the Gentiles stand fast only through faith. While accepting Origen's *praedestinatio post praevisa merita* as a basis for the interpretation of Romans 9:11–13, Erasmus limits it to a *praedestinatio ad gratiam,* not *ad gloriam,* and he passes over Origen's speculations concerning the divine election of

Jacob and rejection of Esau before they were born as signifying their predestination based on merits of their preexistent souls.[30]

As to the third set of passages, concerning the simile of the potter and the clay, Erasmus first emphasizes that their point is not to remove free will, but rather, in the case of the passages from the prophets, to reject the complaint of the people against God, and in the case of Paul, "to repress the wicked murmuring of the Jews against God who on account of their obstinate unbelief were rejected from the grace of the gospel, while the Gentiles were received on the ground of their faith."[31]

Like Origen in his *Peri Archon* and his commentary on Romans,[32] Erasmus places Romans 9:21–23 over and against 2 Timothy 2:20: "In a great house there are not only vessels of gold and silver, but also of wood and earthenware, and some for noble use, some for ignoble. If anyone purifies himself from these, then he will be a vessel for noble use, consecrated to honor, and useful to the master of the house, ready for any good work." If both passages are interpreted literally, says Erasmus, Paul would seem to be contradicting himself, but such a contradiction is disallowed on the basis of the principle, set forth earlier in the treatise, that "Scripture cannot be in conflict with itself, since the whole proceeds from the same spirit."[33] However, they may be harmonized because each has a different function: the Romans passage "to shut the mouth which murmurs against God," and the passage in 2 Timothy "to encourage industry and discourage carelessness or despair."[34] The meaning of Romans 9:21–23, as interpreted with the help of 2 Timothy 2:20, must be that the potter makes of some Jews vessels for dishonor on account of preceding merits—namely, their unbelief—and he makes out of the Gentiles vessels of honor on account of their belief.[35]

Once more like Origen, Erasmus argues for election on the basis of preceding merits, except that he limits it to *praedestinatio ad gratiam* and does not take up from the *Peri Archon* what is absent in the commentary on Romans—the speculative cosmology of preexistent souls and the eschatology concerning the possibility of the unending change in future ages of vessels of wrath into vessels of mercy, and vice versa.[36]

Finally, the exegesis of that central verse in Romans 9, namely, verse

16, is Origenistic just as it was in the paraphrase, as Erasmus had admitted to Marcus Laurinus. Though they both think that verses 14–19 are the words of the impious interrogator, both adopt the backup position that Romans 9:16 can be interpreted in a synergistic manner. Our efforts are not excluded by Paul's words, "so it depends not upon man's will or exertion but upon God's mercy." Their meaning is rather that our work is aided by the mercy of God, which "precedes our will, accompanies it in its endeavor, and grants to it a happy outcome. And yet meanwhile we will, we run, we pursue."[37]

Erasmus treats Romans 9 yet again in *Hyperaspistae II* (1527), his answer to Luther's attack in *De servo arbitrio* (1525). Erasmus's argument is rambling, repetitious, and prolix. Some fifty-five folio columns in the Leiden edition are devoted to refuting Luther's exegesis of this Pauline text and presenting his own.[38] I am concerned only with ferreting out Erasmus's own exegesis of the text from the mire of his argument against Luther, not with his confutation of Luther as such.

The main thrust of his exegesis is that the Pauline text has to do not with the question of eternal predestination and damnation but with the rejection of the Jews and the election of the Gentiles. In one section of his argument Erasmus sets the verses of chapter 9 into the context of Paul's overall theme in Romans, which he explains as follows. In the first part of Romans Paul is concerned to destroy the foolish confidence of the Gentiles in their philosophy and of the Jews in their observance of the law. He teaches that salvation is not bestowed on the basis of the observance of the ceremonies of the law, to which the Jews attribute more than to the spiritual precepts, which are fulfilled, not removed, by the gospel. Erasmus makes it clear here, as in his paraphrase of Romans, that he understands the gospel to be negating only the ceremonial aspects of the law.[39]

Then Paul shows that neither Jews nor Gentiles are righteous, but equally stand in need of the grace of the gospel, which is available to all, not on the basis of preceding merits but on the basis of the promise of God, who saves whoever repents and believes in the gospel regardless of national origin. The promise made to the Jews would be of no advantage to them unless they believed the gospel. They are to be considered heirs of Abraham only if they share in Abraham's faith. The Jews, however, resist the gospel because of their zeal for the old law, and the Gentiles, through faith, suddenly become true sons of

Abraham. God foreknew that the Jews would forsake the gospel and that the gates would be opened to the Gentiles.[40]

Turning then specifically to the question of chapter 9, namely, why God has rejected his people, Erasmus explains that the story of Jacob and Esau is intended to illustrate God's foreknowledge and his election; God rejected the Jews on the basis of his foreknowledge that they would resist the gospel, and he chose the Gentiles for the reward of the gospel's grace on the basis of his foreknowledge of their faith, just as, before they were born, he chose Jacob rather than Esau because he foreknew Jacob's future piety. He brought forth against the Jews examples of his severity, just as he did against Pharaoh, and to the Gentiles he proclaimed examples of his mercy, just as he did to the children of Israel who were freed from Egyptian bondage. But Erasmus emphasizes vis-à-vis Luther that God did not himself forcibly repulse the Jews; they themselves obstinately resisted the gospel in spite of all the miracles they had witnessed and the benefits they received. They are therefore vessels of wrath prepared for destruction, which Paul sets forth as "the most horrible illustration of all in order to show how dangerous it is to spurn the offered grace of God."[41] But God made use of the obstinacy of the Jews for his own glory and the salvation of the Gentiles, and he now makes use of the faith of the Gentiles to declare his kindness to all who believe in the gospel.

As opposed to Luther, Erasmus intends to stress that whether the benefit is received or not depends not entirely upon the divine initiative but also upon the free response of faith, in spite of what might seem to be suggested by the language of Romans 9. "The whole of this benefit," Erasmus says, "depends upon the liberality of God and the faith of men."[42] Romans 9 must be interpreted in the light of Romans 11, which describes how the Jews have been cut off from the olive tree because of their unbelief and the Gentiles have been grafted on because of their belief.[43] Romans 11:20 is therefore an important proof text for Erasmus's contention concerning the participation of free will in the reception of divine grace. He likewise points to 9:30–32: "What shall we say, then? That Gentiles who did not pursue righteousness have attained it, that is, righteousness through faith, [while] Israel by pursuing the law of righteousness did not reach the law of righteousness. Why? Because they pursued it not as based on faith but as if it were based on works." Erasmus comments further, "You see the Jews have been rejected not without cause, namely on account of their confidence in legal works, puffed up by which, they resisted the gospel. Neither have those from the Gentiles been saved without cause, but rather because of simple belief."[44]

He goes on to what he knows would be Luther's difficulty with such an interpretation: "But faith is a gift of God, it is not in our power. I admit it, if you are thinking of justifying faith by grace; but just as there is a certain knowledge which prepares for the light of faith, so there is a certain human faith preparing man for justifying faith."[45] Though he does not mention the term here, Erasmus has in mind the scholastic *fides acquisita*—the faith obtained by natural means that is the necessary condition for the reception of the *fides infusa,* justifying grace.[46] His thought here is entirely in line with the Occamistic point of view expressed elsewhere in the *Hyperaspistae II* concerning the necessity of a *meritum de congruo* in preparation for receiving justifying grace.[47]

But if one retorts to Erasmus that he neglects 9:15–16: "I will have mercy on whom I have mercy, and will have compassion upon whom I have compassion," and also verse 18: "So then he has mercy upon whomever he wills and he hardens the heart of whomever he wills," Erasmus responds that the Fathers attributed these words not to Paul but to an impious opponent of Paul.[48] However, even if they are Paul's words they present no difficulty, for they can be interpreted along the lines of Origen, as Erasmus now expressly notes: "man wills in vain, he labors in vain unless assisting grace is added," just as in the meaning of the psalm: "Unless the Lord has watched over the city, he is vigilant in vain who watches over it" (Psalm 127:1); as well as the statement of Paul: "Neither he who plants nor he who waters is anything, but God who gives the growth" (1 Corinthians 3:7).[49]

But one might press Erasmus further concerning the interpretation of verses 19 and 20: "You will say to me then, 'Why does he still find fault? For who can resist his will?' But who are you, a man, to answer back to God? Will what is molded say to its molder, 'Why have you made me thus?'" Do not these verses and the simile of the potter and the clay which follows demolish free will? As Luther asks Erasmus: "But if God works in such a way that he takes account of merits, why do they murmur and protest? Why do they say: 'Why does he find fault? Who can resist his will?' Why is there need for Paul to silence them? For who is surprised, let alone indignant or moved to protest, when anyone who has deserved it is damned?"[50] But Erasmus answers that these questions—Why does he still find fault? For who can resist his will?—represent the murmurings of the impious Jews against God. As with the story of Jacob and Esau, so with the simile of the potter and the clay; Paul's intention is to repress that murmuring which has as its cause the fact "that they envied the Gentiles to whom the kindness of God was granted, that they seemed to themselves righteous although they were wicked, and that they were puffed up with boasting of the law, which they did not preserve."[51] The story of Jacob and Esau and the simile of the potter and the clay therefore do not properly concern the questions of free will, eternal salvation, and damnation. Chapter 11 makes it clear that Paul is speaking here in chapter 9 about the *temporary* punishment of the Jews, not about their eternal rejection, because he talks there about their ultimate salvation.[52]

Erasmus thus seems to have a double line of interpretation for these passages in Romans 9 that appear to ascribe all to the divine sovereign grace and nothing to free will. The first is to argue that, properly speaking, they do not pertain to a discourse on grace and free will, but rather to repressing the arrogance of the Jews and to explaining God's temporary punishment of the Jews and his gift of grace to the Gentiles. But second, insofar as they concern the question of grace and free will, they have not to do with a *praedestinatio ad gloriam* but a *praedestinatio ad gratiam,* which, however, is grounded not only in the divine but also in the human will—that is, on the basis of a *praedestinatio post praevisa merita.* He makes full use of Romans 11 not only to reject an eternal damnation as the subject of chapter 9 but also to try to show that it is on the basis of faith or unfaith that Jews and Gentiles are ultimately accepted or rejected.

Finally, in order to buttress his view of a participation of free will in the process of salvation, Erasmus marshals the arguments of the Fathers. Though he both explicitly and implicitly referred to the Fathers, especially Origen and Jerome, in *On Free Will,* in spite of the fact that he announced at the outset that he was adopting only Luther's terrain for the argument (namely, Scripture), his references to and citations of the Fathers in the *Hyperaspistae* are far more numerous, extensive, and varied. Perhaps because Luther had criticized his use of

Origen and Jerome in the *Diatribe,* those Fathers now take a back seat to Chrysostom, who receives a far greater number of references and citations; one single citation exceeds four folio columns in length.[53] The ample use of Chrysostom can probably also be explained by Erasmus's involvement with the edition of that Greek Father in the late 1520s.[54] Of course, the introduction of Chrysostom did not signify any change in position, because the Antiochian Father entirely agreed with Origen and Jerome on the central issues of exegesis in Romans 9. Other Fathers cited include Ambrosiaster, Pseudo-Jerome (that is, Pelagius), and even Augustine.

In addition, Erasmus draws on Occamistic thinking concerning the relation of grace and free will, as near the end of his discussion of Romans 9 where he talks about three kinds of merits and three kinds of grace, and here he goes beyond the question of a *praedestinatio ad gratiam* to a *praedestinatio ad gloriam.* First, there is a certain kind of merit based on a life lived not without sins, to be sure, but without malice and commended by many good deeds which render a man worthy to a certain extent of vocational grace. Second, the embracing rather than repulsing of this impelling grace (*gratia pulsans*) constitutes a merit deserving of justifying grace. Third, the strenuous striving for eternal life through pious deeds under the influence of grace in some measure merits the kingdom of heaven. And Erasmus immediately connects this scheme with divine predestination: "God, moreover, who from all eternity has determined for them his graces and eternal life, has made his determination for the reason that he foreknew that his grace would not be fruitless in them."[55]

This is the opinion called Scotist in the *De libero arbitrio* and the *Hyperaspistae I,* but it is really Occamist.[56] Erasmus describes it as holding that free will of its own natural power through morally good works can merit *de congruo* but not *de condigno* justifying grace. He names this as the second of five possible positions on the question of grace and free will. The first is that of Pelagius, who taught that once the will was healed and freed by Christ, no new grace was needed, but free will on its own could attain salvation; the third, that of Augustine and Aquinas, attributes much to grace, without, however, denying free will and thinks that man can only amend his life, progress, and reach the goal of salvation by the continuous aid of divine grace; the fourth, the harsher view of Carlstadt, takes the position that grace produces good not *through* or *with* but only *in* free will as wax in the hands of the molder; and the fifth, the harshest of all, is that of Luther, who taught that free will is an empty name since the free will can accomplish nothing and all that happens is by mere necessity.[57]

Current scholarly opinion still debates Erasmus's own stance among these positions. The first, he knows, is clearly heterodox; the last two he rejects as repugnant to right reason, moral sense, and the teachings of Scripture and tradition. The third, the Augustinian-Thomistic, he calls "probable enough" (*satis probabilis*) in the *De libero arbitrio.*[58] The second, "Scotistic," opinion is set forth in the *Hyperaspistae I* and *II* as one which the church has neither accepted nor rejected and which Erasmus has neither approved nor disapproved,[59] although toward the end of the *Hyperaspistae II* he says he is more inclined to approve than disapprove of this opinion.[60] The choice lies between the second and third opinions—the "Scotistic"-Occamistic and the Augustinian-Thomistic. Some scholars place him in one or the other of these two camps;[61] others see him as fluctuating between these positions;[62] yet another interprets him as closer to the later Lutheran synergists than to either of these two scholastic opinions.[63] My own view remains that in spite of much hesitation and fluctuation, Erasmus's true sympathies were with the Occamistic view, because while it acknowledged a certain incommensurability between human merit and divine grace, it stressed the dignity of man even after the Fall and granted an important role to free will before and after the reception of both vocational and justifying grace. Not only his acknowledgment near the end of the *Hyperaspistae II* that he is more inclined to approve than disapprove of this opinion, but also his actual use of it in his effort to show that the Pauline doctrine of grace need not be interpreted as denying free will attest to its appeal for him.

In a most interesting and important letter to Thomas More written March 30, 1527, just as he was about to begin work on *Hyperaspistae II,*[64] Erasmus reveals his continued wrestling with the Pauline doctrine of grace and its relation to free will:

If I shall have treated the material with the soul of monks and theologians, who attribute too much to the merits of men on account of the gain returning to them, I shall speak indeed against my conscience, and knowingly I shall obscure the glory of Christ. But if I shall have so tempered my style that I attribute something to free will, much to grace, I shall offend both sides, as I found by experience in the *Diatribe.* But if I follow Paul and Augustine, there is very little which is left to free will. . . . To me the opinion is not displeasing which thinks that we *ex meris nature viribus* apart from special grace can *de congruo,* as they say, establish grace, unless Paul is resisted, although not even the scholastics receive this opinion.[65]

In this candid statement Erasmus divulges to his friend what he will not own to Luther—that the Pauline doctrine of grace is not easily harmonized with free will and merit. He also recognizes that Augustine is close to Paul in his championing of the sovereignty of divine grace, whereas to Luther he tries to show that even the late Augustine who wrote to Valentinus "On Grace and Free Will" accords a role to free will.[66] Finally, in advance of his writing of *Hyperaspistae II,* he reveals his pleasure with the Occamist position on grace and free will but acknowledges what again he will not admit to Luther—that it may be contradictory to Paul's teaching.

This Pauline check on his own predilections appears in his revision of the paraphrase of Romans published in 1532. As I pointed out in a previous essay, Erasmus makes several changes throughout the paraphrase that give a greater stress to grace and faith. None is more significant than the revisions of and additions to the paraphrase of Romans 9.

The backup position of Origen and Chrysostom—that even if Romans 9:15–16 is regarded as Paul's words, it can be explained in a synergistic manner—one which Erasmus had adopted not only in the 1517 paraphrase but also in the 1524 *Diatribe* and the 1527 *Hyperaspistae,* is eliminated from the 1532 paraphrase. The statement "And yet some part of it depends on our own will and effort, although this part is so minor that it seems like nothing at all in comparison with the free kindness of God," drops out entirely and is replaced by "However, it does not follow that God is unjust to anyone, but that he is merciful toward many."[67]

Furthermore, he makes an extensive addition to his paraphrase of 9:20–21 concerning the potter and the clay, the most important part of which surprises us by stating in an Augustinian, even a Lutheran, manner:

Therefore, if God abandons someone in his sins, thus he was born, there is no injustice. But if he calls someone to righteousness, his mercy is a free gift. In the case of the former, God declares his own righteousness so that he may be feared. To the latter he discloses his own goodness so that he may be loved. It is not the part of a man to require a reason from God for his decision—why he calls this man later and that one earlier, why he accepts one who has done nothing to deserve it and abandons a man who has incurred no guilt.[68]

Is it possible that during the course of the free-will debate Erasmus was persuaded by renewed study of Paul and Augustine or even by Luther himself to modify his interpretation of Romans 9:15–16 and 20–21? Or did he finally decide, in these passages at least, that Paul must be allowed to speak for himself, however much what he says here may seem to collide with what he says elsewhere—in Romans 11, for example—and however much it may go counter to Erasmus's own deeply held opinion and that of the Fathers he usually followed?

There are other occasions in his exegesis of Romans (to be sure, more in his annotations than in his paraphrase) where his philological, historical perception of the Pauline sense overrules his patristic authorities and his own fundamental predilections. I give just four examples. Erasmus differs from all the patristic authorities except Ambrosiaster in judging the indicative *ἔχομεν* rather than the hortatory subjunctive *ἔχωμεν* to be the correct reading of 5:1 because he thinks the Pauline sense here is that peace is a condition already possessed by those justified through faith rather than a good to be sought.[69] Similarly, he argues on the basis of the probable Pauline sense that *ἔιπερ* in 8:9 has a confirmative, not a conditional, meaning, and here he is at variance with Origen and Ambrosiaster, two of his favorites, and sides with Chrysostom.[70] Moreover, in his annotation of 8:28 Erasmus goes against most of the Fathers, including Origen and Ambrosiaster, whose interpretation he rightly judges to be ambiguous, with his exegesis that *κατὰ πρόθεσιν* refers not to the human but to the divine will.[71] A final example of his perception of Pauline sense and his independence of mind in contrast to most of the Fathers upon whom he usually relies is the proper understanding of *ἀγάπης τοῦ Χριστοῦ* in 8:35 as a subjective rather than an objective genitive, though he remarks in both his annotation and his paraphrase that Christ's love for man should prompt man to love him in return.[72]

It is thus possible to take the position that Erasmus in his paraphrase of 9:15–16 and 20–21 is finally permitting his historical perception of the Pauline sense to set aside his usual patristic authorities and his own personal predisposition. Such an interpretation is not finally satisfactory, however, because Erasmus has by no means eliminated the stress on free will from his exegesis of Romans 9—even of 9:15–16 and 20–21. On 9:20–21 he retains his paraphrase, with its allusion to 2 Timothy 2:20–21: "God has not made you into a filthy vessel. You have defiled yourself, and you have devoted yourself to ignoble purposes."[73] And on verses 15–16 he makes an addition that underlines human responsibility at least for sin, which contrasts with his expanded paraphrase of verses 20–21. On 20–21 he writes in 1532: "It is not the part of a man to require a reason from God for his decision—why he calls this man later and that one earlier, why he accepts a man who has done nothing to deserve it, and abandons a man who has incurred no guilt,"[74] whereas on 15–16 he adds in 1532, "If you have been abandoned to your own obduracy," in order to complete the meaning of "you have no reason to complain."[75] He retains also the numerous other statements that it is Pharaoh's, the Jews', or man's own acts that are the cause of their destruction, not God's.

Rather than a substantial change of interpretation or a foolish inconsistency on Erasmus's part, these changes, along with others in different parts of his Romans paraphrase which give greater weight to grace and faith as trust, represent, as I have argued elsewhere,[76] his effort to arrive at a more balanced view for the sake of Christian unity in the 1530s. I have also argued that he may well have been moved to adopt this somewhat more evangelical exegesis of Romans on behalf of ecumenical peace by Melanchthon's mitigation of his own position on free will and justification in the late 1520s, his renewed goodwill toward Erasmus, and his efforts on behalf of Christian unity at Augsburg. In the same year in which Erasmus released his modified interpretation of Romans as a contribution to ecclesiastical concord, Melanchthon published his full commentary on Romans, which reveals changes in an Erasmian direction in the exegesis of chapter 9 as well as elsewhere. In sharp difference with the 1522 *Annotationes* Melanchthon, like Erasmus, rejects predestination as the subject of this chapter, which concerns rather the identity of the true church. To be sure, Paul does touch upon predestination here, but his intention is not speculation but consolation of the pious. And in fundamental contrast to the 1521 *Loci Communes* and the 1522 *Annotationes,* Melanchthon teaches that the will is not entirely negated by divine predestination; that the will, not God, is the cause of sin; that the words about the hardening of Pharaoh's heart must be interpreted figuratively as meaning that God permitted Pharaoh's heart to be hardened. Furthermore, he seems to look favorably upon the opinion of the early Augustine that although God's mercy is the true cause of salvation, nevertheless there is some cause in the one who receives insofar as he does not refuse the offered grace.[77]

If Erasmus had ecumenical peace as his aim with the publication of his 1532 paraphrases, it is clear from Melanchthon's dedicatory preface to Albert of Mainz that he had the same purpose in mind: "Now I pray that you will graciously receive this lucubration which I indeed hope will be not useless for peace."[78] It seems altogether likely that Erasmus and Melanchthon consciously collaborated for the peace of the church through the publication of their new interpretations of Romans.

Erasmus's exegesis of Romans 9 thus betrays four sets of hermeneutical factors which stand in uneasy tension with one another: (1) his own deep-seated disposition toward the affirmation of free will against any form of determinism or necessitarianism; (2) the theological tradition: in the use of the Fathers Origen, Jerome, Ambrosiaster, and Pseudo-Jerome in the 1517 *Paraphrasis* and the 1524 *Diatribe;* and in the 1527 *Hyperaspistae* the additional use of Chrysostom, the early Augustine, and late-medieval scholastic thinking on the relation of grace and free will, namely, Occamism, all of which provided him with ample authorities to support his basic inclination; (3) his own perception of the Pauline intention and meaning based on a keen philological and historical sense, which noted that Romans 9 concerns, in the first place, not eternal predestination but the temporary rejection of the Jews, but which may have also recognized, against his own predilection and preferred authorities, that God's grace must here be given its due, and so may have played a role in the 1532 revised paraphrase; and (4) the current religious climate, which in 1517 gave rise to the concern about excessive ceremonialism and monkish righteousness, on the one hand, and religious and moral lethargy, on the other; in 1524–27 to a concern for affirming the freedom and dignity of man against a divine determinism; and in 1532, in the midst of the conflict between Protestants and Catholics, to a concern for the unity of the church.

JEAN-CLAUDE MARGOLIN
Translated by John L. Farthing

The Epistle to the Romans (Chapter 11) According to the Versions and/or Commentaries of Valla, Colet, Lefèvre, and Erasmus

In an article published in 1974[1] John B. Payne called attention to the fact that modern historians of humanism had paid far less attention to the exegesis of Saint Paul in the closing decades of the fifteenth century and the first two decades of the sixteenth century than had historians of the Reformation, who had devoted considerable energy to an analysis of the commentaries of the great Reformers—Luther, above all, but Melanchthon, Zwingli, and Calvin as well. Three years later, Jerry H. Bentley[2] decried the abandonment or semiabandonment of the field of biblical philology, as much by theologians and historians of religion as by specialists in philology or the Renaissance. Both Payne and Bentley have attempted repeatedly—and, in the case of the former, again in this colloquy[3]—to fill this lacuna by means of papers and articles that are carefully documented and constructed with finesse and relevance to the topic at hand.[4] Indeed, as their own bibliographies make clear, scholarly interest in the question is largely a phenomenon of the last twenty or twenty-five years. Among the major contributors to the field (particularly specialists in the study of Erasmus) are Rudolf Padberg, Albert Rabil, Bo Reicke, Catherine A. L. Jarrott, Marvin A. Anderson, Wilhelm Kohls, Georges Chantraine, and Michael A. Screech.[5] Still more recent is the work of Jacques Chomarat, particularly his lecture given in Geneva in 1976[6] and his 1981 doctoral dissertation,[7] and André Godin's various works on Erasmus and Origen, including his doctoral dissertation.[8] Concerning Lorenzo Valla and his work as a New Testament critic, the attitude among scholars has changed recently in favor of the view that Valla exemplifies a philology profoundly engaged in the most fundamental debates of his time; this shift of attitude is clearly seen in the works of Salvatore I. Camporeale,[9] for instance, and above all in the writings of Mario Fois,[10] but also in the recent study by Jerry Bentley.[11] The Paulinism of Colet is emphasized, along with his Ficinism, by Sears Jayne.[12] With regard to Lefèvre d'Étaples, whose reformist spirit and connections with the movement of Meaux have been highlighted by Renaudet, publications such as those by Eugene R. Rice,[13] Michael Screech,[14] and especially Guy Bedouelle,[15] John B. Payne,[16] and Helmut Feld,[17] have stimulated the study of the exegetical thought in a band of Parisian Christian humanists, especially in the Collège du Cardinal-Lemoine, during the decades immediately preceding the Lutheran Reformation.

An abundance of evidence shows that the epistles of Saint Paul—the Epistle to the Romans in particular—had become objects of special and energetic attention on the part of scholars during these decades. It is well known that from the time of his return from Italy in 1496 John Colet liked to designate the quasi-revolutionary teaching of the University of Oxford by the phrase "the return to Paul"[18]—the rallying cry of the Oxford Reformers.[19] Throughout 1497 and in the years immediately thereafter, Colet gave several series of lectures and commentaries on all the Pauline Epistles. Later, called back to London and named dean of the Cathedral of Saint Paul—"with a commission [according to a comment by Erasmus][20] to take charge of the chapter dedicated to the Apostle whose Epistles he loved so much"—he had the opportunity to preach a famous sermon on 2 March 1513[21] before the highest personages of the city, including the king and the royal family, and the sermon was distinctly Pauline in inspiration. It is well known, furthermore, that the school that Colet founded in 1509[22] in the shadow of the cathedral—which would be associated with his name for centuries to come—was called, quite naturally, Saint Paul's School.[23]

It hardly needs to be emphasized that Pauline themes are present in the works of Erasmus. Saint Paul's epistles held a special fascination for him from the time of his first sojourn in England to the last version (in 1535) of his translation and commentary on the Bible, not to mention the place of Paul in the *Enchiridion* and the various paraphrases. In the famous portrait by Metsys—or at least a version produced in the Metsys studio[24]—Erasmus is pictured in his study preparing to write on the first page of a voluminous notebook (with a script modeled perfectly after his own) the opening lines of his *Paraphrase of the Epistle to the Romans:* "Paulus ego ille e Saulo factus, e turbulente pacificus, nuper obnoxius Legi mosaice, nunc Moisi libertus, servus autem factus Jesu." Thus the artist sought to bear timeless witness to the crucial significance of the spiritual encounter with Saint Paul, not only for Erasmus but also for Metsys himself.

With regard to Valla, whose commentary on the New Testament in two versions (the *Collatio,*[25] written toward the end of 1443 and the beginning of 1444, and the *Annotationes,* edited by Erasmus in 1505)[26] gives no hint, either quantitatively or stylistically, of any special predilection for the Epistles of Saint Paul, we may say nonetheless that the crucial problem that never ceased to haunt Valla—namely, the problem of the relation between divine foreknowledge and human free will—finds at certain points in the Epistle to the Romans materials for probing that issue in a remarkably profound way. With regard to Lefèvre d'Étaples—editor, commentator, and translator (into French) of the four Gospels[27]—it is worth noting that he wrote, *prior* to these other works of Biblical scholarship, a translation of the entire Pauline corpus, along with a commentary.[28]

In proposing here a study of the exegesis of the Epistle to the Romans—or rather a study of the methodology and the nature of the interpretations offered by these great witnesses to and participants in biblical humanism on the eve of the Lutheran Reformation—my intention is simple: In criticism of the analyses and conclusions of some recent studies, I examine the similarities and the differences that characterize these four commentaries. For that purpose I will focus on one of the most impassioned of the epistle's sixteen chapters. It is also one of the most controversial in the history of the interpretation of Saint Paul, from the commentaries of the church fathers to those of contemporary theologians, both Catholic and Protestant.[29] Chapter 11 deals with the relations between God, Israel, and the Gentiles who have been converted to the new faith, and these relations are discussed from the special vantage point that Paul had assumed in addressing himself to the Christian community in Rome. The subject is a rather painful one for Paul, and it requires all the dialectical skill at his command (or, as some would suggest, the inspiration of the Holy Spirit), for he is dealing with nothing more nor less than the point of connection between the Old Testament and the New, between the old law and the new faith, between the old Adam and the new Adam (a figure of speech for which Lefèvre d'Étaples had a special fondness). This web of relationships is made all the more complex by the fact that Israel is at one and the same time the people chosen and loved by God and the people who rejected Christ, refusing to recognize Christ as Messiah, and in that way, ironically, making possible the salvation of the Gentiles. Rejection of the gospel by the Jews made possible its expansion, although its acceptance would have done so to an even greater extent. In this eleventh chapter is found, at least in embryo, the entire doctrine of the church in relation to Israel—the connections between the church and Israel *hic et nunc,* Paul's hope for Israel's conversion, and, as a consequence, its final salvation. At any moment God can bring about this engrafting of converted Jews into the tree to which they once belonged, for unlike the Gentiles, who had to undergo a veritable mutation of their nature, the Jews, however stubborn or hardened they may be in their unbelief, have never ceased to be the children of God. It was a neuralgic point for Saint Paul; dealing with this set of questions involved some degree of metaphysical audacity in an age when social life and daily relationships—or the absence of such connections—between the Christian community and the Jewish communities dispersed throughout Europe were not characterized by harmony or even tolerance (not to mention charity).[30] In 1492 Spain's Jews had been either forced to convert at the point of a sword or expelled; the nations of Europe that had not banished the Jews were shutting them up in ghettos, while in Germany and the countries of the Danube there were intermittent periods of active persecution. The Reuchlin Affair[31] in the years 1510–15 revealed a total lack of understanding of the "mystery of Israel" that is at the heart of this chapter by Saint Paul. The Dominicans of Cologne,[32] aroused by Pfefferkorn, were drawing no distinctions: they held in the same contempt—and persecuted with the same vehemence—flesh-and-blood Jews, the Hebrew language, and all the writings that had been expressed in Hebrew, including not only the Talmud but even the Old Testament. Yet this was far from Saint Paul's interpretation of the mystery of Israel, and far from the commentaries to which this chapter gave rise in the period that we are now considering. The explicit anti-Semitism that was revealed in the Reuchlin Affair lacked the note of ambivalence that was far more typical of the actual attitude of most Christians toward the Jews. Erasmus himself, whose *Annotations* and *Paraphrase of Romans* reveal a remarkable loftiness of views concerning this "mystery," sometimes let himself indulge in verbal excesses against the Jews or "the Judaizers"[33] through a rather blind fidelity to a kind of Paulinism which contrasts, in an irreconcilable or definitive way, those who live (in their thoughts, as in their actions) "according to the spirit" and those who, as prisoners of their flesh and passions, are bound, like slaves, to the letter—that is, to matter.

What method shall we adopt for this comparative study? A first requirement will be to orient our analyses of the methods employed by Valla, Colet, and Lefèvre to that of Erasmus. There are two reasons for this. The first is that Erasmus's text of the new version of the New Testament (*Novum Instrumentum*), along with his annotations, is the more recent (published by Frobenius in February 1516). We will not consider here the years of preparatory work that preceded this translation,[34] but it is possible to set up the following approximate sequence: the *Collatio Novi Testamenti* by Lorenzo Valla (first redaction, 1442–43; second redaction, 1453–57); John Colet's lectures on the Epistles of Saint Paul—first a commentary, or *Expositio,*[35] on Romans, then a commentary on 1 Corinthians,[36] and a second and third commentary on Romans,[37] which Lupton, in his edition of 1873–, calls the "Lectures" (1497); and the *Epistolae Pauli,* by Jacques Lefèvre d'Étaples (first edition published in Paris by Henri Estienne, 15 December 1512).[38] While Erasmus may not have had Colet's manuscripts at his disposal, he knew full well the general tenor of Colet's commentaries on the Pauline Epistles—and especially his commentary on the Epistle to the Romans—since during this period of his life (from the time of his first visit to England to the end of 1499, and especially during his stay in Oxford, when he was closely associated with Colet) he was constantly in touch with his English friends. His own correspondence with Colet throughout these years reveals a thoroughly Pauline orientation.[39] We know that he was familiar with Valla's work as an exegete, for he discovered, to his great excitement, a manuscript of Valla's commentary on the New Testament in the library of a convent near

Louvain,[40] which he published, with annotations, in 1505. With regard to the text by Lefèvre, which underwent a second edition at Cologne in 1515 under the auspices of Martinus Werdensis[41]—or rather a reprinting based on the Paris edition of 1512—it was impossible for Erasmus to be unfamiliar with his work, as is clear from his allusions to the Picard theologian from the time of the first edition of his *Annotationes*[42] (in other words, from the time of his edition of the *Novum Instrumentum*). The second reason for choosing Erasmus as our basic point of reference is the nature of his connections to the other three. While it is true that he did not know Valla the man, it is also true that the author of the *Elegantiae*[43] and the *Annotationes* helped him, more than anyone else, to actualize in himself and for all time the sacred union of grammar and theology. His friendship and his spiritual and moral affinities with John Colet are nowhere revealed more brilliantly than in his funeral eulogy—or better, his living portrait—addressed to Josse Jonas on 13 June 1521.[44] His relations with Lefèvre were more uneven. They included mutual respect and affection, no doubt, but also numerous divergences in opinion, related, perhaps, to differences in personality and temperament. The famous controversy about the three Madeleines[45] and the controversy over the interpretation of several passages of the Bible (and of Saint Paul in particular),[46] which extended to the *Apologia ad Jacobum Fabrum Stapulensem* (Louvain: T. Martens, 1517), illustrate this point sufficiently.

Another comparative method might be to take our point of departure from the passages in Erasmus's works—i.e., those of 1516, 1519, 1522, 1527, and 1535—that were censured by the Spanish Index and the Roman Index (as reproduced by Le Clerc at the end of volume 10).[47] This censure and its underlying reasons may be easily surmised from a quantitative analysis of the passages that were suppressed. Their pin-point precision—a word, an adverb, an extenuation, an expression that was deemed too questioning (or, on the contrary, too affirmative)—will be found to coincide generally, though not always, with the crucial, burning points of the Epistle to the Romans. These are the points—such as justification by faith, original sin, man's freedom, and God's foreknowledge, inter alia—that were at the heart of the great theological controversies of the time (and of times to come). It is in divergent interpretations at these crucial points that one of the most obvious roots of the Reformation is to be found. Is it not true that most historians of Lutheranism, and, more generally, historians of the sixteenth century, trace Luther's conversion and his rupture with the church back to his own lectures and commentaries on Romans during the years 1513–16?[48]

If we turn now to Lorenzo Valla, annotator and interpreter of the New Testament[49] (we will see a bit later whether or not these two terms are synonyms), what observations are suggested by his *Annotationes* on chapter 11 of the Epistle to the Romans? First of all, two observations concerning method are in order. In spite of the textual difficulties and the lack of versification in the text as we have it now, it is from the second version (the only one that Erasmus would have known), which was edited by the Dutch humanist and published by Badius at Paris in 1505, that I intend to draw my commentary. If necessary, I shall refer in the notes to the text of the *Collatio Novi Testamenti* (first version), following the Perosa edition.[50] Similarly, in dealing with later editions of the *Annotationes,* I will make reference to the Cratander edition (Basel, 1526), the Lasio edition (Basel, 1541), and the Revius edition (Amsterdam, 1630). The second observation is that Valla, as I have already suggested, did not study and comment on Saint Paul in isolation: the Epistle to the Romans, and its eleventh chapter in particular, simply make up one aspect of his philological work, subordinated to his larger enterprise, which was nothing less than a critical examination of the New Testament as a whole.

The first notation by Valla deals with verse 11 ("Sed illorum delicto, salus Gentibus est ut illos aemulentur," Vulgate). As we have already observed, what is at stake here for Erasmus, in his *Annotationes* and *Paraphrases,* is the central mystery concerning the destiny of the Jews and the salvation of the Gentiles, and in particular the jealousy (*aemulatio*) that the one can come to hold for the other. But the crucial question remains: Who is jealous of whom? It is well known—especially in light of the citation of Deuteronomy 10:19—that the conversion of pagans aroused among the Jews a form of jealousy in which the Jews felt threatened with the loss of the exclusive love of God. Valla examines this text in minute detail, paying special attention to the gender of the pronouns *illorum* and *illos* (Erasmus translates the latter with *eos*) in relation to the gender of *gentibus,* corresponding to the Greek τοῖς ἔθνεσιν, "Qui aemulentur? An Israelitae aemulentur gentes? Atqui dicendum erat *illas* quod fieri nequit, quia graece est *illos* sive *eos:* nam *gentes* est generis neutri [because *people* or *nation* is rendered in Greek as τὸ ἔθνον]. An gentes aemulentur Israelitas: at hoc indignum est." Let us linger for a moment on this early section of the commentary. Valla is expressing himself primarily as a *grammaticus;* he focuses on the problems involved in translating a Greek noun that is neuter in its grammatical gender with a Latin noun whose gender is feminine (*gens*). The masculine pronoun in the plural is not permitted by the grammar, but how is it to be avoided, since it seems to fit the sense of the passage ("the Gentiles" being taken generically in the masculine)? At this point the *grammaticus* gives way to the *theologus* (even if this term is understood in the broadest sense, the same sense in which Jacques Chomarat applied it to Erasmus: that is, a man who speaks on religious questions and sacred texts). As a theologian he is indignant at the notion that the Gentiles could be jealous of the people of Israel. Erasmus, commenting in his *Annotationes* (623F–24B) and in his *Paraphrases* (814A–B), refers to another passage by Saint Paul and to a passage from Psalm 77. Valla is content to give his own opinion, which at the same time clarifies the text; or rather he translates it in his own way: "Ego accipio id sic interpretandum fuisse puto: *ut adduceret eos ad aemulationem,* hoc est deus, nam graece est infinitivum εἰς τὸ παραζηλῶσαι, quod infinitivum incommode transfertur per gerundium quod Graeci carent: transferturque sic ad verbum = ad deducendum eos in aemulationem: quae sententia congruit cum illa superiori: *Ad aemulationem vos adducam,* et cum sequenti paulo post. Si quo modo provocem carnem meam ad aemulandum suam vocat Israelitas qui sunt ex eodem progenitore Abraam παραζηλώσω." At this point, clearly, the comparative method is being used. By examining the use of the same word—here the Greek verb which means "to make jealous" or "to make envious"—in two or three adjacent passages, the passage in which the sense is somewhat obscure is clarified at once by being juxtaposed with the two others. Erasmus was later to recall this annotation: he himself rendered the Greek verb by the Latin phrase "ut eos ad aemulandum provocaret."

The second notation has to do with the words of Romans 11:16: "Quod si delibatio sancta et massa." The same notation is made by Erasmus in the *Annotationes* (6:624E). Both Valla and Erasmus focus on the meaning of the same term, corresponding to the Greek ἀπαρχὴ, which signifies the offering by which a sacrifice is begun, i.e., "the offering of the first fruits," which Erasmus follows Valla in translating by the Latin phrase *primitiae sanctae.* Here is the text from Valla (fol. XXVIIIv): "Quod hic *delibationem* saepius alibi *primitias* vocat, ut ibi: Sed et ipsi primitias *spiritus*[51] habentes ἀπαρχὴν." He also sees fit to replace the term *massa* in the Vulgate with the term *conspersio* (the act of pouring out), as Erasmus also was to do (*sancta est et conspersio*): "et quod nunc *massam,* alibi *conspersionem,* ut ibi: Ut sitis nova *conspersio: φύραμα.*" Here is the same utilization of the comparative method: just as *primitiae* expresses the exact technical term, so *conspersio* (the act of pouring)—a term that is found in the writings of the agronomist Palladius—is preferred to *massa* for reasons of precision and elegance to which the author of the *Elegantiae latinae linguae* was always sensitive, as was his disciple Erasmus, and that all the more in view of other passages in the Vulgate which employ the term *conspersio* (the act of moistening or diluting a lump of dough) and not the term *massa* (the dough itself,[52] i.e., the result of the moistening, the diluting of the dough by the water): "Nec proprie puto nunc dici massam quod nomen ad multa generale est, quodque haud scio an huic loco conveniat." Of course, one might turn the argument around on Valla by observing that the Greek word *φύραμα* itself designates precisely a lump of kneaded dough, including both the water and the dough, and that the Latin *massa* is not such a bad term for translating it. But let us see again the point Valla makes in justifying his view of the matter: "*Conspersio* autem proprie significat farinam cum aqua sive farinam et aquam invicem conspersa, quae est graeci verbi significatio."

I will not enter into a controversy with Valla—or with Erasmus—concerning the appropriateness of substituting *conspersio* for *massa,* even though the second term corresponds more to the action of *conspergere* and the first to the moistened material, and even though Greek words ending in -*μα* ordinarily designate the result or object of an action. (For instance, *ποίημα*, the poem, is the outcome of a *ποίησις*; *ὅραμα*, the object of the faculty of vision, the thing seen, is the result of a *ὅρασις*, and not the action itself.) Moreover, it should be noted that almost all modern translations of this passage have adopted the term *lump,* which is equivalent to *massa:* "If the first fruits are holy, the lump is holy also; and if the root is holy, the branches are holy also," as it is expressed by Andre Viard (p. 242 of his edition of the Epistle to the Romans).[53] What I do maintain is that Valla, open to philological correction in this double comparison (roots and branches, on the one hand, the first fruits and the lump, on the other), does not adopt a definite interpretation, such as an allegorical interpretation in which the first fruits represent ancient Israel. Such an exegesis fails to take into account the fact that it was not simply a question of the first Jewish converts who would constitute, by the same qualification as the first fruits offered to God (see Numbers 15:17–21), a kind of down payment: Their consecration would suffice to sanctify their brothers in the whole Jewish nation, who are always joined to them as the offshoots of the same branches, the same trunk, even if in some respects they are separated from one another. No matter which word is used, the terms *massa* and *conspersio* as translations for the Greek *φύραμα* are not the clearest way of expressing the matter; but as is often the case in such a situation, in an equivalence of relationships when three terms are known and the fourth is unknown, the unknown term is knowable in relationship to the other three. "First fruits" and "roots" are equivalent representations of the Jewish people; "branches" represent the offshoots of this tree. Consequently, *conspersio* is found on the same level as *rami* (branches). But it is interesting to note the explanation of *conspersio* offered by Erasmus, an explanation that differs significantly from Valla's purely lexicographical definition: "Conspersionem *non* ad farinam humore temperatam referri puto, sed magis ad molas, sive collyridas [the first of these terms designating, in a derivative sense—for *mola* is primarily the millstone[54]—the sacred flour, made from toasted wheat, that was poured on the heads of the victims, while the second of these terms designates a cake,[55] as in Leviticus 7:12]: ea erat farina oleo conspersa, quae olim juxta ritum Mosaicae Legis immolabantur, unde et *sanctum* vocat." Erasmus wants to associate the action of *conspergere* so closely with the object of this sprinkling that the epithet *sancta* or *sanctum* becomes almost redundant.

The third notation is "Tu autem oleaster . . . illis" (Romans 11:17). Valla's comment has to do with the past participle *insitus* (from *insero, inserere, insevi, insitum*), which means "to sow," "to implant," but also "to engraft." Valla believes that the "old interpreters" have confused *insitus* with *insertus,* the past participle of *insero, inserere, inserui, insertum,* which means "to insert" or "to introduce one thing into another." Valla expresses himself with somewhat less brutality than did Erasmus in a similar case: "pro *insitus* dixit interpres contra rationem *insertum* ἐνεκεντρίσθης." In fact, what we are dealing with here is the image of the wild olive tree and the cultivated olive tree, and the engrafting of the former into the latter (*in illis,* or simply *illis*)—i.e., "in them" (in the cultivated olive tree), not just "among them." (Erasmus emphasizes the same point when he writes, "Ridiculum est autem quod quidam interpretatur, *in illis,* pro eo quod erat *in locum illorum.*" While Erasmus comments on the double metaphor of the cultivated olive tree (the Jews) and the wild olive tree (the Gentiles), who were incapable in themselves of bringing forth good fruits, the author of the *Elegantiae* limits himself to drawing the attention of Latin scholars, both teachers and students, to the ambiguity resident in the fact that there are *two* verbs—*insero* and *inserere*—which are in one respect quite close in meaning (since to insert by engrafting is one modality of the general action of inserting), and yet in another respect quite distant from one another in meaning (since the operation of engrafting is neither an introduction nor an interpolation).

The fourth notation is "Noli altum sapere, sed time" (Romans 11:20). With an eye fixed on the Greek text (which he has reconstituted according to the "Greek codices" of which he speaks in the preface to his *Collatio,* just as Erasmus does in his own preface to the *Novum Instrumentum*), Valla writes: "Usitatius et magis proprium est *sentire* quam *sapere* juxta graeci verbi sensum: est enim unum ὑψηλοφρόνει.[56] Veteres sic exprimebant *tollere spiritum,* hoc est de se magnifice sentire." Erasmus translated the same passage as follows: "Ne efferaris animo, sed timeas," changing at once the grammatical construction and replacing the Vulgate's *sapere altum*—which seemed to him too intellectual because it was too closely associated with *sapientia*—with an expression that was more affective and at the same time more classical: in the passive, the verb *effero* signifies, in effect, "to be transported by passion," "to be swept away by emotion," or "to be elevated by powerful tendencies or feelings"; here it is a question of pride, or rather of vanity. In fact, both Valla's and Erasmus's translations correspond quite closely to the image suggested by the Greek verb. I do not think that their stylistic remarks are aimed at anything other than psychological accuracy and Latin "elegance."

The fifth notation is "Ut non sitis vobis ipsis sapientes" (Romans 11:25). This notation was taken up again by Erasmus (who does not cite Valla, his general procedure when he happens to agree with Valla's opinion). What is at stake here is again a question of translation. The Greek, Valla notes (apud vos ipsos prudentes), is "*παρ' ἑαυτοῖς φρόνιμοι*."[57] Valla explains: "id est ne de vobis plus aequo sentiatis. Quod probat alter locus paulo post sequens, eisdem quibus nunc ego transfero verbis." (Actually, the third verse of chapter 12 is what confirms the position taken by Valla in his interpretation.) Erasmus has taken up again the remarks of his predecessor, translating the idea of "sentire de vobis plus aequo" (to have excessive feelings toward yourselves) with "apud vosmetipsos elati animo," thus reiterating his translation of verse 20. Here again the interpretation of the biblical text stresses various aspects of what is meant to be a psychological and moral agent. It also emphasizes a distinction between the realm of knowledge and that of affectivity. It is not unfair to ask whether this dichotomy may not be a bit forced in the biblical interpretation by our two Hellinists-Latinists, nourished as they were on the ancient writers. Some modern translators of the Bible or of Saint Paul, such as A. Viard, who takes the word *wisdom* in a less intellectualist sense, do not hesitate to suggest a rendering such as "in order that they may not be wise in themselves," which is rather different from "in order that you may not have too lofty an idea of yourselves." (We assume that "idea" in this context could be replaced by "feeling.")

The sixth notation, "Ita et isti nunc non crediderunt in vestram misericordiam" (Romans 11:31), as A. Viard translates it, means "They also in their turn have now disobeyed in proportion to the mercy of which you are the recipients and beneficiaries" ("Eux aussi à leur tour ont maintenant désobéi en raison de la miséricorde dont vous bénéficiez"). Valla simply observes: "Graece est, vestrae misericordiae, *τῷ ἡμετέρῳ ἐλέει*." For his part, Erasmus translates as follows: "Sic et isti nunc increduli facti sunt, ex eo quod misericordiam estis adepti" (626B–27A), which has the merit of providing a good rendering for the idea of unbelief. (The adjective *incredulus*—referring to one who does not have faith or has lost it—is borrowed as much from classical Latin authors as from ecclesiastical sources, and it provides a better rendering of the condition of unbelief than does the Vulgate's use of the verb *crediderunt.* On the other hand, the idea of cause—which the Greek dative as well as the Latin translation by Valla, who underscores the Latin dative dependent on the verb *crediderunt,* does not render with sufficient clarity—is quite well expressed by the phrase "*ex eo quod.*" As will often be noted in a study of the long interpretive notes by Erasmus, the new and bold translations that he proposes are related to the Greek text primarily in the sense that the Greek text "posts bail" for Erasmus's fairly free renderings, as De Jonge has shown in a recent study.[58] Erasmus carefully defends his translations with long glosses, including, when possible, appeals to patristic commentaries. In the present case, when the Vulgate's Latin expression "*in vestram misericordiam*" is in effect the point at issue, he invokes Ambrose, Thomas Aquinas, Chrysostom, Theophylact, and Origen over the course of the successive editions of the *Annotationes,* the final text of which was reproduced by Le Clerc.[59] The text is quite ambiguous, but what is principally at stake in it is nothing less than the heart of the *mysterium* in relation to the conversion or repentance of the Jews and in relation to the psychological/theological interplay—a balance, or seesaw—between the faith of the Gentiles and that of the Jews according to Saint Paul and the Christian tradition, in the sight of God and according to his plan, foreseen from all eternity. Erasmus's long notation (which takes up more than a column in the Clericus edition, pp. 616D–17D) contains a complete theological essay in which are mingled literal/historical, anagogical, and allegorical interpretations, although from beginning to end he stresses the Greek and Latin dative forms and the sense in which he believes they should be taken. (Clearly it is not possible for me to surmise what may have been Valla's opinion or attitude in regard to this metaphysical play of alternation between the belief and unbelief of Jews and Gentiles.) Such is the thrust of Erasmus's exegesis: He grounds his perspective in various authors whom he abundantly quotes and interprets, drawing what seems to him the best interpretation in light of the polysemant Greek dative and Origen's commentary, and deciding in the final analysis for the simpler sense (*sensus simplicior*) according to a criterion that often recurs in his work as a critic of both sacred and profane texts ("although," he adds *in fine,* "none of the other meanings deviates from piety").

The seventh notation is "Conclusit enim Deus . . . misereatur" (Romans 11:32). Valla (whom Erasmus repeats without citing by name) writes: "*omnes,* non *omnia, τοὺς πάντας.*" This is a simple, marginal, quasi-professorial adjustment, because in fact what is involved here is an indefinite pronoun in the masculine plural, not in the neuter. Its meaning is, "In reality God has shut up everyone in unbelief, in order to show his mercy toward all." In 1 Timothy 2:4 we find "He wishes to save all men." God first shut up the pagans in disobedience (that is, nonobservance of the law, unbelief), then the Jews. Erasmus does not accuse the "old interpreters" (*vetus interpres*) of error in having written *omnia,* and he even writes that this word is more forceful ("Sensus idem est, nisi quod *omnia* vehementius est"). It is unclear what Valla the purist would propose for the equivalents (with only an affective nuance distinguishing them) *omnes* and *omnia.* He does not comment further on the equivalence or nonequivalence between *incredulitas* and *inobedientia* (corresponding to the Greek ἀπείθεια), although, as Erasmus noted, both meanings may be included: "The act of not believing in the law of God or in his commandment amounts to an act of disobedience. It is even an act of unbelief, in all the richness and ambiguity of that word: how can one betray a faith that one does not share and has never shared?"

The eighth notation is "Et investigabiles viae ejus" (Romans 11:33). Valla—always in the background of Erasmus's comments but not explicitly quoted—noted the mistake of the interpreter who is misled by the preposition *in* to confuse a positive term (i.e., what one may discover) with a negative term (i.e., the impenetrable, the inaccessible). He correctly emends the reading to "puto legendum cum negatione *ininvestigabiles viae ejus,* quae videlicet nequeant investigari, id est per vestigia inveniri. Nam *vestigari* est per vestigia quaerere, nisi hoc velimus intelligere quae nec *inquiri* viae Dei possint."[60] It is well known that French words such as *inflammable* and *ininflammable* are easily confused by those who are just learning the language, but at first glance this seems less outrageous than confusing *intelligent* and *inintelligent!* There is nothing theological about all this. Erasmus renders the word as *impervestigabiles.* Does this arise from a concern for variety, or is it precisely in order to avoid a possible confusion between two uses of the prefix *in-,* which do not have the same meaning at all? In appealing to Hilary and to the ancient manuscripts consulted by him—thus appealing to Theophylact or Jerome—Erasmus deepens the idea, underlining this nuance of meanings suggested by the prefixes *in-* or *per-.* There is more in *investigare* than in *vestigare,* a suggestion of scrutiny and profundity: lexicographical and stylistic observations turn out to be, in reality, comments about meaning.

The ninth notation is "Quis enim cognovit sensum Domini?" (Romans 11:34). Here we note something new in the vocabulary dealing with the realms of affectivity and intelligence, which take on a new dimension by virtue of the fact that the subject of the action or representation is God. "Mallem ego dicere *mentem domini* (νοῦν)," writes Valla. Erasmus also substitutes the word *mentem* for the Vulgate's *sensum:* "Quis enim cognovit mentem Domini?" In an extremely brief note he suggests the synonym *cogitationem.* In any case, the interpretation of the meaning of the text is unaffected. This theme recalls a passage from the Old Testament (LXX), Isaiah 40:13.

The tenth, and final, notation is: "Quoniam ex ipso . . . omnia" (Romans 11:36): "Graece est *in ipsum* (εἰς αὐτὸν), etsi nonnunquam actus hujusmodi apud Graecos habet vim dativi, qui est instar ablativi apud nos, tamen magis puto significari *in quem* quam *in quo omnia,* ut sit idem, *unde omnia* et *per quem omnia,* et *in quem omnia;*[61] quasi idem sit principium, medium et finis rerum omnium."[62] This is a difficult and important passage in which grammatical observations (involving comparisons of the Greek and the Latin) merge into theological positions. Elsewhere (p. 628B, n. 44) Erasmus touches on this subject: "In his tribus propositionibus [all things are from him, by him, and for him] philosophantur theologi veteres." He begins by citing Saint Thomas, who, in the framework of the Aristotelian theory of the four causes, interprets this text in terms of the schema of the first cause, the final one, and the fourth one, the operative, or efficient, cause. Then he draws connections with Origen and Augustine, two authors (especially the former) who accompany him almost everywhere on his exegetical itinerary. While expressing himself more discreetly than Erasmus, Valla in the closing words of his commentary on this verse is hardly less clear in affirming the absolute sovereignty of God in the unfolding of the history of the world from Creation to the final salvation of all believers. The Origenism of Erasmus has been abundantly demonstrated by the works of André Godin;[63] in this case, though, the citation from Origen hardly differs in its basic content and glosses from Augustine's commentary in the *De natura boni* or from that of Thomas.

We will reserve for the conclusion a discussion of the teaching that can be drawn from the parallel commentaries of the *Annotationes* of Valla and those of Erasmus. Here it is sufficient to note, along with other students of these two great humanists, that they posed the question of the relation between grammar and theology, which Erasmus raised, moreover, in his dedicatory epistle to Christopher Fisher,[64] after Valla himself had already included in his *Antidotum in Poggium*[65] a response to the attack that Poggio had launched against his version of the *Collatio:* "So if I correct (*emendo*) something in the Vulgate, I am not correcting Holy Scripture but its translation; I am not hostile but on the contrary reverent with regard to Scripture; all I am trying to do is to improve on the work of previous translators. In this way, to the extent that my translation is exact, it should be designated as Holy Scripture rather than the less exact Vulgate—although, strictly speaking, Holy Scripture is what the saints themselves have written in Hebrew or in Greek, and by this standard nothing in Latin qualifies as Holy Scripture."[66] As Chomarat, the translator of this text, notes,[67] this was nothing less than a revolutionary proposition in the era in which it was stated, as was the image—so often repeated by Erasmus—of "the Latin stream" that carries along so many impurities that it has become necessary to return to the "Greek source." In his *Annotationes* of 1516, commenting on a passage from the Acts of the Apostles (*LB* 6:519D–E, n. 11), he renders a glowing tribute to Valla that sums up quite well his constant attitude toward him: "As for me, I cannot fail to speak in praise of the zeal of Lorenzo Valla; although he was a specialist in rhetoric (*homo Rhetoricus*), at least in the judgment of the masses, and although he was not a professional theologian, still he brought to bear the utmost care in investigating whatever in Sacred Literature is in disagreement with the Greek text, what is in harmony with it, what has been corrupted, whereas many theologians today . . . have so little competence in comparisons and inquiries of this sort that they do not even know in what language the Apostles wrote."[68]

Turning to John Colet of Oxford and London, we may observe that it is the preacher—the *ecclesiastes,* but also the teacher and specialized commentator[69] (if we may put it that way) on Saint Paul—that Erasmus lifts up in his correspondence, and especially in the portrait to which I referred in the beginning. In contrast to Valla, Colet devoted himself to the exciting task of expounding—in the strict sense of the Latin *expositio*—the ideas of his favorite saint, whether on the occasion of his Oxford "lectures" in 1497 or in his sermons at Saint Paul's

Cathedral. Unfortunately, only a portion of Colet's writings are still extant.[70] In particular Colet's commentary (which goes by the name of the *Expositio*) remains silent on the eleventh chapter of Romans for the simple reason that only his comments or paraphrases in relation to the five preceding chapters seem to have survived.[71] But the nature of these expositions makes it possible for us to extrapolate and surmise the likely outline of Colet's commentary on the other chapters. In discussing the art of the preacher—an office that Colet himself held—and the art of paraphrasing, Colet places us again in an Erasmian atmosphere, though on what is clearly a different level: it is the level of Erasmus's own *Paraphrases,* but also that of a theorist of the art of speaking, and above all, the art of sacred eloquence (whose principal rules the *Ecclesiastes*[72] would set forth in a definitive way in 1535). The exacting and meticulous philologist, like Valla, who devoted himself to comparing Greek terms and their Latin counterparts, rarely allowing himself a personal opinion in the arena of religious controversy (in the strict sense of the word *religious*), now gives way to a man of the Word—a Word that is both warm and engaging. Colet wants above all to persuade, to arouse the hearer as best he can; for him, the Scriptures, and especially the Epistles of Saint Paul, are models of preaching. Here again one might invoke Augustine and Origen as theorists and practitioners of the art of preaching. We might read, for instance, those magnificent bits of oral rhetoric—even in Lupton's modern English translation—that were the famous Saint Paul sermons, such as the sermon of 6 February 1512 (known as the "convocation sermon"),[73] which marks a key date in the history of the Church of England, since it may be considered as the opening of the grand drama of the Anglican Reformation, or the sermon preached in the presence of the king and his court just before the expedition to France in the spring of 1513.[74] The citations from Saint Paul—and especially from the Epistle to the Romans—are like dikes that provide channels for the torrents of his eloquence. For like the Erasmus of the *Annotationes,* whose intensity and tone are often far removed from Valla's laconicism and verbal moderation, and who sometimes bears a resemblance to the continuous discourse of the *Paraphrases,* Colet as an interpreter of Saint Paul is also a man of flesh and blood and spirit who raises his voice against the crying abuses within the civil society and the religious society in which he lives, who calls for the indispensable reforms in the name of its affirmations—and sometimes in the name of its groanings. In a word, Colet at his most original, most vibrant, and most riveting is the Colet of his personal digressions—appealing or attacking ad hominen (or ad populum)—for whom the Bible is a viaticum, an instrument of understanding and love, a veritable prayer book given for all the seasons and all the hours in the lives of a people or an individual. This text, which I cite in English, following Lupton,[75] includes reminiscences of Cicero (especially *De Oratore* 1:55), and at times one senses allusions to the *Verrines* or the *Discourse against Catillina:* "O tempora! O mores!" But let us listen to his digression from his commentary on Saint Paul (Romans 12:2):

> Atrocious race of men! deadliest plague to the Church of Christ! very devils transformed into angels of light! in their respect worse than the devils themselves, and more hurtful to Christian people; seeing that, on account of the position they falsely hold in the church, none can openly despise them with safety; but everyone must put his neck beneath their sword—the sword of bad example, the sword of pecuniary fine and extortion. . . .
>
> How much more justly and becomingly would the practitioners of our days be acting, these adepts in the law, these reciters of formulas, and watchers for syllables, ever spinning their toils, ensnaring the unwary, extorting money, heaping together riches.

This passage brings Cicero to mind; one might also mention similar passages from *In Praise of Folly,* which, after all, is also a sermon or a homily.

The text by Colet that I will use to analyze his reactions to Romans 11 is found in the bilingual edition obtained by Lupton in 1873; it is taken from a work entitled *Ioannis Coleti A. M. Enarratio in Epistolam B. Pauli ad Romanos.* Let us take note of the term *enarratio,* which was the standard way of designating what we call commentary, and which is quite different from the term *expositio.* An *expositio* is closely associated with oratorical presentation, with oral preaching, to speak a bit redundantly. It is indeed a kind of commentary, but it is a continuous, running commentary, rather like the Erasmian *Paraphrases* (for the first five chapters of what we possess only a condensed version, but which is considerably enlarged beginning with the sixth chapter).

How, then, is Romans 11 presented in the nearly three pages in which Colet comments on it? The first thing to note is that one finds here no comments reflecting a deep mastery of philology or a concern for technical precision. The mediocrity of Colet's knowledge of Greek[76] would not have allowed him to venture into the field of philology, and even less into the field of comparative philology. He had some misfortune in the realm of Latin philology, which does not diminish his stature as a theologian, preacher, and educator: his lack of philological acumen is seen, for instance, in his abortive attempt to explain the Latin *praevaricator* (i.e., transgressor)—a term which functions in a basically juridical context—in medical terms, deriving the word from *varix* (a varicose vein) or from the adjective *varicosus* (having varicose veins), and bending over backward to show that there is a straight line from the physiological sense to an ethicojuridical sense of the term![77] There are no personal digressions in the commentary on Saint Paul contained in this *Enarratio*—or at any rate they are quickly suppressed. The author limits himself to a more continuous reading of his text while throwing into sharp relief its general import, which is fundamentally ethical. It is not too much to say that he pours his soul into that of Saint Paul, returning to Pauline expressions (according to the Latin of the Vulgate) but also speaking his own language. A slow process of assimilation finally results in an uninterrupted verbal fabric from which the difficulties are suppressed or smoothed away, without giving references to other ecclesiastical writers, explaining Saint Paul in reference to materials from the Pauline corpus or from the Gospels, as can be seen from the numerous marginal references: Isaiah 1:18, John 3:8, 1 Peter 5:5, 2 Corinthians 3:5.

It will be instructive to notice the way in which Colet deals with a number of passages that held the attention of Valla (or Erasmus), as well as some additional passages on which Valla did not see fit to make extended comments.

First of all, he presents Paul as a prophet ("*agitatus prophetia*"), one who is animated by the Holy Spirit ("*divino spiritu instructus*"), and this way of speaking raises again the central issue of the apostasy of the Jews and their relationship with God (who has not rejected them). The term *vaticinatur,* often taken by Erasmus in a pejorative sense, corresponds here to the gift of prophecy. This recalls the prophetic sense of Scripture and the prophetic interpretation of the Old Testament: Paul's prophecy is thus connected to that of Isaiah and the other prophets, and the Bible is viewed as forming a seamless tunic (parallel to the catholicity of Christ's church): the "obstinacy" and "unbelief" of the Jews with regard to the prophets of the Old Testament continue in their rejection of the message of the New Testament, because they were not able—or willing—to recognize the Messiah in the person of the Christ. The questions of divine foreknowledge and predestination, along with the questions of grace and the role of faith and works in salvation—matters that were as crucial for Catholic theology as for Protestant thought and concerning which there quickly arose in both camps dialectical argumentation and polemical instruments—are not passed by in silence, as was the case with Valla. As employed by Colet, the Latin *praedestinati* corresponds to the English term *the elect.* This term is also employed by Erasmus, who devotes a long paragraph to a gloss on the term *praescivit*[78] (a form of *praescire*) as used in the Vulgate: he admits that he prefers the phrase *ante agnoverat* as a rendering of the Greek *προέγνω*. The allusion to Origen ("*ut ait Origenes*")—which is also taken up by Erasmus—is all the more remarkable in view of the fact that Colet only rarely refers to the patristic literature. In Colet's commentary on Romans 11 everything is arranged for the purpose of facilitating an understanding of the profound sense of Scripture and making us familiar with the preacher-prophet who is the author of the epistle—thus making it possible to underline clearly these lines of continuity (which we just discussed) between the Old Testament and the New, between the prophets of Israel and the prophets of Christ.

Another characteristic uniting the biblical commentary of Colet with that of Erasmus is the concern to present a central person—in the one case, Paul of Tarsus, in the other, Jesus of Nazareth—in his full humanity: humanity at its highest level, but humanity nonetheless. We know what a heavy price Erasmus paid at the hands of inquisitorial censors for portraying Christ as a Christian Epicurean[79] or as a schoolmaster, or for presenting Christ in all his human anguish on the Mount of Olives on the night before his crucifixion.[80] When Colet speaks of Paul's "amazing insight" (*mira prudencia*) or of the "skill" (*ars*) with which he tempers his discourse in his epistle (p. 173), when he praises (p. 174) this alliance between *brevitas* and *fecunditas* (which he describes as "*quasi in angustum coacta,*" that is, "a condensed richness"), when he cannot hold back from calling him admirable ("*admirandi Pauli,*" p. 174), one cannot help but recall Erasmus's numerous human portraits of the Fathers of the church, or the great personalities of pagan antiquity (Cicero, Seneca, Socrates), or his contemporaries (such as Vitrier and Colet himself).[81] Moreover, the joining of *brevitas* and *fecunditas* brings clearly to mind the Erasmian conception of the *copia verborum,* which involves precisely this kind of joining of terms that are apparently contradictory, like sobriety and opulence; it is the endowment of the great orator or the great preacher, who knows how to find in every situation just the right word that will be appropriate to the circumstances, time, and place in which a word must be spoken and to the particular exigencies of the ones to whom that word is addressed.[82] Here it is a question of the language employed in addressing the Christian community in Rome. Most modern commentators on the Pauline Epistles[83]—and especially the Epistle to the Romans—have underlined the fact that the significance of these letters is both very general and very determinate, because in each instance it is a singular historic community that is being addressed, except when an epistle is directed to a single person, such as Timothy. It is easy to understand that a commentary by his friend (who was also his mentor from the time of Erasmus's first sojourn in England) must have held a deep fascination for Colet when he in his turn became a translator of and commentator on the Bible. (Erasmus found in Colet's hired copyist, the Belgian Pierre Meghen, the transcriber of the second (1519) version of his own translation.)[84]

Colet interprets his text from the inside, seeking to illuminate it in a way that brings out the basic contours of the argument, much as a bright flash of lightning sketches or scours the angles and surfaces of a landscape. So far from giving the impression of being useless pegs, the adjectives of which I was speaking, or the adverb *sapientissime* (p. 172), which Colet uses to characterize a verbal attitude of Saint Paul, enable us to come to a better understanding of the thrust of Paul's proclamation of a message that includes, for example, such ideas as the call or election of the Jews (*illorum vocationem*).

From the pen of Colet come Latin expressions that are later found in the writings of Erasmus (*se efferent,* made more specific in *superbiant,* p. 173, l. 1), and key words such as *gracia* that are repeated in virtually every line in order to create an almost hypnotic effect, causing us literally to live and breathe in an atmosphere of grace. There is nothing of the sort in Valla, who makes no comments on the term *gracia* for the simple reason that it corresponds to the Greek χαρὶς—

and, as a result, he has nothing to say about it. The first paragraph of Colet's exposition of chapter 11 closes magnificently with a citation from the First Epistle of Peter, "*princeps apostolorum*": "God resists the proud but gives grace to the humble" (Deus superbis resistit, humilibus autem dat graciam).

With a remarkable sense of synthesis, Colet summarizes in a few sentences the schema of historicometaphysical and psychotheological alternation between the faithfulness of the Jews and that of the Gentiles. But the predetermination established by God must be recognized by the Christian people: So the whole exposition unfolds as if Paul's discourse—the terms of the oratorical communication multiply themselves, beginning with *oracio*—were intended to promote a certain equilibrium, expressed metaphorically by the image of balance ("eam quasi librat tam pari lance"). While remaining in the background of the text that he explains (by shedding light on it and polishing its surface), Colet gives evidence of his considerable pedagogical gifts. He offers an example of the *praelectiones,* whose theoretical characteristics Erasmus outlined in his *De ratione studii*[85] (written at the behest of the dean of Saint Paul and the director of the new Latin school), before furnishing one or two concrete examples. It is not a question of repetition or paraphrase—in the pejorative sense in which these terms are often used—but rather of a stylistic and psychological refitting of the text. If Colet is a theologian, he yields to no one in his opposition to scholastic theology; he comments on each word of the text in a radically discontinuous discourse. He writes for a congregation, putting words together in such a way that the main ideas will remain engraved on the memory: hence the repetitions of *gracia, misericordia, fidelitas,* which occur more frequently in Colet's exposition than in the text on which he is commenting.

So goes the expository discourse of Colet, who cannot resist the temptation to quote a lovely passage from Paul (according to the Vulgate) because it functions precisely as commentary. For the preacher, apparently, a certain way of reading Saint Paul is worth more than all the commentaries!

If now, following our method of bipolar comparison, we bring into the picture—side by side with Erasmus and his *Annotationes* and *Paraphrases*—Jacques Lefèvre d'Étaples and his *Sancti Pauli Epistolae*

XIV ex vulgata editione, adjecta intelligentia ex graeco, cum commentariis [Jacobi Fabri Stapulensis] (Paris, H. Estienne, 1512), we will find in his discussion and method of interpretation of Romans 11 several new elements that are of great interest for our study. For reasons that I made clear at the outset, Erasmus will always be the final point of reference in this comparison; in a close examination of the relevant texts we will exclude all value judgments, including those of a polemical nature (which do sometimes arise in the interactions between the French humanist and the Dutch humanist). The edition of Lefèvre on which I have relied is the original Parisian edition of 1512,[86] with occasional incursions into the Parisian edition of 1517[87] (according to the copy that is found in the Library of Saint Andrews University),[88] which, after all, involves no alteration of what is found in the first edition or the editions of 1515. Let us examine for a moment the title of Lefèvre's work: by indicating from the very first line that the fourteen Epistles of Saint Paul (of which the first is the Epistle to the Romans) are taken from the Vulgate ("*ex Vulgata*"), he warns the reader that he has not attempted to produce a completely new Latin translation (like Erasmus, three or four years later, with his truly revolutionary *Novum Instrumentum*). And indeed, all those who have closely examined the edition of Lefèvre—and above all John B. Payne[89]—recognize a rather substantial conformity (though I will not say reproduction, since there are occasional differences) between Lefèvre's text and that of the Vulgate. But let us take care not to be misled at this point. If we turn from the first part of this work (which contains the text of the fourteen Pauline Epistles) to the second (which contains the commentary), a reading of several articles of Lefèvre's commentary, especially his Latin interpretations of various Greek terms, will be enough to show that on more than one occasion he takes fairly significant liberties with the text (in comparison with the Vulgate). To be sure, his departures from the Vulgate are not as substantial as those of Erasmus. It is true that in the margins of his *Paraphrases* Erasmus and his editors reproduced not his own translation of the New Testament but rather the traditional text of the Vulgate. And yet, except for a few instances in which he modified his original stance because of his concern for harmony, he never renounced his corrections to the Vulgate! In drawing conclusions we will be especially attentive to Lefèvre's commentary, and not just to the running text of the Epistles. One other observation drawn from the title: *adjecta intelligentia ex graeco, cum commentariis.* Here again—as in the case of Valla and, somewhat later, Erasmus[90]—the superiority of the *veritas graeca* over any Latin version is not only affirmed but practically demonstrated: one recalls the Erasmian metaphor of the pure source and the impure tributaries. A professor at the Collège du Cardinal-Lemoine and editor of the works of Aristotle, Lefèvre possessed a competence in Greek which made possible an understanding (*intelligentia*) of the thought and feelings of Saint Paul as they could be revealed only in the Greek manuscripts that he consulted. Finally, the term that he uses for his notations is neither *annotationes* nor *enarratio* nor *expositio* but *commentarii,* a rather general term that, depending on the individual case, can designate a running commentary,[91] a long digression (such as is often seen in the *Cornucopiae* of Perotti[92] or in the *Commentarii* of Budé or Dolet[93]—which, incidentally, is what justifies the designation *commentarius*[94] as that term is applied in Robert Estienne's dictionary), or a series of pointed remarks, fragmentary and discontinuous. Indeed, what becomes clear from a close reading of Lefèvre's commentaries is that he reconciles, or rather juxtaposes, two methods of interpretation that correspond to two ways of approaching Scripture. The first is an interpretation that one might describe as all-encompassing or synthetic, and more often than not it results in a short essay, resembling on the surface Erasmus's more fully developed *Annotationes* and *Paraphrases.* This is an all-encompassing interpretation that seeks to resolve the meaning of a sentence, a discourse, or a term into rich connotations—*gratia, fides, principium, lux, mens,* or *spiritus*—by way of spiritual, allegorical, or mystical interpretation. The second kind of interpretation, which is explicitly announced by the words "*Examinatio nonnullorum circa literam,*" and which always follows the first way of reading the text, would correspond to the short *annotationes* of Valla or Erasmus in dealing principally with the proper translation of such and such a Greek term. This is a systematic exposition in clear, fragmentary discourse, sometimes made a bit awkward by constant repetitions such as *"Vulgata aeditio," "potius," "Paulus,"* etc. But here Lefèvre is not aiming at an aesthetic effect: he is doing his work as a philologist and as a theologian trying to reestablish a text that is more in conformity with the truth of the original documents. Do we expect the one who produces a critical edition of some text to create a work of literature while showing the textual variants at the bottom of the page and arguing in favor of the choice of one reading over another?

With regard to Lefèvre's exegetical method in comparison to that of Erasmus, I mentioned earlier the excellent article by John B. Payne, whose conclusions I myself share. There is a contrast, for instance, between the defensive attitude of Erasmus—who is primarily interested in defending the bold departures or simply the novelties of his translation and who, for that purpose, refers constantly to the Greek but also to the Fathers of the church—and the more traditional character of the commentary by Lefèvre, who—having placed in parallel columns the text of the Vulgate and his own translation—proceeds systematically with a twofold interpretive reading of each of the chapters of each of the Epistles. Erasmus's elaborate exploitation of the resources of patristic thought is matched by Lefèvre's reserve in this respect. From the very important preface that he dedicated to Guillaume Briçonnet, dated December 1512,[95] we know how Lefèvre felt about the Vulgate and the tradition that Jerome was its translator:

> Some will perhaps be surprised that I have had the boldness to add to Jerome's translation the understanding of the Greek text, deeming me to have conducted myself with too much insolence; they will condemn me less for rashness and audacity in the actual work that I have produced than for daring to challenge Jerome's authority. I have no ill feelings toward those who raise this objection, because they would have a good point if things were as they, along with a vast number of people, believe them to be. But they will extend to us a full pardon when they come to understand that I have undertaken nothing audacious against St. Jerome's translation, since I have dealt only with the Vulgate, which dates from a time quite a bit earlier than that blessed and glorious light of the Church, Jerome.[96]

On this point Valla, Lefèvre, Erasmus, and even Colet are in full agreement: the Vulgate, insofar as it may have been transcribed in different periods by scribes who were more or less ignorant or more or less careful in their work, has nothing about it that is sacred. Rationally, the point seems quite banal, but putting it into writing was a daring act, all the same!

I also think, along with Payne, that Lefèvre's commentary—in spite of its philological notes and its emendations—is less intellectual than spiritual and homiletical in character: Arousing and edifying his readers' hearts is more his intention than persuading their minds. Everything we know about the life and work of Lefèvre points toward this interpretation: His numerous friends, colleagues, and disciples at the University of Paris have offered abundant witness in this respect. On this point one may see a certain similarity between Lefèvre and Colet, although the style of the *enarratio* or *expositio* produced by the dean of Saint Paul's is quite different from that of Lefèvre's *commentarius* in both spiritual interpretation and literal commentary.

Lefèvre's discretion with regard to patristic commentaries may be due, as John Payne suggests,[97] to a feeling of conscientiousness, which did not inhibit him from constantly justifying his translations with indisputable references that warranted rendering Greek expressions in certain ways. His way of using patristic sources may also reflect a pedagogical desire for clarity and simplicity: why multiply the reasons for a choice if a terse, precise explanation is sufficient? And might not references to all these Fathers of the primitive church obstruct the reader's meditation or contemplation—becoming, in effect, a barrier between him and Saint Paul, or between him and Christ?

Let us turn now to Romans 11 in order to verify these general remarks and to evaluate *in concreto* the method and the final product of Lefèvre's exegesis, both in relation to Erasmus and in relation to Valla and Colet.

The commentary on this chapter occupies about six and one-half pages in the folio edition of 1512 (fol. 93v–96v); the text of the Vulgate and that of Lefèvre's translation take up about two pages (fol. 8r–9r), placed in two parallel columns.

The fact that God has not rejected the Jewish people in spite of their unbelief (Romans 11:2) quite obviously attracts Lefèvre's attention, as does, a bit later (verses 2–7), the reality of salvation by grace and by works. It is not too much to say that only Lefèvre undertakes to give, in light of Scripture (to which he refers often—and more eagerly than to the patristic commentaries), a continuous theological exposé, a reading of Scripture that is clearly the work of a master in divinity. Whereas Erasmus makes repeated references to Chrysostom, Origen, Theophylact (from 1522 onward), Nicolas of Lyra, etc.,[98] Lefèvre gives a continuous commentary, attempting to penetrate to the interior of the most intimate thoughts of Saint Paul. He neatly separates the two interpretations: the exposition of the "Greek understanding," or spiritual meaning, on the one hand, and the examination of certain points concerning the literal meaning, on the other;[99] as a result, it is not difficult to get a clear understanding of his thought. He prefers to make use of *praecognovit* rather than the Vulgate's *praescivit,* in this resembling Erasmus,[100] who translates the Greek verb *προαγνώσκω* with *ante cognoverat* in order to express the idea of divine foreknowledge. In his exposition number 1 he makes reference to the preaching of Saint Peter and to the Acts of the Apostles in order to specify the number of three thousand "righteous" who did not bow the knee to Baal. Lefèvre finds words that are most precise and illuminating—which he may or may not borrow from the formulas of the Epistle to the Romans—in order to characterize the unbelief of the Jews: "voluntaria et pertinax aversio." A whole section of Lefèvre's commentary precedes the opening words of the chapter (Dico igitur, Numquid repulit deus populum suum?), as if the interpreter wished to step back and take into account the various stages in the development of the thought and the unfolding of the word sequences.

Let us now focus our attention on the first fourteen verses of Romans 11[101] for the "*Examinatio nonnullorum circa literam.*" From this examination, which represents a little more than a third of the chapter, we will be able to derive some information on Lefèvre's exegetical method. His commentary gives the impression of waves following close upon one another, often overlapping one another: the same expressions recur again and again, hammer strokes in the reader's consciousness. The same expressions are used repeatedly, but always they go further, deeper. The cardinal questions of the salvation of the Jews, and the opposition or complementarity between faith and the law, grace and works, become the object of a lengthy development, regularly punctuated by references to Paul, who is cited textually but in various presentations: "Quae et Paulus insinuat, dicens . . . ," "Ideo subiungit Paulus . . . ," "Recurrit enim apud Paulum iste sermo . . . ," "Ad quod audi Paulum dicentem . . . ," and so on.

It would be fair to say that Lefèvre's commentary is both an expansion and at the same time an explanation of the words of the apostle. His commentary has absorbed or integrated the totality of the words of Saint Paul, but he establishes harmonies, sharpens oppositions, clarifies obscure points—all with consummate pedagogical skill. His choice of words is remarkable, as is his striving for logical explanation. In order to designate the contrast between saving faith and the works that are connected to salvation, he introduces the notion of what is owed or due (*debitum*), which is found neither in the text by Saint Paul nor in Erasmus's commentary. He opposes the debt (*debitum*) to the gift (*donum*), and the obligation of repaying a debt is contrasted with the gratuity of a gift. In the same way the concept of the will (*voluntas*) passes again and again before our eyes, and by virtue of the association that he establishes between the notions of grace (*gratia*) and election (*electio*), Lefèvre causes us to sense the dimensions of the chasm that separates the omnipotent and free (i.e., gracious) will of God from the will of man, bound to works and determinate actions. In his commentary everything is directed toward a theodicy, on the one hand, according to which God is not responsible for the perversion of man and has no duty toward his creation, and, on the other hand, a conception of the free will of man. Closer to Luther than to Erasmus in his emphasis on the transcendence of grace, he is closer to Erasmus in recognizing that "there are works joined to salvation" ("*saluti opera sunt conjuncta*").

A reading of Lefèvre's continuous commentary conveys an impression of flawless demonstrative logic and, at the same time, musical incantation. The repetition, at lengthy intervals, of certain key words—*gratia, electio, debitum, voluntas, donum, opera, caecitas, incurvatio*—provides the leitmotif of the melody. Turning at the end of his commentary from the literal examination of certain philological points, he does not become entangled in his paraphrase with long grammatical or syntactical digressions like Erasmus did when commenting in his lengthy note 14 (verse 11) on the stylistic value of the conjunction *ut*. Did the Jews commit an offense (Vulgate: "*Numquid sic offenderunt . . .*"; Erasmus: "*Num ideo impegerunt . . .*"; Lefèvre: "*Numquid deliquerunt . . .*") *in order to* fall—which would imply an evil will on the part of God—or did they commit an offense which had *as its result* their downfall, leaving the responsibility to the Jews themselves? Assimilating but at the same time transcending this philological ambiguity, Lefèvre is content to interpret the passage in the sense that is most in harmony with the spirit of the gospel: God did not positively will the disobedience of the Jews, but his will and his foreknowledge operated in such a way as to bring it about that this offense and this fall would take place in order that the gospel might be preached and humanity might be saved thereby.

This "fabrist" theodicy reminds us of Descartes's famous parable in a letter to the princess Elizabeth. He poses the case of two nobles whom the king arranges to encounter one another, and who confront one another in a duel, even though duels are expressly forbidden by law. Who is responsible for the consequences of this ill-fated encounter? The king, or the two men?

With its logical, incantatory commentary, this "fabrist" exegesis is more clearly allegorical than that of Erasmus (in spite of the importance of Origen as a source for Erasmus's exegesis), but it is also more allegorical than are the commentaries by Valla and Colet. An example is provided in Lefèvre's comments on verse 9 (with reference to Psalm 69 [Psalm 68, Vulg.], verses 22ff.), in connection with the word *mensa:* "Let their table be a trap, a snare, a pitfall, an occasion of falling, so that they may receive their due recompense." Whereas Erasmus is content to compare the translation of the Septuagint and Origen's commentary in connection with David's imprecation, Lefèvre deliberately and audaciously pursues an allegorical interpretation in which the table becomes a metaphorical image of books ("libri eorum ex quibus credunt se legere pastum animae"). It would be a question, then, of good things that have been diverted from their original ontological purposes, good things granted by God to his people, or the law, written in books. The expression *pastum animae* (food for the soul) is found in neither Saint Paul nor the patristic commentaries.

The literal examination of the text, which forms the second part of Lefèvre's commentary, gives a philological explanation of certain points in the text, comparing, term by term, his own translation with that of the Vulgate. Far from striking us as redundant, this literal/philological section puts the finishing touch on Lefèvre's pedagogical work.

We have attempted to compare four exegetes, always presenting them in pairs, the second member of each pair always being Erasmus. The crucial position of Erasmus in this study is justified both by the fact that he is exceptionally renowned and by the fact that his exegetical work is posterior to that of the other three (at least in terms of dates of publication). What conclusions may we now draw from these comparisons?

If it were necessary to come to a swift and general verdict on the exegetical enterprise of these four representatives of the European Renaissance and humanist Christianity on the eve of the Renaissance (and of the cultural revolution that the Renaissance unleashed), I would say that they were all personally involved in a widespread desire to return to the actual text of the Scripture, which implies a powerful and audacious attempt to disentangle the text itself from all philological corruptions, from all the obscurities that conceal its light, from all the scholastic and pseudo-dialectical glosses that twist or distort its meaning. Two of these interpreters—Valla and Lefèvre—were fairly good scholars of Greek (and more or less competent in the study of Hebrew) who knew how to deal relevantly and effectively with the Greek source that was available in the manuscripts at their disposal, along with the Vulgate; thus they were in a position to justify their own translations and their own annotations or commentaries. As for Erasmus, he needed the help of friends (such as Wolfgang Capito) when facing Hebrew texts. One thing that these three have in common is that they were all led to propose a fresh translation of the New Testament. This was a revolutionary undertaking, for it presupposed a sharp distinction between the inspiration of the divine Word and the fallibility of the human enterprise of translation. The same impulse is seen in their desire to analyze the relevant documents with a view toward establishing a more adequate text, in which and by which the words (*verba*) would correspond in reality to the things (*res*) signified by them, i.e., to their meaning.

Colet—whose culture and learning (especially his Neoplatonic and, of course, biblical culture) are by no means negligible—did not have sufficient mastery of the tools of philology to use them in producing a new translation. Yet his intuition and enthusiasm enabled him to find the accent and the words to sustain his listeners as they traveled on the path of the imitation of Christ. The major difference between the three other commentaries and that of Colet lies in the fact that Valla, Lefèvre, and Erasmus all wrote for eager readers who followed the text with pen in hand and with minds alert, while Colet addressed a community of persons, a congregation. As we have seen, he practiced in a consummate way the art of the *ecclesiastes.*

There is, however, one common denominator linking Colet's *enarratio* with Lefèvre's *commentarius:* Lefèvre's pedagogical experience enabled him to discover a style of exposition that was capable of holding the attention of his readers—and some of these readers could, in addition, hear his lectures at the Collège du Cardinal-Lemoine.

The commentary that appears to be the most neutral, the most purely and exclusively grammatical, is that of Valla. It is also the most discontinuous. But—as we have seen—its theological significance is no less assured.

The Epistles of Saint Paul clearly played a more fundamental or normative role in the life and work of Colet and Erasmus (and, to a lesser extent, of Lefèvre as well) than they did in the life and work of Valla. Finally, if I were asked to point out the sociocultural roots of these interpretations of the New Testament, and more specifically of the Pauline Epistles, especially the central problem of Romans 11 (viz., election and salvation by grace, as applied in particular to the question of salvation of Jews and Gentiles according to the *veritas Christiana*), I would say that Colet and Erasmus were more engaged with their era and the twofold society—lay and ecclesiastical—in which they lived and which they labored to reform. More mystical and also more philosophical, Lefèvre's commentary rises to a greater extent above sociohistorical contingencies to reach "a certain likeness of the eternal" ("*quamdam speciem aeterni*").

With these four prototypical commentaries, spanning a period of sixty years, the way was paved for the double movement—parallel or interwoven—of the great translators and/or commentators of the Bible during the era of the Reformation and Counter-Reformation.

IRENA BACKUS

Polemic, Exegetical Tradition, and Ontology

Bucer's Interpretation of John 6: 52, 53, and 64 Before and After the Wittenberg Concord

Bucer's commentary on the Fourth Gospel went through three editions in the author's lifetime. The first appeared in April 1528,[1] over a year after the first edition of Bucer's commentary on the Synoptics.[2] It followed immediately upon a short commentary on the Epistle to the Ephesians and Bucer's defense of his translation of Bugenhagen's Psalter, both published toward the end of 1527.[3] There is little doubt, however, that it was the Berne disputation of 6–26 January 1528 which provided the occasion for the composition of the commentary on John. In his preface to the Bernese ministers Bucer states: "Equidem ut testarer, quanti mihi sit, viri fratres observantissimi, vestra ad Deum tam plena conversio, nuncupare vobis decrevi quam, hisce diebus, in Evangelion Iohannis enarrationem scripsi, sperans non omnino absque fructu legendam a plerisque ecclesiarum vestrarum ministris, qui in Scripturis nondum adeo sunt exerciti."[4] Thus one of Bucer's aims in writing the commentary was to provide a manual for preachers, particularly Bernese preachers. It is worth bearing in mind that such a manual would not only acquaint preachers with biblical exegesis but also would provide them with an outline of doctrine and some answers to their religious opponents. We must also bear in mind that the fourth thesis of the Berne disputation concerned the question of real presence,[5] and that the debate around it amounted to a confrontation between the "Lutheran" and the "Zwinglian" factions, even though the disputation as a whole was intended primarily against the Roman Catholics. We may thus expect a continuation of the eucharistic dispute within the commentary itself.

The second edition of Bucer's commentaries on John appeared in March 1530 together with the second edition of his commentary on the *Synoptics.*[6] This version came shortly after the Marburg colloquy of 1529, during which the Lutheran and Zwinglian parties reached no agreement about the doctrine of the Eucharist, as Bucer himself points out in his dedicatory epistle to the Marburg Academy.[7] The third edition of the commentary was printed, again with the Synoptics,[8] in 1536, after the Wittenberg Concord, which was concluded on 29 May of that year. As might be expected, this edition contains several changes made by the author in an apparent attempt to reconcile the eucharistic pronouncements of his commentary with the recently concluded agreement.

My object here is to trace the textual changes introduced by Bucer between 1528 and 1536 into his exegesis of John 6:52, 53, and 64.[9] My choice of these verses was dictated by the following criteria: First, verse 52 was interpreted by some as a promise or foreshadowing of the institution. Second, verse 64 was an object of controversy, with some taking the term *caro* to refer to Christ's flesh conjoined with the Holy Spirit—i.e., his divine nature—and others taking the *caro* to refer to carnal, human, understanding of Christ's words. Third, verse 53 was understood by practically the entire exegetical tradition to refer to the Jews' horror at the suggestion of eating Christ's flesh literally. Only Chrysostom took it to refer to their inability to comprehend Christ's divine nature. Bucer adopted Chrysostom's exegesis in 1530 and, as we shall see, used it in conjunction with verse 64 in a way that left his own Christology unchanged in 1536. Our aims in analyzing the textual changes in Bucer's interpretation of these three verses will be, first, to see how exegetical tradition is used for polemical purposes within the framework of a biblical commentary, and second, to isolate Bucer's and Luther's ontological positions, which made any real agreement impossible even after the apparent reconciliation of 1536.

VERSE 52: "*PANIS QUEM EGO DABO CARO MEA EST [QUAM DABO] PRO MUNDI VITA*"

This verse first became an object of theological controversy with the publication of Luther's *De captivitate* in 1520. There Luther asserts that "[John 6] in totum est seponendum ut quod nec syllaba quidem de sacramento loquitur, non modo quod sacramentum nondum esset institutum, sed multo magis quod ipsa sermonis et sententiarum consequentia de fide, ut dixi, incarnati Verbi Christum loqui clare ostendunt."[10] Luther does not refer to verse 52 specifically, and neither does Henry VIII in his *Assertio septem sacramentorum* of 1521.[11] The verse, however, is discussed by John Fisher in his *Defensio* of the king's book published in 1525.[12] There Fisher, arguing against Luther's view that Christ in John is referring to faith in the incarnate Word or food for the spirit, interprets John 6:52 as follows:

> Primum illud quod dicit [Lutherus] Christum de solo spirituali pane loqui pro nobis facit. Nam ibi quoque de sacramento isto loquitur, quod et veteres abunde testantur sed et ipsa quoque verba Christi palam docent. Dicit enim: *Panis enim quem ego dabo, caro mea est quam dabo pro mundi vita* [John 6:52]. Hic lector adverte dixisse Christum bis *dabo,* semel pro pane quem esset daturus in sacramentum, quemque carnem affirmavit esse suam; atque iterum pro carne quam esset daturus pro mundi vita.[13]

The reading adding *ἥν ἐγὼ δώσω* after *ἡ σάρξ μού ἐστιν* occurs in most koiné manuscripts, but not in the Vulgate. Erasmus incorporated it into his New Testament of 1516[14] but drew no exegetical conclusions from it. About a year before the publication of Fisher's *Defensio,* however, Oecolampadius's translation of Theophylactus's commentaries on the four Gospels came out in Basel.[15] Theophylactus also adds *quam ego dabo* (*ἥν ἐγὼ δώσω*) after *caro mea est* (*ἡ σάρξ μού ἐστιν*). Commenting on the text, he emphasizes that Christ here refers, first and foremost, to the giving of his body in the Eucharist and, second, to the sacrifice of his body on the cross, which will obtain resurrection and salvation for man.[16] It seems indisputable that Fisher is using Theophylactus to combat Luther's view of John 6, given that no other patristic or medieval commentary contains *both* the reading with *δώσω* repeated and the explanation of the two "givings" as referring to the Eucharist (transsubstantiation) and to the Crucifixion, respectively.[17] By 1525 the Lutheran position on John 6 and the Eucharist had undergone a change. Iohannes Bugenhagen, in his *Contra novum errorem de sacramento corporis et sanguinis . . . epistola* (1525), argues against the Zwinglians that Christ's body must be really present in the Eucharist "alioqui seipsum mendacem faceret, quia dixerat: *Caro mea est pro mundi vita*" (fol. 3v).

Bucer's exegesis of John 6:52 constitutes an interesting blend of apparently disparate components. As we shall see, in spite of certain textual changes his doctrinal position remained unaltered between 1528 and 1536. Let us first consider the passage as it stood in 1528.

Echoing Fisher, whose works were known to him,[18] Bucer emphasizes that Christ repeats *dabo* twice. The first *dabo,* affirms the Reformer against Fisher (and indeed Theophylactus), refers to the awareness of redemption or to faith which Christ imparts to his believers. Bucer thus applies to John 6:52 Luther's interpretation of John 6 as a whole. The second *dabo* refers to the giving of Christ's own body for the sins of the world.[19] Bucer thus alters radically the significance of Fisher's double giving, and we can isolate two likely sources for his exegesis here. First, Cyril of Alexandria, available to Bucer in the Latin translation of George of Trebizond,[20] repeats *dabo* in the text and does not interpret the verse as foreshadowing the Eucharist.[21] Cyril's commentary makes no reference to the double giving in the text, but places strong emphasis, first, on Christ's sacrifice for the sins of the world and, second, on the resurrection to eternal life of those who have faith in Christ.[22] Second, Zwingli in the *Commentarius* of 1525 takes John 6:51–52 as one of the supporting texts for his attack against any form of real presence in the Eucharist. According to him, *panis* means *evangelium,* and *edere* means *credere.* Thus Christ, by his words, is inculcating faith in the saving nature of the sacrifice of his body. This sacrifice will save men, but only because Christ is divine as well as human.[23] Zwingli, like Bucer, adopts the double *dabo*[24] reading (presumably from Erasmus) but does not refer to it in so many words in his interpretation of the verse.

It might be said at this point that Bucer's exegesis of this verse takes its basic structure from Fisher and its contents to some extent from Cyril but largely from Zwingli. It might also be said that Bucer's chief aim here is to combat, with Zwingli, any eucharistic interpretation of the passage, be it Roman Catholic or Lutheran. This aim is not really attenuated by a certain Lutheranizing of what seems at first a hard-and-fast Zwinglian line. Already in 1528 Bucer, referring to the first *dabo,* uses the terms *satiare* and *pascere* in the context of "fides," whereas Zwingli is careful to avoid such direct association. On the other hand, the link is made perfectly clear by Iohannes Brenz in his commentary on the Fourth Gospel, ad loc.[25] The latter adopts a eucharistic interpretation of John 6:52, as might be fully expected, and uses a biblical text with only one *dabo*. This does not prevent Bucer from paraphrasing Brenz's "nam caro Christi, morti tradita, est panis, fides vero vescitur hoc pane, hoc est credit carnem Christi pro se traditam"[26] as "ipse Christus, reficiens et satians mentem in aeternam vitam, hoc nos ordine reficit et satiat, quod primum dat suam carnem dum donat fidem qua scimus pro nobis morte eius satisfactum, pro nostris peccatis carnem eius immolatam." But Bucer avoids any explicit identification of *caro* with *panis* and thus maintains his refusal to interpret John 6:52 as referring to the Eucharist.

The few changes he introduces in his exegesis of this verse in 1536 do little to moderate this categorical refusal. In his explanation of the first *dabo* Bucer adds to the sentence "Ipse namque panis vitae et vivificans est qui aeternum satiat ubi editur, id est cognoscitur" the phrase "et in os vera fide summitur." This phrase is a borrowing from Brenz's commentary to John 6:64, where he speaks of "os fidei," which "accipit suo etiam sensu corpus et sanguinem."[27] Yet, given that Bucer does not alter the basic meaning of his sentence, which is Zwinglian in its identification of eating with recognition or faith, the Brenzian addition constitutes a merely stylistic concession to the Lutheran doctrine.

The same can be said of two further changes introduced into the passage in 1536. After a sentence in which he emphasizes, after Zwingli, the saving nature of Christ's divinity: "Hinc eo perducimur ut et ipso Deo, hoc est divinitate eius, qua idem est cum Patre, pascamur," Bucer adds: "Ista omnia ipse nobis efficit seque ita nobis impertit, ita se nobis immittit, ita vivit agitque in nobis ut simus item caro de *carne eius* et os de *ossibus eius* [Ephesians 5:30] et vivamus in illo." This statement, which at first reading appears to allude not only to the Eucharist but also to the doctrine of ubiquity, is in fact a paraphrase of a comment by Chrysostom on John 6:52. There is nothing unusual in Bucer's paraphrasing Chrysostom, whose homilies on the Fourth Gospel he acknowledges as one of his models.[28] What is worth noting is that Bucer, in his paraphrase, omits all explicit mentions of the Eucharist that occur in the Chrysostom passage. The Chrysostom/Aretinus version reads as follows: "Unum corpus sumus et membra ex carne et ossibus eius. Quare initiati eius praeceptis parere debent. Ut autem non solum per dilectionem sed reipsa in illam carnem convertamur, per cibum id efficitur, quem nobis largitus est. Cum enim suum in nos amorem vellet, per corpus suum se nobis commiscuit et in unum nobiscum redegit ut corpus cum capite uniretur."[29] Bucer, as we have seen, adopts Ephesians 5:30, but only after condensing the Chrysostom/Aretinus passage so as to exclude any reference to *cibus.* The eucharistic reference in Bucer's interpolation is thus much weaker than in his source, and it remains unclear whether Bucer is talking about the communion of the faithful in Christ (i.e., the Eucharist) or solely about the benefits that Christ imparted to the faithful through his incarnation and death.

The sentence immediately following the Chrysostom addition is also only an apparent emendation. In the versions of 1528 and 1530 it reads: "Haec autem perfruitio divinitatis hic nondum plena est." If we take this statement together with the statement about our participation in Christ's divinity (which immediately precedes it in the 1528 and 1530 editions), it is plain that Bucer is elaborating upon the point made by Zwingli in his *Commentarius.* Whereas there the Zurich reformer stops short at affirming that the saving power of Christ's divinity will not take full effect until he has accomplished the sacrifice of his human nature,[30] Bucer here adds that *our* participation in this divinity will not be complete until the Spirit of Christ abolishes all sin in us (and here he cites 1 Corinthians 15:28), in other words, until the last judgment. In 1536 the same sentence is altered to "Haec autem Christi communio et perfruitio hic nondum plena est." "Christi communio" evokes the Eucharist at 1 Corinthians 11:26, and this allusion is reinforced by the omission of "divinitatis" after "perfruitio." This later version of the sentence echoes a eucharistic passage in the *Libellus* of Paschasius Radbertus, which was edited by Hiob Gast (with a dedication to Brenz) in 1528.[31] However, as in the Chrysostom "borrowing," all explicit mention of the Eucharist is omitted by Bucer. Paschasius, referring to 1 Corinthians 11:26, makes it quite plain that in celebrating the Eucharist, we commemorate Christ's death and participate in his body and blood. This participation, however, will not be complete until the last judgment.[32]

The pro-Lutheran tone of the 1536 version is by no means strengthened by Bucer's interpretation of the future tense of *dabo.* According to him, it refers to the increase of faith after Christ's Resurrection and the giving of the Holy Spirit. This interpretation undergoes only one modification in 1536, when the phrase "quia fides in mortem eius a resurrectione eius primum revelari debuit" is expanded to "quia fides in mortem eius illa amplior et Christi communio plenior a resurrectione eius primum revelari debuit." Despite the interpolation of "Christi communio," Bucer's original meaning remains unchanged here. He makes it plain in 1536, as in 1528, that Christ here is *not* promising to give his body in any form of bread. Thus Bucer's objections to both Fisher's and Bugenhagen's interpretations of *dabo* remain unchanged. What is removed in 1536, however, is a long passage of controversy which immediately follows Bucer's exposition of *dabo* in the 1528 and 1530 editions. This passage made explicit what the surviving text leaves implicit, with Bucer stating: (1) those who think that Christ at John 6:52 promised the presence of his body in the bread (i.e., Fisher and Bugenhagen) are wrong; (2) Christ is bread insofar as he is food for the soul in being the Son of God (we see here a direct allusion to Zwingli's *Commentarius*);[33] (3) eating Christ means having faith in Christ; (4) he is surprised that certain Lutherans (i.e., Bugenhagen and Brenz)[34] interpret Christ's words as a promise of the Eucharist, since Luther himself claims "et non ingenue" that Christ makes no mention of it in John 6; (5) according to the Lutheran interpretation, the sacrament itself brings about salvation. They thus deny the truth of Christ's repeated promise: *Qui credit in me habet vitam aeternam* (John 6:35, 47). What is moderated in 1536 is the polemical tone of Bucer's comments on John 6:52; neither his theology nor his exegesis undergoes any change as a result of the Wittenberg Concord.

VERSE 53: "*QUOMODO POTEST HIC DARE NOBIS CARNEM EDENDAM?*" AND VERSE 64: "*SPIRITUS EST QUI VIVIFICAT*"

The same, as we shall see, goes for Bucer's exegesis of these verses. It is only in 1530 that Bucer comments at length on verse 53.[35] The Jews' reaction here appears to suggest that they were offended by Christ offering them his flesh as if they were cannibals. However, Bucer continues, if we examine the context of their words, it will become plain that what offended them was not the eating allegory (which they understood perfectly) but the idea that Christ, whom they saw as a mere man, dared claim such power. Bucer then establishes a parallel between the Jews' behavior here and the behavior of the Samaritan woman at John 4:7–29. She too had no difficulty understanding the water allegory but mocked Christ's claim that he had the power to give her eternal life. The Samaritans, like the Jews, were used to allegories, and particularly to allegories of food as representing spiritual salvation. Had they had difficulties in understanding the bread allegory at John 6:35, they would have asked, for example, why does he call himself "bread" when he is a man? Instead, they insisted that Christ could not have descended from heaven because they knew him to be the son of Joseph and Mary. Then, following Chrysostom, Bucer establishes a parallel between the Jews' lack of understanding here and the disciples' protest at John 6:62. His explanation of Christ's reply in both cases is also taken from Chrysostom's forty-seventh homily: the Jews (at 6:53) and the disciples (at 6:62) doubted Christ's divine power. His retort in both cases was intended to quell their doubts, which, Chrysostom specifies, were due to the fallibility of carnal (or human) powers of comprehension.[36]

This exegesis is retained by Bucer in 1536 with only a few grammatical emendations and the addition of one sentence where Bucer expressly cites Chrysostom's forty-sixth (i.e., forty-seventh) homily in support of his interpretation.[37] Its aim in 1530 and in 1536 was at least partly polemical. In saying that the Jews' reaction only *appears* to suggest that they were offended by the notion of eating human flesh, Bucer goes against practically all the exegetes of the passage who follow Augustine. The latter makes it quite clear in his commentary to John 6:53 that the Jews could not understand *how* Christ's flesh (and blood) could be consumed by man and were outraged at the suggestion.[38] He then harmonizes this exegesis with John 6:64, interpreting this latter verse not as a failure of human powers of understanding but as Christ's continuing explanation of the exact nature of the usefulness of his flesh: "Sic etiam nunc *caro non prodest quidquam* sed sola caro; accedit spiritus ad carnem, quomodo accedit caritas ad scientiam et prodest plurimum. . . . Sicut illi intellexerunt carnem, non sic ego do ad manducandum carnem meam."[39]

Carnem edendam in John 6:53 is interpreted in the Augustinian sense by Aquinas,[40] the Gloss, Erasmus,[41] Luther,[42] Oecolampadius,[43] Zwingli,[44] and Brenz.[45] This consensus is surprising, as Luther and

Brenz both adopt Chrysostom's exegesis of John 6:64. On the other hand, Bucer in 1530 apparently follows Augustine's interpretation of the latter verse. What were his reasons for making what seems a deliberate effort in 1530 to expound Chrysostom's exegesis of 6:53? Before attempting to answer that question, it is worth noting that Bucer elaborates upon and supports Chrysostom with information culled from other sources.

The Greek Father does not state in his commentary that allegories, especially allegorical representations of salvation by food, were familiar to the Jews. Bucer's contention that this was so appears to be based on Lactantius, who in his *Divinae institutiones* describes the entire Jewish law as a series of carnal (including dietary) prohibitions and rules which lead to spiritual improvement.[46] It is also Lactantius who affirms (without reference to John 6, however) that the Jews' principal fault lay in their inability to see Jesus as anything other than human because of his humble origins and appearance.[47] Bucer makes the same point in his comments on John 6:53, but with specific reference to John 6:42. It is thus quite likely that Bucer here refers to Albert the Great's commentary on John as well as to Lactantius. Albert's commentary is the only one (of those available to Bucer) to state at John 6:42: "Murmurabant autem maxime de ista parte quod dixit *qui de coelo descendi* de coelo dicens suam originem esse, cum ipsi suam originem humilem in terra et a terra cognoverunt."[48]

On the other hand, Bucer's parallel between the Jews' and the Samaritan woman's reaction (which does not occur in Chrysostom's commentary) is aimed expressly against Brenz, who in his commentary at John 4:11 emphasizes the woman's carnal (i.e., literal) understanding of Christ's words by paraphrasing her: "Domine, inquit istam aquam ego peto, quae sitim in aeternum sedat; nam quod ex hoc puteo aquam feram magno me labore constat. Itaque si mihi talem aquam dederis facies mihi admodum pigrae rem gratissimam."[49] Yet, while contradicting Brenz on the nature of the woman's understanding, Bucer is quite content to adopt tacitly the Lutheran's view that it is mockery that motivates her words. All the other commentators take the woman's request at John 4:11 to indicate a simple lack of understanding, with no connotations of malice. These apparently extraneous elements introduced by Bucer into his interpretation of John 6:53—the Jews' understanding of allegories in general, their inability to comprehend Christ's divinity, their similarity in this respect to the Samaritan woman—serve to reinforce Chrysostom's point about the Jews' (and the disciples') inability to see Christ as the Son of God. Bucer thus distances himself from Luther's theology and uses Chrysostom so as to reaffirm the distinction between Christ's human and divine natures and to avoid making any explicit connection between John 6:53 and the Eucharist.

How does this exegesis of verse 53, which, as we have said, remained unchanged between 1530 and 1536, balance out Bucer's comments on 6:64, which were emended radically in 1536? In order to answer this question we begin by analyzing the 1528 and 1530 versions of Bucer's exegesis of 6:64.[50]

He begins it by saying that Christ's body cannot be really in the bread because—and here he cites the Nicene Creed—"ipse a nobis abierit, caelos ascenderit, sedeat ad dexteram Dei ad iudicium demum inde rediturus."[51] He then replies to Brenz's accusation leveled against the Zwinglians in his commentary at 6:63–64: "Licebit vobis impune fidei nostrae simplicitati imponere? An nos fungos existimatis, qui hos astus non queamus depraehendere?"[52] by paraphrasing and negating it: "Neque fidei vestrae, o fratres, imponimus neque fungos vos existimamus."[53] But it is only in countering Luther's arguments that Bucer defines, in the same passage, the ontological difference between his own and the Lutheran position. Luther asserts in his *Sermon von dem Sakrament* (1526) that Christ after his Resurrection "ist nicht allein nach der Gottheit, sondern auch nach der menscheit ein Herr aller ding, hat alles ynn der hand und ist uberal gegenwertig."[54] Bucer replies that Christ's human nature is not "in divinam mutata sed glorificata" and, that being the case, "non poterit esse in tot panibus corruptibilibus et simul in diversis locis."[55] He thus touches on the basic point of division between Luther and himself, which can be traced back to patristic and medieval theology.

The question of how Christ's body can be present in several pieces of bread had been raised before, notably by Augustine in his *Sermo* 28, 4 (at Psalm 104:3). There the Bishop of Hippo draws an analogy between the eucharistic presence and the human voice which can be heard in several ears at once. It is pointless, according to him, to take the question further.[56] This very solution to the problem of real presence is proposed by Innocent III in *De sacro altaris mysterio,*[57] by

Johannes von Paltz in *De coelifodina,*[58] and indeed by Luther himself in *Ein Sermon.*[59] The latter is attacked by Zwingli in the *Amica exegesis* of 1527, but Zwingli does not state as explicitly as Bucer that it is *impossible* for Christ's body to be present in several places at once, objecting rather to the idea of the body being *eaten.*[60] We can, however, establish a definite link between Bucer's eucharistic ontology and that of Saint Thomas Aquinas. The latter, without denying real presence, asserts in the *Summa* that it is impossible for the flesh of Christ to be in the sacrament "sicut corpus in loco, quod suis dimensionibus loco commensuratur; sed quodam speciali modo, qui est proprius huic sacramento." To support this contention Thomas refers to Augustine's commentary of John 6:53, 64 and explains that the Jews and the disciples objected to Christ's words because they understood him to be offering his flesh physically and locally.[61] He himself rejects any position that admits of Christ's presence in the sacrament "per motum localem," as this would mean him deserting his place in heaven. Moreover, he affirms, "impossibile est quod unus motus eiusdem corporis localiter moti terminetur simul ad diversa loca."[62] Bucer put forward the identical argument in his contribution to the dispute on the fourth thesis during the Berne disputation as a reply to the "one voice in many ears" argument. There he stated, "Es ist gar wyt von einandern, das ein oug zůmal viler gestalt fasse, und ein wort vō vilen oren empfangen werde: dañ das ein warer natürlicher lyb der sin eigne grösse unnd lydmass haben sol, sye zůmal an vilen orten."[63] This "Thomist" position causes Bucer to reject *Deo sunt omnia possibila* (cf. Matthew 19:26) as an argument in favor of ubiquity and real presence in his comments on John 6:64 in 1528 and 1530.[64] This argument is put forward by Luther in the *Sermon*[65] and had already been used by Paltz in the eucharistic context.[66] Bucer admits that all things are possible to God but repeats, after Zwingli, that God is truthful[67] and himself testifies that his Son was made real flesh.

It is only after refuting Luther's ontology of the Eucharist and affirming his own that Bucer proceeds to give an exegesis of John 6:64, which turns out to be a compilation of Chrysostom's and Augustine's interpretations of that verse. Bucer says:

Nulla igitur alia ratione hic *Dominus carnem* suam *inutilem* [John 6:64] pronunciavit, quam ut usque in humili illa, qua tum erat conditione relinqueretur. Ut enim mihi dubium non est intellexisse et Iudaeos et discipulos quod allegoricos dixisset carnem suam *vere* et vivificum *cibum* [John 6:56] et ideo offensos quod sibi tam humili atque abiecto vivificatricem virtutem arrogaret . . . ita non videtur ideo dixisse Dominum suam *carnem nihil prodesse* [John 6:64] ut significaret nihil conducere dentibus laniatam et corporaliter comesam, sed ut significaret fructum illum propter quem eam assumpsisset non posse, illa ita humiliter versante in terris provenire, ideo subvehendam esse in caelum [cf. John 6:63] ut qualis caro esset palam fieret et tum Spiritum vivificatorem mittendum.[68]

There follows a sharp criticism of those (i.e., Luther and Brenz)[69] who take *caro* at John 6:64 to refer to the inadequacy of human understanding. Bucer does not say in 1528 or 1530 that this is Chrysostom's interpretation. He himself follows Augustine in referring *caro* to the flesh of Christ, but he also contradicts Augustine by asserting that Christ's audience did *not* take his words to imply cannibalism, but that their difficulty lay in recognizing divinity in such a frail human body. This basic idea is reinforced, as we have seen, in the 1530 edition by Bucer's exegesis of John 6:53. Here, as there, Bucer uses Chrysostom as his source. The Greek Father asserts in his homily on John 6:64 that the spiritual understanding amounts to perceiving the divine nature of Christ in spite of his human form.[70] Augustine, on the other hand, emphasizes that Christ's flesh is of no avail in the sense of being literally eaten, and that his audience "carnem quippe sic intellexerunt, quomodo in cadavere dilaniatur aut in macello venditur, non quomodo Spiritu vegetatur."[71] Bucer, as we have seen, paraphrases this phrase of Augustine's in order to contradict it.

So far, it appears that in commenting on John 6:64 in 1528 and 1530, Bucer enters into an active polemic with the Lutherans about the distinction between Christ's human and divine natures. While he has no scruples about using Augustine in order to deny any form of real presence in the Eucharist, he avoids the implication of spiritual manducation that Augustine's exegesis contains by tacitly supplementing Augustine's "*caro* [Christi] *non prodest quidquam*" with Chrysostom's point at 6:64 about Christ's audience being unable to recognize his divinity. This point is reinforced by Bucer's insertion of the same exegesis at John 6:53 in 1530.

In the 1536 edition, however, the polemic disappears and the exegesis undergoes an apparent transformation. As regards *caro non prodest* at 6:64, Bucer explains that he is now following Chrysostom in referring the words to the inadequacy of human (or carnal) understanding. This interpretation is quite appropriate, he continues, as the Lord here is talking about his ascension and the giving of the Paraclete. He admits that previously he had defended Augustine's reading of the passage "non sine stomacho."[72] There follows a *retractatio* in which Bucer emphasizes that the Eucharist contains a real *exhibitio* of Christ's body and blood without, however, containing these elements physically or locally. His *retractatio* thus constitutes no more than a repetition of the Wittenberg Concord.[73]

In fact, there was no change in Bucer's exegesis of John 6:64 as a result of the Wittenberg Concord, especially if we take into account his unaltered interpretation of John 6:53, which emphasizes the distinction between the two natures of Christ. There, Bucer's explicit invocation of Chrysostom in 1536 was very likely intended to serve as a defense against any anticipated accusations of Zwinglianism. Should such accusations occur, the Strasbourger might reply that he is now following Chrysostom at both John 6:53 and 64. At verse 64 all Bucer alters is the reference point of *caro*. Given that already in 1528 and 1530 he emphasized that Christ's *caro* was of no avail if his divine nature was not understood—thus following Chrysostom as against Augustine—the change in 1536 represents no more than a "sharpening up" of his former theological position. It is true that Luther, particularly in the *Bekenntnis* of 1528, followed Chrysostom by understanding *caro* to mean that human flesh is incapable of understanding things spiritual. However, he interpreted Chrysostom as saying that just because humans cannot understand the concept of spiritual eating, it does not follow that Christ's flesh, being spiritual, cannot be eaten in the Eucharist with faith.[74] To Bucer in 1536 (as in 1528 and 1530) the inadequacy of the human flesh means its incapacity to understand the Spirit that Christ will give to the elect after his ascension. Furthermore, Bucer in 1536 does not touch on the crucial ontological question which separated him from Luther—i.e., is it possible for Christ's body to be in several places at once? As at verse 52, so at verse 64 it is only the polemic which Bucer removes in 1536; his theological position remains unchanged.

The following conclusions might be drawn from our examination of Bucer's treatment of these three verses. At John 6:52 Bucer uses

Cyril of Alexandria, Zwingli, *and* John Fisher in order to combat any eucharistic interpretation of the verse, be it Roman Catholic or Lutheran. Any emendations introduced in 1536 leave Bucer's theology unchanged, although all overtly polemical passages are suppressed. At John 6:53, 64 Bucer uses Chrysostom, particularly, in 1536 so as to give "respectability" to his own Christology, which underwent no change after the Wittenberg Concord. At verse 64, however, the 1536 edition suppresses all overtly polemical statements, including the mention of the fundamental ontological difference between him and Luther. Thus between 1528 and 1536 polemical and ontological statements gave way to biblical exegesis *sensu stricto* without the underlying theology[75] altering in any way: Bucer never even approached the view of the ubiquity of Christ's body that was held by Augustine, Innocent III, Paltz, and Luther himself.

KENNETH HAGEN

"De Exegetica Methodo"

Niels Hemmingsen's *De Methodis* (1555)

Exegesis is generally understood to be a modern discipline, and the current literature on the direction of its future is enormous. The history, or "prehistory," of exegesis, regarding the sixteenth century at least, is neither clear nor very accurate. Historical surveys of the historical-critical method, hermeneutics, and the discipline of Einleitung (Introduction) credit various figures and works as the "real beginning" of this and the "father" of that.[1] I suggest, vis-à-vis the sixteenth century, that these terms (historical-critical, hermeneutics, Einleitung) are not very helpful because they were not the terms used at the time. For example, the phrases "medieval hermeneutics" and "Luther's hermeneutics" suggest that the medievals and Luther actually had hermeneutics; whereas they only had "rules" for exposition. As Flacius held and is still accepted today, to use a philosophy (such as is entailed in hermeneutics) is to bring with it a whole host of presuppositions.[2] My point is simply that it would be more helpful to use sixteenth-century terms when discussing the sixteenth-century background to an eighteenth-century discipline (historical hermeneutics).

"De exegetica methodo" is the phrase Niels Hemmingsen used in 1555 in his first work, *De methodis libri duo* (the first book was for philosophy and the second for theological method).[3] My thesis is that Hemmingsen belongs in the historical surveys of so-called historical criticism, hermeneutics, and Einleitung—or, to use his term, the development of exegetical method. This thesis is based on a word study of exegesis, Hemmingsen's work of 1555 and his subsequent commentaries on the New Testament Epistles, and on secondary literature, that is, accounts of who does qualify for these surveys and why.

People who write about historical exegetica do not seem to know about Hemmingsen, and, on the other hand, those who write about Hemmingsen do not seem to know about his work on exegetical method.[4] Carl von Kaltenborn's book *Forerunners of Hugo Grotius on Ius naturae et gentium* praises Hemmingsen as "epoch making" for considering the scientific form of law according to mathematical sciences. After all, it is Grotius's scientific method that is important rather than the content of his work. It is the science of the principles of law for which he is important but completely unknown.[5] I would like to make the same claim for Hemmingsen regarding the rise of exegetical method. I will not use "forerunner" or "father" language, but I will contend that he is important for the methodical framework in which he placed "exegesis," and for that he is unknown.

Hemmingsen (1513–1600) was not unknown in sixteenth-century Europe. He was at the center of university and church life in Denmark. The *praeceptor universalis Daniae* was also the leader in the Philipist period of power. The "brilliant young Dane" was with Melanchthon in Wittenberg, 1537–42; then in Copenhagen (1542) as professor of Greek (1543), dialectic (1545), and theology (1553), until his dismissal in 1579 on grounds of Crypto-Calvinism regarding the Lord's Supper. Trygve Skarsten says that "his fame and reputation throughout the learned circles of Europe brought renown and glory to the University of Copenhagen. His Latin and Danish works were to be found in the leading libraries in multiple editions and often in Dutch, English, and German translation. As he advanced in age, scholars and dignitaries made their pilgrimage to his door, and kings like James VI of Scotland counted it an honor to have talked with the famous Danish theologian."[6]

He published in the areas of exegetics, dogmatics, ethics, and pastoral theology. He published commentaries on individual epistles, beginning with Romans in 1562 and continuing to write one or more every year until 1569. The bulk were published between 1564 and 1566. His *Commentaria in omnes epistolas apostolorum* appeared in 1572 (Leipzig), 1579 (Frankfurt), and 1586 (Strasbourg).

The reasons for this study on exegetical method for the Second International Colloquy on the History of Biblical Exegesis in the

Sixteenth Century were twofold. First, in my study *Hebrews Commenting from Erasmus to Bèze, 1516–1598,* it seemed to me that "introductions" to Pauline Epistles in the second half of the century were quite different from those earlier in the century, particularly after Calvin's 1549 commentary on Hebrews. M. E. Schild also sees a change "near the middle of the century." This change involved the removal of the traditional Vulgate prologues from their places in the Latin Bible of the Roman Catholic church, possibly because of "the new critical literary attitudes."[7] He says no more. My second reason was Hemmingsen's use of the words *method* and *exegesis.*[8] I learned that discussion of "method" (Methodenlehre) was already under way earlier in the century. So Hemmingsen could be seen as a part of that transition to what Reinhard Kirste calls "methodological thinking in Orthodoxy."[9] What is significant is Hemmingsen's use of *exegesis,* particularly within a philosophical and theological framework.

EXEGESIS: MEANING AND HISTORY OF THE WORD

Hemmingsen's use of the word *exegesis* prompted an investigation into the meaning and history of the word itself. Independent lexicographical work confirmed the overview given in the *Allgemeines Real-Wörterbuch* of 1784. The word *exegesis* is both an ancient and a relatively modern word. As far as I can tell, it was not used in ecclesiastical Latin in the ancient or medieval period, but it was used in the seventeenth century, and certainly in the eighteenth century and afterward. In the modern period it is connected with the "art of interpreting Scripture" (*Auslegungskunst der heiligen Schrift*). Regarding the ancient period it is related to grammar and interpretation of poetry. In classical Greek, exegetes were interpreters or expounders of sacred lore. With the Romans they were the augurs and *interpretes,* often meaning "translator" or "mediator" of some kind. In Christian theology well into the sixteenth century, work on the Bible was done in the genre of commentary, explanation, exposition, and annotation, but not in the more modern sense of interpretation. *Intepretatio* at that time referred more to translation and explanation of obscure and enigmatic words or dreams.[10] For Luther, Scripture was its own interpreter.[11]

A comparison of two types of lexicons—the sixteenth-century edition with the later seventeenth- and eighteenth-century versions—

confirms the above overview. The types are the *Thesaurus linguae Latinae* and the *Vocabularium,* as classified in the subject catalog of the Herzog-August-Bibliothek in Wolfenbüttel. Within each type one can compare the various editions of the *Thesaurus* of Robert Estienne (Stephanus) (the 1740 edition versus the 1573 edition) and the various editions of Ambrosio Calepino's *Dictionarium latinarum* (the 1647 edition versus the 1598, 1542, and [1510] editions). In the later editions (seventeenth and eighteenth century) *exegesis* appears, while in the sixteenth-century ones it does not.

Minimally, it seems to me that Hemmingsen certainly played a role in development in the area of exegesis as well as in the area of *Methodenlehre.* Can one get at the beginnings of the discipline of exegesis? If so, I suggest that Hemmingsen was at least a part of it.

DE METHODIS LIBRI DUO (1555)

The Context of Hemmingsen's Book

Lutz Geldsetzer's introduction to Jacobus Acontius's work on method (*De methodo,* 1558) sets that work in the context of Erasmus's *Ratio seu methodus* (1520), Erasmus Sarcerius's ... *ad certam methodum* (1547), and Hemmingsen's *De methodis libri duo* (1555). These works, however, are not all in the same genre. Hemmingsen's is *De methodis;* but Sarcerius's is a *loci communes,* beginning with *De trinitate* and ending with *de sepultura,* and is *ad certam methodum,* and not *de methodo.* Erasmus's "pedagogical methodology"[12] is concerned, as he says, with "true theology" (*incipit, explicit*).

One might say, as Hemmingsen himself intended and as the Danish scholar E. Munch Madsen believes, that Hemmingsen's exegetical method came from Melanchthon. Hemmingsen regarded his *Enchiridion theologicum* of 1557 as an introduction to Melanchthon, a resource for a deeper understanding of Melanchthon's *opus sacrosanctum.*[13] And in *De methodis* he defers to Melanchthon's *Loci.* The only person who discusses *De methodis* in the secondary literature is Madsen, who accepts Hemmingsen's word about his faithfulness to Melanchthon.[14] Madsen's thesis is that on method and dogmatics Melanchthon was Hemmingsen's teacher, but on exegetical particulars he turned to others (e.g., Calvin). Madsen's contention that Hemmingsen's method is "hardly original" is offered without proof, except to say that that is what one would expect.[15] I disagree. As to Hemmingsen's dependence in dogmatics on Melanchthon, in the Five Hundredth Jubilee of the University of Copenhagen Nils Andersen describes Hemmingsen's claim that his *Enchiridion* is an introduction to Melanchthon as "grossly exaggerated."[16] It is true that in the beginning of the second period of the *Loci* (1533) Melanchthon discusses method. But he does so in terms of the *ordo locorum* (*Corpus Reformatorum* 21:253); so he is not talking *about* method as such. Further, I would point to the beginning of the third period of the *Loci* (1543), where Melanchthon says that method has no place in theology. Method belongs to philosophy, which proceeds from experience, principles, and proofs. The doctrine of the church, however, proceeds from what God has said, from revelation (*CR* 21:603–4). It may well be that Hemmingsen thought he was carrying out Melanchthon's wishes, for it "seems" to N. W. Gilbert, who thinks Melanchthon's reputation as *artifex methodi* is ill-founded, that Melanchthon emphasized the importance of method more in "oral teaching" than in his books.[17]

Taking my cue from Wilhelm Risse, a contemporary historian of logic covering the period from 1500 to 1640,[18] and Jodocus Willich, an earlier dialectician in the sixteenth century and principal independent of Melanchthon, it is clear that method was being discussed earlier in terms of dialectic. The context for Hemmingsen's *De methodis* is his own work, including teaching, in dialectics. This then concurs with the standard biography and treatment of Hemmingsen's theology (Kjell Barnekow's *Niels Hemmingsens teologiska åskådning*) as far as book 1 is concerned. Barnekow relegates it to a footnote and classifies it as a philosophy textbook,[19] as does the *Danish Biographical Lexicon* (vols. 1 and 2).[20] The problem with this is that book 2 is overlooked. Book 2, which parallels book 1, contains exegetical method for theology and method for spiritual rhetoric (hermeneutics and homiletics, in our terms). Hemmingsen's connection of dialectics (book 1) with theological method (book 2) could well have come from Melanchthon. But according to Risse, given Melanchthon's direction toward *Lehrunterricht,* his followers in logic tended either to go their own ways or to simplify Melanchthon for school purposes.[21] Also according to Risse, using some terms also found in Willich, Hemmingsen was his own person.[22] *Methodus* as a technical term came into medicine before the middle of the sixteenth century, and by the second half of the century lawyers were discussing *Methodus* as well.[23] Hemmingsen, then, was a part of the contemporary discussion of method. From Melanchthon he turned to Galen and Aristotle and the dialectical and rhetorical traditions. With this context in mind, we turn to the book.

Book I, Definition of Method and the Methodological Framework for De Exegetica Methodo

Before defining method, Hemmingsen gives high praise to *ordo* and *methodus* for teaching and learning. Since the "little book" is on method, it seems "commodius" to Hemmingsen that one should indicate what particular method will be followed in the discussion "of methods" (method for method). His is διαίρεσιν—the method of definition and division (pp. 2–3, 1570 ed.). Method is defined, following the ancient Greek methodists, as *via docendi certa cum ratione.* It is the *via* or *ratio docendi* (p. 3). Synonyms include *via, ratio, forma, methodus,* and *ordo.*

The overall division of methods is between universal, which is the *via integrarum* (p. 4), and particular (pp. 21–23), which is divided into *simplex* and *composita* (plus rhetoric) with further definitions and divisions. At the end of Hemmingsen's discussion of universal methods, he asks whether one is preferable. The answer, contra Ramus, is no; each has its strengths and place (p. 19).

As with the universal, the subdivisions of *simplex particularis* are synthetic, analytic, and "definitive." This comes from Galen and is also the format of Flacius's well-known "*tabula* of theological methods."[24]

The section on exegetical method is in the second cluster of three methods in the *composita particularis.* "This second part especially helps the zeal for discovery, confirms the memory, and shows the way to read the best authors" (p. 40). It consists of *disputatio, collatio,* and *examen. Examen* is the exegetical method: "examination of those things written by others" (p. 22). The exegetical method is then divided into four aspects (pp. 89–108).

The first aspect, which is all-inclusive, is *forma,* or *ratio interpretandi authores.* Just as there are many ends of interpretation, so there are many forms. The grammatical pays attention to words and phrases, the dialectical to things, the rhetorical to the *accidentia* of words and things, and the *interpretationis genus* to all these things *simul.* All these genera are to be found in the great disciplines of theology, mathematics, law, physics, and ethics. So far, then, exegesis is the examination or interpretation of other authors and includes the grammatical, dialectical, and rhetorical methods; it is the examination of the words, the thing itself, and the accidental.

The second aspect of exegesis prescribes the way of reducing to dialectical brevity the dialectical forms of interpretation. Included in this section, which is anything but brief, are the different forms of speech (*expositio, argumentatio,* or both), rules for dialectics, oratorical forms, examples, and more rules. At the end of this second section is a summary of the dialectical *via* that discusses the question of whether it comes from some firm principle, is a hypothesis, is absurd, or whatever, and whether the proposition follows dialectical precepts.

The third aspect examines *quae tradita sunt,* and they are (again) grammar, dialectic, and rhetoric.

The fourth is the method for learning to remember: know the thing well, count the parts, note the order of the parts and the "adornment."

Perhaps Kaltenborn could be repeated at this point to the effect that *what* Hemmingsen is saying is not as important, vis-à-vis Melanchthon or Willich, Hyperius or Flacius, as the fact that he discusses "exegetical method" as such, and then carries it over from philosophy into theological method in book 2. That is significant and at least deserves notice. Or, to put my thesis in other words, Hemmingsen puts together method-exegesis-theology in such a way that neither Luther nor Melanchthon would be happy—i.e., independently. Luther, Melanchthon (at least in the preface to the third edition), Hyperius, and Flacius would not (in Luther's case) or did not (in the other cases) want to talk about method, and certainly not from the dialectical tradition. They would rather talk about Scripture (Luther and Flacius), revelation (Melanchthon), or a particular locus (Hyperius). Hemmingsen is also independent of the dialecticians in the areas of *Methodenfrage* and theology.

Book 2 and Theological Method

Whenever we look at what God has made, we see the most beautiful order; so too in sacred theology. The *ratio* for observing this order is, with a very apt metaphor, called *methodus*. Those who have a method become *periti* more quickly than those who become fatigued from reading the Bible without order or method (pp. 119–20). Vis-à-vis book 1, "methodum Theologicam" comprises spiritual dialectic (*ratio interpretandi scripturam*) and spiritual rhetoric (*ratio formandi sacras conciones*). Theological method, then, is the *ratio* "et interpretandi scripturam et formadi sacras conciones" (p. 120). Theological method is the procedure or principle for interpreting Scripture and forming sacred speeches (i.e., sermons). The purpose of the former is that we might more easily understand other interpreters and grasp the interpretive forms. The latter's purpose is that we might be able to discuss (i.e., preach) the thing proposed (in Scripture) in ecclesiastical contexts.[25] The second part, then, is Hemmingsen's method for preaching (which we will not treat).[26]

The section on method for interpreting Scripture is divided into two parts: "division of Scripture" and "forms of interpretation" (pp. 122–40). Hemmingsen acknowledges the common division: Old Testament/New Testament, Law/Prophets/Gospels/Epistles, and so on. Moderns define the historical-critical method as concerning first and foremost the origin of individual books, but also the canon. In the light of such concerns, it should be noted that in dividing the New Testament into Gospels, Acts, twenty-one Epistles, and the Apocalypse, Hemmingsen comments on the canon: "All these books of the New Testament are in the canon except Second Peter, Second and Third John, the Epistles of James and Jude along with the Apocalypse. Some also place the Epistle to the Hebrews outside the canon" (p. 124). Such lists of inclusion/exclusion were not uncommon at the time.

Hemmingsen dismisses immediately the scholastic division of law-history-wisdom-prophecy. He offers the "most suitable" division: history and doctrine (p. 126). History is both old and new, dividing at Christ. The *doctrina rerum* is law and gospel; the *doctrina signorum* is ceremonies and sacraments. A further distinction is important lest law and gospel be confused, as the Papists do by defining the gospel as a new law. The prophets and apostles teach nothing that Moses did not teach; but in the *modus tradendi* there is a great difference. Moses received the doctrine from God, and the Fathers passed it down from hand to hand, but it is more obscure than the prophets. The prophets are interpreters of Moses. What is an aphorism in Moses, the prophets explain fully. But what the prophets predict, the apostles see clearly. The apostles are clearer interpreters of Moses and the prophets. Note the medieval distinction of *clarior* just after his criticism of the Papists for calling the gospel a new law. With this distinction of *clarior,* Scripture can be read with greater fruit. At the outset Hemmingsen claims that the purpose of knowing the parts of Scripture is twofold: The parts may be recognized more easily, and the use of the individual parts may be seen more clearly (p. 121). What is important for theological method is that these distinctions are necessary for clarity. In other words, there is some historical perception here of a process of interpretation.

Concerning the *forms* of interpretation (*De formis enarrationum*)—the other part of his method for interpreting Scripture—there are four (pp. 129–40): (1) aids for the interpreter, (2) causes of interpretation, (3) the kinds of interpretations, and (4) the use of commentators.

1. *Aids for the interpreter.* The interpreter of Scripture is treating sacred mysteries, or, as Hemmingsen also says, "the mind of the interpreter ought always to be attentive to the first axioms of our religion" (p. 132). Such being the case, care is incumbent on one wishing to be free from error, one wishing not to deviate from *pietas.* He must, first, seek God and his will; second, have the word of God *pro regula;* third, compare Scripture so that the consensus of Moses-prophets-Christ-apostles appears, diligently observing the circumstances of the places (texts) lest they be taken out of context; and, fourth, refer every true interpretation "ad analogian fidei." Even if one is in error regarding the scope and mind of the author, so long as one is in agreement with the faith, one's salvation is not endangered. The analogy of faith means with respect to the first axioms of religion, which are law and gospel (pp. 130–33). Since the eighteenth century these four would be considered not aids but hindrances to biblical criticism. For Hemmingsen, every interpretation hangs on the constant word of God (p. 133), hence the consensus. In this section on aids I find Hemmingsen close to Augustine (book 3 of *De doctrina*).

2. *Causes of interpretation.* Hemmingsen refers here to the preface of Melanchthon's *Loci.* Again, the subdivision is four. (He is surely following his announced method for method.) The first is to understand the kind of language so as to retain its sense. The second is an examination of the order. The third is to bear witness to the true

interpretation. The fourth is to refute false opinions (pp. 133–34). A comparison between Melanchthon (*Loci,* preface to third period, 1543) and Hemmingsen on this point shows a further differentiation between the two. On language and interpretation Melanchthon says, "Because the untrained do not everywhere know the *genus sermoni* nor immediately see the order of things, they are to be admonished by the voice of the interpreters concerning the genus of words and the order of things," and, because there are corrupters around, pious pastors and theologians are witnesses of the truth and refuters of false interpretations. On account of these "causes" God has restored the ministry of the gospel with studies in schools and temples so that we are keepers (*custodes*) of sacred books (*CR* 21:606). Hemmingsen's analysis, I submit, is very aware of the problem of translation and interpretation. For Hemmingsen, we must understand the *genus sermonis,* "for hearers or readers do not always understand the phrases of another language, even the most learned of men sometimes are lacking very much in this *palaestra.*" He goes on to say that it often happens that where a speech is translated with words of another language, while corresponding in *significatio* they often do not retain the same sense in both languages, on account of dialect or the variety of phrases; thus, lest we be deceived, the work is to be done by an "expert interpreter" (pp. 133–34). Whereas Melanchthon's "pious pastors and theologians" are custodians of Scripture, Hemmingsen's "expert interpreters" must pay attention to meaning, sense, and translation.

3. *Kinds of interpretation (interpretandi genera).* Hemmingsen wants to be as clear as possible here because these genera are quite distinct. Reading the commentaries of others, he finds four kinds of interpretation: grammatical, dialectical, oratorical, and mixed. We will look particularly at the dialectical and its various subdivisions. The first is grammatical "exegesis" (p. 135), for which one needs to know Hebrew, Greek, and Latin (pp. 135–36). The second is dialectical, for which there are four canons. First canon: In the beginning of a commentary it is fitting to discuss the kind of doctrine in general and its authority, certainty, necessity, and utility. Second canon: Following the dialectical genus of interpretation, there are four questions with regard to any particular writing. These four questions will structure the *argumenta* to Hemmingsen's commentaries, beginning with Romans in 1562. Here the former professor of dialectic lays out the methodology for

interpretation that he will follow in his later commentaries. The first question, authorship, determines the authority of the writing. The second, occasion, leads to an understanding of the literary structures ("*tractationis ordinem*"). The third, the status or principal question, leads to a perception of the ultimate goal and scope of the whole writing. Without the fourth, method or *ordo tractationis,* the effort will be to little or no advantage (pp. 137–38).

The third canon, what is being taught, follows on the question of method and is a part of it. The doctrine is often "dispersed" in admonition, praise, threat, consolation, etc., by which the author accommodates the doctrine to the hearer (p. 138). The fourth canon is on the explication of particular commentaries. There is a necessary order among as well as within these canons. The first is a summary of the whole commentary; next is how the commentary fits into the preceding and following commentaries; then is "*exegesis textus*" (pp. 138–39). In his commentaries on the Epistles, beginning with *ad Romanos,* Hemmingsen follows the format detailed in the final canon of the dialectical genus: first a summary of the whole commentary, then its *ordo,* then "*exegesis*"—again the actual word.

4. The final form is on the use of commentaries (p. 140), which completes Hemmingsen's theological method for interpreting Scripture, divided into the division of Scripture and forms of interpretation.

The point I want to emphasize regarding *De methodis libri duo* is that "exegesis of the text" is grounded in dialectic, a part of philosophy. There is a definite method for exegesis or interpretation; in fact, there is a method for the method, which Hemmingsen consistently follows, with its definitions, divisions, and subdivisions. The purpose of method is clarity in exegesis. The interpretation of Scripture is grounded in *de exegetica methodo.*

COMMENTARIES ON NEW TESTAMENT EPISTLES

In his *argumenta,* or introductions, to the New Testament Epistles, Hemmingsen announces that in order to understand them better, four items have to be discussed: authorship, occasion, principle question, and method. "In order that the *Argumentum* or general *Periocha* of this noble epistle written to the Romans be understood more explicitly by readers, four things need to be explicated by us in order."[27] On James

(1563), these four "*introducunt*" skillfully and correctly the innermost reaches of Scripture as a light held before the reader.[28] On Galatians (1564), "In order that entrance (*ad-itus*) to this epistle be had more easily."[29]

The year that Flacius prefaced and published the *Clavis,* 1567, is the same year Hemmingsen prefaced his *Commentarius* on Hebrews (published in Wittenberg, 1568). What stands out in Hemmingsen's introduction, or *Argumentum in Epistolam ad Hebraeos,* is his explicit statement about what an introduction is supposed to accomplish and what questions should be asked in order to prepare the way for understanding the epistle: "But omitting these [questions of authorship] let us talk about the things which the argument of this epistle opens up to us: let us see what the occasion was for writing, what the principal point or question was, and what was the order of proceeding or method. For knowing these things well, we will have the way prepared for understanding this epistle more clearly" (p. 830).

For Hemmingsen, Beza (1556), and others at this time, questions of authorship—and not only of Hebrews—were regarded as "useless disputations" (Hemmingsen). They continue to discuss authorship, but one has the strong impression that the reason why the long-standing authorship question was regarded as useless is that no consensus regarding Hebrews had emerged from Erasmus on through Calvin, where the question was vigorously discussed. Hemmingsen does raise the authorship question in other introductions. The growing tendency regarding Hebrews was to emphasize that the Holy Spirit is the real author, anyway. Besides, for Hemmingsen, other questions—the occasion, point, and method—were more important. After all, the purpose of an introduction is to prepare the way for understanding.

My point here is that because Hemmingsen reflects on the function of an introduction, even using the verb "to introduce" at one point, in his *argumenta* to the Epistles, he deserves notice in the history of exegetical method.

SECONDARY LITERATURE

Who, then, does receive the attention in histories of historical criticism, hermeneutics, and so on, and on what basis? We began with the question of how Hemmingsen compares with his contemporaries. In the literature, the sixteenth century and the first half of the seventeenth are treated as background to the eighteenth century, when historical criticism "won out."[30] The picture presented is that the sixteenth and seventeenth centuries were a time of transition between the Dark Ages and the dawn of historical consciousness in the eighteenth century.

In order to compare Hemmingsen with contemporary material, the Complutensian, Erasmus, Calvin, Karlstadt, Santes Pagnino, and Flacius were checked because of the claims made on their behalf and because, except for Flacius, all are earlier than Hemmingsen.

In his commentary on "Biblical Scholarship" in the *The Cambridge History of the Bible,* Basil Hall praises "the great Complutensian Polyglot of Alcalá, 1514–17." In discussing its content, he notes that it contains two statements about the method of studying Scripture.[31] After Brevard Childs evaluates Pagnino's *Isagogae* (1536) and Sixtus Senensis's *Bibliotheca sancta* (1566) as traditional, he says, "However, the major contribution to the discipline of Introduction was the publication of the Complutensian Polyglot Bible (1514–17) which dramatized the new philological interest and set the stage for critical biblical scholarship in the field of Old Testament."[32] Early in the Complutensian (vol. 1) there appears a short section on "Modi intelligendi sacram scripturam," which turns out to be a discussion of the famous medieval *quadriga.* At the end is a section on "Introductiones artis grammatice hebraice." It is strictly grammatical—consonants, vowels, Hebrew sounds, vowel points, word order, nouns, and pronouns. A comparison of the Complutensian introduction to Hebrews with medieval introductions reveals that the Complutensian is a reprint of the medieval *Glossa ordinaria.* Certainly this is a "contribution," but it is not "the major contribution to the discipline of Introduction."

H. J. Kraus assesses Calvin and his discussion of the intention of the biblical author as an *Ansatz zur Kritik.* Calvin insists on investigating "the history, geography, and institutional *circumstances* which are determinative for the author's situation."[33] Then Kraus states, "He is clearly following the lead of Erasmus" (Greek and Latin New Testament, 1516). Erasmus also insists on study of the history and geographical setting, the customs, and institutions. "Then a marvelous light and, I might say, life, is given to what is being read" (Erasmus).[34] A check of Erasmus's introduction and the context of Kraus's quote reveals that Erasmus is actually citing Augustine's *De doctrina chris-*

tiana (2:16, also 2:28). This suggests that one should be very careful about such words as *historical* and *critical.* Consider the words *historical, geographical,* and *institutional circumstances.* Do you think they had the same meaning for Augustine, Erasmus, Calvin, and Kraus?

Another kind of misjudgment, e.g., by Kraus and Otto Kaiser, is made about the importance of Karlstadt's *De canonicis scripturis* (1520). Kaiser evaluates the work as "at least the beginnings of a modern science of Old Testament introduction,"[35] and Kraus considers Karlstadt the first precursor of literary historical research on the Old Testament within Protestant theology.[36] I do not see it. What I see is a series of quotations, principally from Augustine and Jerome. Occasionally Karlstadt will argue with the Fathers (with Jerome on the Apocrypha, for example), but he gets permission to do so from Augustine.[37] An early section on the majesty of Scripture is reminiscent of Lyra's prologues. One way I can account for the misjudgment about Karlstadt is that these authors were misled by the title, which sounded scientific.

Some have listed Pagnino's *Isagogae* (1536) as a part of the history of the discipline of *Einleitung.*[38] Even as the full title indicates, it is very traditional and mystical. The first brief book discusses topical questions; for example, the four modes of expounding the law (from Augustine). The second, much longer, section is concerned with the mystical meaning of various words, listed alphabetically from *abyssus* to *uxor.*[39]

Almost everyone considers Flacius's *Clavis Scripturae Sacrae*[40] key to the development of the modern discipline of historical criticism. It has been described as the "real beginning of scholarly hermeneutics" (Werner Kümmel);[41] the first of a scientific biblical discipline;[42] for Hans Frei, it is the "first writing on hermeneutics."[43] The *Clavis* is a general and special (hermeneutical) guide to Scripture. Flacius lists fifty-plus causes for difficulty with regard to Scripture (which Olivier Fatio argues were plagiarized from Hyperius).[44] There are fifty-plus rules from Scripture for understanding Scripture (treatise 1); for example, the distinction between law and gospel is the "clavis" to "true religion." In addition, treatise 1 considers the *ratio* for understanding Scripture (largely from Scripture, with a long section on multiple senses of Scripture). Treatise 2 contains rules from the Fathers for understanding Scripture; 3 and 4 are grammatical, 5 is literary (*de*

Stylo), 6 is both grammatical and literary, and 7 is mostly on tradition. The *Clavis* is impressive in its ordering of detail. Karl von Schwartz, however, thought the same details could be found in Luther.[45] A work that I would also cite relative to the beginning, or prehistory, of scientific biblical criticism is Flacius's *Glossa Compendiaria* on the New Testament (1570) with its introductions.[46]

In his introduction to Matthew, Flacius says that questions of language are of no little moment. He also discusses the "occasion of the writing" (pp. 1–3, 1570 ed.). In his introductions to several Epistles, the occasion is one of four things that should be known ("praenoscenda esse," p. 748) or given to the reader before one begins to speak of the writing. The others are author, scope or argument, and status. Method and sequence (*series*), the "order of the parts" (pp. 640, 748, 873–74, 915, 959, 984–85, 1105–7), are important also. Here, then, Flacius is commenting on issues that a *praefatio* or *argumentum* should deal with. On Ephesians and Philippians he is also interested in the situation of the city (pp. 915, 959); on Colossians about the time of writing (p. 985). On Hebrews his argument for Pauline authorship is among the most extensive I have seen, for or against. His responses to two traditional arguments against Pauline authorship are nuanced and unusual, and basically literary. For one, the reason the language of Hebrews is clearer and more splendid is that Paul is not writing to one church or one person but to the whole Hebrew nation. Is not the Holy Spirit able to vary the style out of "the necessity of things, times, and hearers"? Besides, Cicero and Aristotle altered their styles (pp. 1101–3). Among his fifteen reasons for Pauline authorship, some historical or circumstantial "evidence" is used; for example, it had to have been written before the fall of the temple and Jerusalem, and no disciple of the apostles would have dared to write it or would have gotten by with it if he had (pp. 1103–5).

My perspective is that Flacius is the continuation, albeit also a synthesizer, of trends under way for some decades. I have in mind the literary-grammatical character of the *Clavis* and the concerns of the *Glossa Compendiaria* with author, occasion, argument, and method, and his reflection on the purpose of a preface.

With reference to secondary literature, two conclusions are offered. First, some sloppy work has been done relative to early sixteenth-century exegetica, perhaps due to ignorance of medieval forms. A good example would be the place of Luther, who is often credited with separating Scripture and churchly tradition, using the former to attack the latter, and then singling out Scripture for study (Kümmel, Hendricus Boers).[47] But the same thing happened in the fifteenth century (with Hus, Gerson, D'Ailly, and Erasmus) and probably earlier. Without medieval background, sloppy conclusions arise. Second, histories—especially histories of hermeneutics—have been misled by concentrating on seemingly methodological works without checking the theory in practice or finding theory in the actual commentaries.

CONCLUSION

The field is wide open for a specialist in the sixteenth century to write a history of exegetical method. Hemmingsen's *De methodis libri duo* (1555) should be included because of his discussion of exegetical method for philosophy and theology. Certainly Hemmingsen deserves as much attention as others from his time who are credited with beginning modern critical trends in biblical interpretation. He deserves attention not only for his actual discussion of exegesis and method but also for his explicit discussion of the function of an introduction to a biblical book. The Danes are certainly correct in the assessment of *De methodis* as "en gylden Bog."[48]

Notes

H. C. ERIK MIDELFORT
Social History and Biblical Exegesis

1. See Fernand Braudel, "History and the Social Sciences," in *Economy and Society in Early Modern Europe. Essays from "Annales,"* ed. Peter Burke (London, 1972), 11–42; and Emmanuel LeRoy Ladurie, "History that Stands Still," in his *The Mind and Method of the Historian,* trans. Sian Reynolds and Ben Reynolds (Chicago, 1978), 1–27.

2. Lawrence Stone, *The Past and the Present* (Boston, 1981); Emmanuel LeRoy Ladurie, *Montaillou. The Promised Land of Error* (New York, 1978); idem, *Carneval in Romans* (New York, 1979). One could object that these excursions into story telling are still so concerned with extracting large social lessons that the recovery of narrative is far from complete.

3. John Bossy, "Some Elementary Forms of Durkheim," *Past and Present* 95 (May 1982): 3–18.

4. *Witch Hunting in Southwestern Germany, 1562–1684: The Social and Intellectual Foundations* (Stanford, 1972).

5. Philipp Dietz, *Wörterbuch zu Dr. Martin Luthers Deutschen Schriften,* 2 vols. (Leipzig, 1870–72; reprint, Hildesheim, 1973), 2:73. Luther did use the word to express the union of Christians with Christ in the Sacrament; cf. Luther, *Werke: Kritische Gesammtausgabe (Weimarer Ausgabe)* (Weimar, 1883–), 2:743 [hereinafter cited as *WA*]: "communicare auff latein heyst diss gemeynschafft empfahen, wilches wir auff deutsch sagen zum sacrament gehen."

6. Dietz, *Wörterbuch,* 2:77, 99.

7. Heinz Holeczek, *Humanistische Bibelphilologie als Reformproblem bis Erasmus von Rotterdam, Thomas More und William Tyndale* (Leiden, 1975), 331–42.

8. Dietz, *Wörterbuch,* 2:72.

9. "Sermon von dem hochwirdigen Sacrament" (1519), in *WA* 2:747.

10. "Von dem bapstum zu Rom" (1520), in *WA* 6:293; cf. p. 295 for Luther's discussion of the "leyplich gemein."

11. The origin of *Kirche* goes back to *kyriakon,* Greek for "house of the Lord."

12. Jacob Grimm and Wilhelm Grimm, *Deutsches Wörterbuch* (Leipzig, 1854–1954), vol. 3, cols. 1305–6.

13. *Mishpachah* as in Genesis 10:5, 26:14; *bayith* as in Genesis 50:4; 2 Chronicles 35:5; *eleph* as in Judges 6:15; *patria* as in Ephesians 3:15; or *oikodespotes* as in Matthew 13:27; Luke 14:21, 22:11.

14. Grimm is eloquent in his regret over this development: *Wörterbuch,* vol. 3, col. 1305.

15. Philippe Ariès, *Centuries of Childhood* (New York, 1962); Lawrence Stone, *The Family, Sex, and Marriage in England, 1500–1800* (London, 1977).

16. Otto Brunner, *Adeliges Landleben und europäischer Geist. Leben und Werk Wolf Helmhards von Hohberg* (Salzburg, 1949), esp. 240–58; see also Brunner's "Das 'ganze Hans' und die alteuropäische Ökonomik," in his *Neue Wege der Sozialgeschichte* (Göttingen, 1956), 33–61; H. L. Stoltenberg, "Zur Geschichte des Wortes Wirtschaft," *Jahrbücher für Nationalökonomik und Statistik* 148 (1938): 556–61. I am in deep sympathy with M. I. Finley, "The Ancients and Their Economy," in his *The Ancient Economy* (Berkeley, 1973), 17–34.

17. "For the belief of the Old Testament sorcery means trafficking with strange divine powers or those hostile to God," Martin Noth, *Exodus. A Commentary* (Philadelphia, 1962), 185. Witchcraft "implied a use of supernatural power outside of, and hostile to, the power of the Lord" (Ronald E. Clements, *Exodus* [Cambridge, 1972], 145). See also Frank Michaeli, *Le livre de l'Exode* (Neuchâtel, 1974), 209; and U. Cassuto, *A Commentary on the Book of the Exodus,* trans. I. Abrahams (Jerusalem, 1967), 95–96, 289–90.

18. See also Deuteronomy 18:10, 2 Chronicles 33:6; Exodus 7:11; Daniel 2:2; Malachi 3:5. *Keshaphim* (sorceries) is also found six times: 2 Kings 9:22, Micah 5:12, Nahum 3:4 (twice), Isaiah 47:9, 47:12. *Kashshaph* (sorcerer) is found in Jeremiah 27:9.

19. *Encyclopaedia Judaica,* 16 vols. (Jerusalem, 1971–72), 15:163–64.

20. Ibid., 15:163.

21. Ibid., 11:703.

22. Jeffrey B. Russell, *Witchcraft in the Middle Ages* (Ithaca, 1972); Norman Cohn, *Europe's Inner Demons. An Enquiry Inspired by the Great Witch-Hunt* (New York, 1975).

23. Edward Peters, *The Magician, the Witch, and the Law* (Philadelphia, 1978), 17–18; J.-P. Migne, *Patrologiae cursus completus . . . series latina,* 221 vols. (Paris, 1844–1900), vol. 108, col. 121 (hereinafter cited as *MPL* with volume number and column number).

24. Peters, *The Magician,* 68; Migne, *Patrologia Latina,* vol. 113, col. 261.

25. Peters, *The Magician,* 139; Beryl Smalley, "William of Auvergne, John of La Rochelle, and St. Thomas Aquinas on the Old Law," in *St. Thomas Aquinas,*

1274–1974, Commemorative Studies ed. Etienne Gilson, 2 vols. (Toronto, 1974), 2:11–72.

26. Peters, *The Magician,* 177, n. 5, citing Lyra, *Postillae* (Basel, 1501), vol. 1, fol. 170v.

27. I have used the Anton Koburger edition: Jacob Sprenger and Heinrich Institoris, *Malleus Maleficarum* (Nuremberg, 1494).

28. *WA,* series 3, *Deutsche Bibel,* 5:102.

29. In general, see Joseph Hansen, "Die Zuspitzung des Hexenwahns auf das weibliche Geschlecht," in his *Quellen und Untersuchungen zur Geschichte des Hexenwahns und der Hexenverfolgung im Mittelalter* (Bonn, 1901), 416–44.

30. *WA,* series 3, *Deutsche Bibel,* 8:268–69.

31. Andreas Osiander der Ältere, *Gesamtausgabe,* vol. 3, *Schriften und Briefe 1528 bis April 1530,* ed. Gerhard Müller and Gottfried Seebass (Gütersloh, 1979), 646.

32. Gottfried Maron, "Thomas Müntzer als Theologe des Gerichts. Das 'Urteil': ein Schlüsselbegriff seines Denkens," *Zeitschrift für Kirchengeschichte* 83 (1972): 195–225.

33. From his "Ausgedrückte Entblössung" of 1524: Thomas Müntzer, *Schriften und Briefe. Kritische Gesamtausgabe,* ed. Paul Kirn and Günther Franz (Gütersloh, 1968), 290.

34. "Fürstenpredigt," in ibid., 261–62.

35. See Roland H. Bainton, "Religious Liberty and the Parable of the Tares," in his *Early and Medieval Christianity* (Boston, 1962), 95–121.

36. Müntzer, *Schriften,* 259. The notes incorrectly identify this passage as Exodus 22:2 and the evildoers as thieves.

37. Johann Weyer, *De praestigiis daemonum* (Basel, 1583), book 2, chap. 1, col. 136.

38. Ibid., cols. 136–37.

39. Ibid., col. 143.

40. Ibid., cols. 741–42.

41. Ibid., col. 745, citing Josephus, *Jewish Antiquities,* book 4, chap. 8.

42. Weyer, *De praestigiis,* col. 747.

43. Ibid., col. 748.

44. Ibid., col. 749.

45. Ibid., col. 658.

46. Ibid., cols. 718–31.

47. See George H. Williams, *The Radical Reformation* (Philadelphia, 1962), 489–93, 499–504.

48. George H. Williams and Angel Mergal, eds., *Spiritual and Anabaptist Writers* (Philadelphia, 1957), 253.

49. Bucer, *De Regno Christi, Martini Buceri Opera Latina,* ed. François Wendel

(Paris, 1955), chaps. 22–46; Cyriacus Spangenberg, *Ehespiegel, das ist alles was von dem heyligen Ehestande . . . mag gesagt werden* (Strasbourg, 1570), fol. 194v; Steven Ozment, *When Fathers Ruled. Family Life in Reformation Europe* (Cambridge, 1983), 80–98; François Wendel, *Le mariage à Strasbourg à l'epoque de la Reforme 1520–1692* (Strasbourg, 1928); Williams, *Radical Reformation,* 514–17.

50. Edmund S. Morgan, *The Puritan Family: Religion and Domestic Relations in Seventeenth-Century New England* (Boston, 1944; rev. ed., New York, 1966).

GUY BEDOUELLE

The "Great Matter" of King Henry VIII

Select Bibliography

G. Bedouelle and P. Le Gal, *Le "divorce" du roi Henry VIII. Études et documents.* Travaux d'Humanisme et Renaissance 221. Geneva: Librairie Droz, 1987.

H. A. Kelly, *The Matrimonial Trials of Henry VIII.* Stanford, Calif.: Stanford University Press, 1976.

G. de C. Parmiter, *The King's Great Matter: A Study of Anglo-Papal Relations, 1527–1530.* London: Longmans, 1967.

J. J. Scarisbrick, *Henry VIII.* Berkeley and Los Angeles: University of California Press, 1968.

E. Surtz, *Henry VIII's Great Matter in Italy.* 3 vols. Reprint. Ann Arbor, Mich.: University Microfilms International, 1974.

E. Surtz and V. Murphy, *The Divorce Tracts of Henry VIII.* Angers: Moreana, 1988.

H. Thieme, *Die Ehescheidung Heinrichs VIII. und die europäischen Universitäten.* Juristische Studiengesellschaft Karlsruhe 31. Karlsruhe, 1957.

1. At that time the word *divortium* meant what canon law means by the phrase "the declaration of the nullity" of a marriage. Such "nullity" arises most often because of an impediment from which one has failed to obtain a dispensation (especially consanguinity or blood relationship, and affinity, which in sixteenth-century parlance meant a relationship resulting from consummated marriage or sexual intercourse).

2. This is the consideration that led Henry VIII, even before the annulment of his marriage to Catherine of Aragon, to ask for a new dispensation (in anticipation that the divorce would be granted) to enable him to marry Anne Boleyn: his liaison with Anne's sister, Mary, had established an affinity between them. Clement VII granted this dispensation, which, although it had little effect at the time, does at least indicate that at the time the king's conscience was not burdened by any perceived impediment as far as the law of God was concerned.

3. If the text is indeed applicable to the case of the wife of a deceased brother, it is clear that the germ of a serious challenge to the authority of the pope is implied in Henry's position, since the pope frequently granted dispensations from such impediments.

4. This phrase is found in the correspondence of 1529 as cited by Geoffrey de C. Parmiter, *The King's Great Matter: A Study of Anglo-Papal Relations, 1527–1530* (London: Longmans, 1967), 123, n. 2.

5. Ibid., 121, n. 2.

6. Cf. J. V. Pollet, *Martin Bucer: Études sur sa correspondance,* 2 vols. (Paris, 1962), 2:462ff.

7. Parmiter, *King's Great Matter,* 124; Hans Thieme, *Die Ehescheidung Heinrichs VIII, und die europäischen Universitäten,* Juristische Studiengesellschaft Karlsruhe 31 (Karlsruhe, 1957), 13.

8. H. A. Kelly, *The Matrimonial Trials of Henry VIII* (Stanford: Stanford University Press, 1976), p. 174.

9. Ibid., 180ff.

10. *Gravissimae atque exactissimae illustrissimarum totius Italiae et Galliae academiarum censurae,* dated April 1530, but in fact published in 1531. *The Determinations of the Moste famous and mooste excellent universities of Italy and France,* 7 November 1531. See E. Surtz and V. Murphy, *The Divorce Tracts of Henry VIII* (Angers: Moreana, 1988).

11. *Gravissimae . . . censurae:* "*jam* per matrimonium fiant caro," fol. M4v.

12. "Of these reasons it foloweth that al Christians men, if their private conscience lichtned with the holy ghost and knowledge of holy scripture, as it ought to be, hath moved them unto it," *The Determinations,* fol. 152v.

13. *Gravissimae . . . censurae,* fol. P2r.

14. Thus in 1530 the University of Salamanca and the College of Saint Bartholomew in the same city commented on the case, as did Louvain, whose texts have survived in manuscript form.

15. Amerbach responded with a letter from Basel dated 2 February 1531 (*Opus Epistolarum Erasmi,* ed. P. S. Allen and H. M. Allen [Oxford, 1934], vol. 8, letter 2267, 351–54). It should be noted that Boniface Amerbach was interested not in the question of the validity of the dispensation but rather in the possibility of the marriage being dissolved by a lack of consent on the part of the king. In this paper we shall consider only those examples of special interest for the history of exegesis.

16. This work is signed only by the initials T. W. and bears the title *The practyse of Prelates. Whether the Kynges Grace maye be separated from his Quene because she was his brothers wyfe* (Marburg: H. Luft, 1530).

17. "I did my diligence a longe season to know what reasons oure holey prelates should make for their devorcement but I coude not come by them" (fol. I, ii, v).

18. *Corpus Reformatorum* 98, *Huldreich Zwinglis Sämtliche Werke,* ed. Walther Köhler (Leipzig, 1935), vol. 11, beginning with no. 1259, 567ff.

19. Pollet, *Martin Bucer,* 449. For Luther, *WA, Briefwechsel,* vol. 6, no. 1861, 175–88; for Melanchthon, *Corpus Reformatorum* 2, *Philippi Melanthonis Opera,* ed. C. G. Bretschneider (Halle, 1835), vol. 2, no. 1000, cols. 520–27.

20. Pollet, *Martin Bucer,* 452, letter to Bucer dated 21 October 1531.

21. A letter to Grynaeus dated 9 October 1531.

22. Pollet, *Martin Bucer,* 454–55.

23. Ibid.

24. "Moses nihil ad nos" (Ibid., 450, n. 5).

25. The most famous were Francisco De Vitoria, in his "Relectiones" *De matrimonio;* John Fisher, who became the queen's advocate to the bitter end; Johannes Cochlaeus; Juan Luis Vives, etc.

26. Stephan Ehses, *Römische Dokumente zur Geschichte der Ehescheidung Heinrichs VIII von England* (Paderborn, 1893), no. 146, p. 240.

27. Ibid., 244: "Regula igitur Levitici sano est capienda intellectu; ad uxorem fratris nullus accedat vivente fratre vel defuncto cum liberis. Quibus omnes cessant querelae!" It seems, therefore, that Felix de Prato is more interested in defending the institution of marriage than in demonstrating that there is a certain consanguinity created by it.

28. Jared Wicks, ed. and trans., *Cajetan Responds: A Reader in Reformation Controversy* (Washington, 1978), 39. The text of the *votum (Opuscula Omnia* [Turin, 1582], fol. 442a–46a) is reproduced in English translation on pp. 175–88.

29. Ibid., 180.

30. Ibid., 181.

31. Ibid., 185.

32. Ibid., 187.

33. In 1530 Cajetan was in the process of preparing his commentaries on the Pentateuch. In the preface to that work he penned the famous statement that one may hold to the literal sense of the Bible even if in doing so one sets oneself against "a flood of saintly Doctors" ("a torrente Doctorum sacrorum alienus").

34. As Thieme says, "Cujus regio, ejus opinio" (*Ehescheidung Heinrichs VIII,* 13).

SCOTT H. HENDRIX
The Use of Scripture in Establishing Protestantism

1. The only complete biography of Rhegius is still the older work by Gerhard Uhlhorn, *Urbanus Rhegius: Leben und ausgewählte Schriften* (Elberfeld: Friderichs, 1861). For an updated treatment of many aspects of Rhegius's early career

and a summary of the literary treatment of this Reformer, consult Maximilian Liebmann, *Urbanus Rhegius und die Anfänge der Reformation* (Münster: Aschendorff, 1980). The second part of his career has been studied in several works by Richard Gerecke: "Studien zu Urbanus Rhegius' kirchenregimentlicher Tätigkeit in Norddeutschland," *Jahrbuch der Gesellschaft für niedersächsische Kirchengeschichte* 74 (1976): 131–77 (hereinafter *JGNKG*); "Die Neuordnung des Kirchenwesens in Lüneburg," *JGNKG* 77 (1979): 25–95; "Urbanus Rhegius als Superintendent in Lüneburg (1532–1533)," in *Reformation vor 450 Jahren: Eine Lüneburgische Gedenkschrift* (Lüneburg: Museumsverein für das Fürstentum Lüneburg, 1980), 71–93. Liebmann's book contains the best bibliography of Rhegius's works in both manuscripts and printed editions.

2. For the role of Rhegius in the Reformation in Augsburg see, in addition to Liebmann, Friedrich Roth, *Augsburgs Reformationsgeschichte 1517–1530,* 4 vols., 2d ed. (Munich: Ackermann, 1901–).

3. Liebmann, *Urbanus Rhegius,* 102, n. 239, and 341, Mss 1 and 2.

4. On Reisch, see *Correspondence of Erasmus* (Toronto: University of Toronto Press, 1976), 3:37. Reisch also taught Capito; see Beate Stierle, *Capito als Humanist,* Quellen und Forschungen zur Reformationsgeschichte 42 (Gütersloh: Gerd Mohn, 1974), 30 (hereinafter QFRG). On Reuchlin, see Ludwig Geiger, *Das Studium der Hebräischen Sprache in Deutschland vom Ende des XV. bis zur Mitte des XVI. Jahrhunderts* (Breslau: Schletter'sche Buchhandlung, 1870), 30. Reuchlin, however, did not live in Ingolstadt until late 1519, after Rhegius had left the city; Geiger, *Johann Reuchlin: sein Leben und seine Werke* (Leipzig: Duncker and Humblot, 1871), 461–62.

5. Geiger, *Das Studium,* 41–48, 109. See James Kittelson, *Wolfgang Capito: From Humanist to Reformer,* Studies in Medieval and Reformation Thought 17 (Leiden: Brill, 1975), 21–22 (hereinafter SMRT); see also Stierle, *Capito,* 34–35. On Adrianus, see *Correspondence of Erasmus,* 4:301, 40n; 5:191, 11n.

6. Uhlhorn, *Rhegius: Leben,* 219.

7. A typical case is his discussion of the meaning of "fool" (נָבָל) in Psalm 14:1. For Rhegius the word connotes not a simpleton but a person whose heart is perverted and who has bad intentions. This interpretation includes the sinner in all people according to Paul in Romans 3. *Der XIIII. Psalm inn eil ausgelegt/durch D. Urbanum Regium/an einen guten freund* (Magdeburg: Michael Lotther, 1536), Aiiii verso–B verso.

8. *Perbrevis ratio fructuose studendi in sacris literis . . . ,* in *Opera Urbani Regii latine edita* (Nuremberg: Johannes Montanus and Ulrich Neuber, 1562), pt. 3, XIV verso.

9. Ibid., XV recto: "In Testamento veteri placet, ut legas quotidie caput unum vel duo. Et idiotismos hebręos, quos Monsterus, vel alii eius linguae periti ostendunt, diligenter observabis, et cum septuaginta interpretum versione, vel

communi, quae graeca est, conferes, quae quidem collatio mirum in modum iuvabit te, ut verum scripturae sensum eruas, et dono spiritus sancti consequaris."

10. Liebmann, *Urbanus Rhegius,* 192–93.

11. *Ain kurtze erklärung etlicher leüffiger puncten aim yeden Christen nutz und not zů rechtē verstand der hailigē geschrifft zů dienst; Die zwòlff artickel unsers Christlichē glaubens mit anzaigūg d hailigen geschrifft....* Both of these works were first published in Augsburg in 1523. See Liebmann, *Urbanus Rhegius,* 372–73 (D 41 and D 42).

12. Johannes Freder, *Epistola dedicatoria,* in Rhegius, *Prophetiae veteris testamenti de Christo collectae et explicatae* (Frankfurt: Peter Brubach, 1542), ii verso.

13. Ibid. Rhegius's work: *Dialogus von der schönen predigt die Christus Luc. 24. von Jerusalem bis gen Emaus den zweien j$^{e}_{u}$ngern am Ostertag aus Mose und allen Propheten gethan hat* (Wittenberg: Josef Klug, 1537). See Liebmann, *Urbanus Rhegius,* 396 (D 115).

14. *Eine ungehewre wunderbarliche Absolution der Closterfrawen jm Fürstenthumb Lüneburg...* (Wittenberg: Georg Rhau, 1532), Aii verso.

15. Ibid., Aiii recto.

16. Ibid., B–Bii verso.

17. Ibid., Dii verso.

18. Uhlhorn, *Rhegius: Leben,* 217–18, calls it the chief goal of Rhegius, especially the education of clergy.

19. *Wie man fürsichtiglich und ohne Ärgerniss reden soll von den fürnemesten Artikeln christlicher Lehre (Formulae quaedam caute et citra scandalum loquendi),* ed. Alfred Uckeley (Leipzig: Deichert [Böhme], 1908). The Latin version was printed first by Hans Lufft in Wittenberg in 1535. See Liebmann, *Urbanus Rhegius,* 390 (D 101).

20. *Examen episcopi in Ducatu Luneburgensi* (Erfurt: Sturmer, 1538). For a discussion of the date of the *Examen* and its content, see Ferdinand Cohrs, "Urbanus Rhegius' 'Examen episcopi in ducatu Luneburgensi,' 1536 (?). Ein Beitrag zur Geschichte des Prüfungswesens in der evangelischen Kirche," in *Studien zur Reformationsgeschichte und zur praktischen Theologie. Gustav Kawerau an seinem 70. Geburtstage dargebracht* (Leipzig: M. Heinsius Nachfolger, 1917), 57–69. Cohrs suspected but did not know of the existence of the 1538 Erfurt edition. It was reprinted in Frankfurt in 1545.

21. *Examen,* A2 verso.

22. Ibid., A4 recto, A5 recto.

23. Gerecke, in *Reformation vor 450 Jahren,* 83.

24. *Abdias propheta explanatus commentariolo....* (Magdeburg: Lotther, 1537), A2 verso. See Waldemar Bahrdt, *Geschichte der Reformation der Stadt Hannover* (Hannover: Hahn'sche Buchhandlung, 1891), 101–2.

25. See Hermann Beck, *Die Erbauungsliteratur der evangelischen Kirche Deutschlands. Erster Teil von Dr. M. Luther bis Martin Moller* (Erlangen: Deichert, 1883), 40–41; Bahrdt, *Geschichte,* 106.

26. In *Perbrevis ratio* (see above, n. 5), and in *Alia ratio tractandi scripturas sacras quibusdam verbi ministris praescripta,* in Rhegius, *Opera,* 3:XV verso–XVI verso.

27. *Alia ratio,* XV verso–XVI recto. *Perbrevis ratio,* XIV verso: "Et cum novum testamentum sit expositio veteris et velut clavis." See *Abdias,* D8v: "At novum Testamentum, quod est lux veteris, abunde docet, qualis sit Rex noster Messias in Prophetis promissus."

28. *Perbrevis ratio,* XV recto.

29. *Alia ratio,* XV verso–XVI recto.

30. *Dialogus,* 3v. Citations are from the 1539 edition published in Wittenberg by Josef Klug.

31. Ibid., 1 verso.

32. Ibid., 295 recto–96 recto.

33. *Abdias,* A3 verso: "Diversitas est in tempore, caeterum in doctrina, quantum ad mysteria Christi attinet, nulla est, nisi quod Prophetae cecinere futurum Christum, Nos exhibitum et praesentem docemus. . . . Eadem est docendi ratio, quantum ad doctrinae summam attinet, in Prophetis et Evangelistis. Summa Apostolicae doctrinae haec est, ut Acto. 20. legimus, poenitentia et fides in Christum."

34. *Dialogus,* 9 recto: "Denn Christus wird auff zweierley weis inn der Schrifft verkündiget / Einmal durch tunckele Verheissung / und figuren von ferns her. Zum andern / durch klare Verheissung / und helle ausgedruckte wort."

35. *Alia ratio,* XVI recto. Although the stated purpose of the *Dialogus* was to confirm the truth of the New Testament through the Old, it is likely that Rhegius also had another purpose in mind. The accumulation of messianic passages could be an answer to the anthology of Jewish anti-Christian apologetic called the *Nizzahon,* which was a medieval rebuttal of the messianic interpretation of the Old Testament that Rhegius knew well. For a detailed discussion of this possibility, see my forthcoming article: "Toleration of the Jews in the German Reformation: Urbanus Rhegius and Braunschweig (1535–1540)," *Archiv für Reformationsgeschichte* 81 (1990).

36. *Abdias,* C5 verso: "Caveant igitur et nostri Edomitae Evangelii persecutores, qui palam nunc Edomiticum in nos animum declarant, et dicere non verentur, se male contra nos bella gerere, quam contra Turcas."

37. *Abdias,* D4 verso: "Haec verbosius tractavi propter nostros Anabaptistas Καθα ρῶς et Novatianos, qui reliquiis peccatorum etiamnum in nobis grassantibus ita offenduntur, ut putent nullam esse Ecclesiam nisi plane perfecta adsit sanctitas, in qua porro nihil queat desiderari." Ibid., D5 verso–D6 recto: "Hinc

etiam confunditur pestifera vanitas Pharisaeorum nostrorum id est Monachorum et monacharum, vocant enim ordines suos sanctos formaliter et effective, quasi sancti sint et alios sanctificent."

38. Ibid., D7 recto: "Iam vide Acta et Epistolas Apostolorum, et invenies possessionem illam praeclaram, cuius Abdias meminit. . . . Sicque nationes quae antea iuxta carnem possederunt Iudaeos, tandem a Iudaeis Apostolis et eorum successoribus, factae sunt possessiones domus Iacob, id est, per Evangelii praedicationem in Ecclesiam Christi congregatae sunt. Et hic est verus Prophetae sensus." Ibid., D7 verso–D8 recto: "Et quod horrendum est auditu, etiam hodie velamen cordibus Iudaeorum et Iudaisantium quorundam impositum est, ut legem et Prophetas de Christi regno vaticinantes nequeant intelligere, somniant enim talem Messiam in lege et Prophetis promissum, quo Chanaan occupet et omnes gentes suo subdat imperio. . . . Fuit mihi cum Recutitis acre certamen annis plus minus viginti de Messia et regno eius, qui semper hos et similes locos carnali sensu tractatos mihi obiecerunt." Ibid., D8 verso: "Verum ubi idiotismos Hebraicae linguae et circumstantias omnes exacte animadvertimus, haud difficile fuerit intelligere, Christi servos Prophetas, de rebus longe maioribus nempe spiritualibus et aeternis, non ex ratione humana, sed instinctu spiritus sancti vaticinatos, quam sint omnia huius visibilis mundi regna cum omni potentia, honore, splendore, opulentia et apparatu seculari, quod ut rudioribus planum fiat, recensebo aliquot circumstantias vaticiniorum de regno Christi, ex quibus facile intelligemus, Prophetas de regno spirituali et aeterno non corporali locutos."

39. *Alia ratio,* XVI verso: "Proderit et hoc plurimum in docendo populum, si omnia Evangelia, quae per anni circulum se offerunt enarranda, ita excutiamus, ut semper ad aliquem Catechismi articulum ea referamus. Sic enim non solum Catechismus memoriis hominum firmius insculpetur, sed etiam Evangelia intelligentur clarius, et velut ad usum transferentur, atque in omnes vitae casus, semper velut remedium facilius depromentur."

40. For a detailed discussion of Rhegius's use of the church fathers, see Scott H. Hendrix, "Validating the Reformation: The Use of the Church Fathers by Urbanus Rhegius," in *Ecclesia Militans. Studien zur Konzilien- und Reformationsgeschichte,* ed. Walter Brandmüller, Herbert Immenkötter, and Erwin Iserloh, 2 vols. (Paderborn: Schöningh, 1988), 2:281–305.

41. *Alia ratio,* XVI recto: "Non igitur adferas vel sensum sine scripturis, ut Anabaptistae, vel scripturas in sensu, qui fidei non est analogus, sed adfer scripturas in sensu Ecclesiastico, hoc est, in eo sensu, qui semper a temporibus Apostolorum fuit in Ecclesia orientali et occidentali. Neque enim scripturae intellectus extra Ecclesiam Catholicam invenitur, et spiritus sanctus Ecclesiam, ut suum templum, et suam domum inhabitat, haereticorum Synagogas execratur."

42. Uhlhorn, *Rhegius: Leben,* 220.

43. *Alia ratio,* XV verso.

44. *Ein Sermon von den guten und bösen Engeln/zu Hannover geprediget durch D. Urbanum Rhegium* (Wittenberg: Josef Klug, 1538), E recto: "Derhalben der Christlichen Kirchen glaube allzeit aus der Schrifft gewesen ist / das ein jeglicher seinen eigen Engel habe / Wie Basilius magnus / de spiritu sancto schreibet / als einen Zuchtmeister und hirten / der im sen leben richte." Ibid., Eii verso–F recto: "Die Schrifft leret uns / man sol vertrawen und hoffnung inn niemands setzen / denn inn den einigen / waren Gott / und sollen auch inn der not allein den selbigen / als den waren nothelffer anrüffen / wie wir im ersten und andern gebot lernen / und die Schrifft spricht. . . . Höret aber / was man vor tausend jaren inn der Christenheit von der Engel anbeten gehalten habe / damit ir nicht argwonig seiet / ich lere hierinn etwas newes / Augustinus uber den xcvi. Psalm spricht also."

45. *Alia ratio,* XVI verso.

46. Ibid.

47. *Abdias,* B8 verso–C recto: "Et haec omnia pertinent ad primum praeceptum de fide et spe. In solum enim Deum in omni tribulatione sperandum est, solus enim ex vult et potest nos ex malis omnibus eripere, sicut apud Isaiam ait cap. 43. Ego sum, Ego sum Dominus, et non est absque me salvator, et non est qui de manu mea eruat [Is. 43:11, 13].

48. *Der XIIII. Psalm,* Aii verso: "Ein jeglicher tregt im busen diesen Nabal / das ist / ein solchen Gottlosen thoren. . . . Drück den Nabal mit dem ersten und andern gepott / und frag / ob er trew an seinem trewen Gott gehalten hab / so wirt er bekennen müssen / Es fehle im allenthalb inn Gottes gepoten / und sonderlich inn der ersten tafel Mosi. Denn wiewol er list inn der schrifft / an der predig hört / und inn teglichen gutthaten leibs und der seel von Gott gegeben / erfert und greifft / das ein Gott ist / und das er warhafftig / trew und barmhertzig ist." Ibid., B recto: "Wenn man nu das erst gepot nicht helt / so ists unmöglich / das man die andern halte nach Gottes befehl / denn wer inn seinem hertzen Gott nicht recht kent / nichts nach im fragt / der ist Gottlos odder glaublos / wie kan denn der mund im andern gepott / Gottes namen preisen."

49. Ibid., Ciiii verso.

50. *Kirchenordnung der statt Hannofer durch D. Urbanum Regium,* in *Die evangelischen Kirchenordnungen des XVI. Jahrhunderts,* ed. Emil Sehling (Tübingen: Mohr [Siebeck], 1957), pt. 6/1, vol. 2, p. 1004: "Und dieweil unser widerpart saget, wir predigen neue lere, müssen sich auch unsere prediger befleissen, alle artikel christlicher lere daran unser heil ligt, mit zeugnis der alten kirchen zu befestigen, auf das die einfeltigen klar sehen, wie unser lere nicht neu, sondern die rechte, alte christliche lere ist, wie sie in der christlichen kirchen in der ganzen welt vor tausent jaren gehalten und gepredigt worden ist."

51. *Absolution,* C verso.

52. Uhlhorn, *Rhegius: Leben,* 220.

53. *Alia ratio,* XVI recto.

54. Uckeley (ed.), 63: "Diesen spruch zihe ich nicht vergeblich an, denn er von vielen Ungelehrten gerhümet wird, als werden darin gelobt die, so keine schrifft lernen noch wissen, und meinen, sie haben allhie für sich Gottes wort, dadurch alle löbliche künste, da zu die Heilige Schrifft, verworffen werden."

55. Ibid., 64: "Hie redet Christus von der gemeinen lere des Evangelii, so jederman zur seligkeit von nöten ist, dadurch wir Christum lernen erkennen, das er sey umb unser willen mensch worden, und an in als unsern einigen Heiland gleuben. Durch diese lere werden gewislich alle ausserwelten erleucht, und wer die selbige nicht hat, der mus verloren werden. Aber uber diese gemeine lere und erkenntnis ist ein ander kunst und sonderlicher verstand inn der Christenheit, welchs heisst die gabe der Weissagung, damit nicht on unterscheid alle Christen begnadet werden, sondern ettliche so der Christenheit furstehen sollen inn der lere, das sie die heilige Schrifft auslegen, zur besserung, zur vermanung, zu trostung."

56. *Kirchenordnung,* pt. 6/1, vol. 2, p. 1000: "Erstlich, dieweil Paulus, 1. Corin. 14 (28:26), ordnet, das der in der kirchen schweigen sol, der die schrift nicht kan auslegen, und das alle ding in der gemeine sollen zur besserung geschehen, so hat uns dis gebot gedrungen, die bepstischen priester, die auf ihrem irthum harren abzustellen; denn sie können die schrift in der kirchen nicht auslegen nach der schnur des apostolischen verstands."

57. Liebmann, *Urbanus Rhegius,* 265–67, 279–85.

58. Rhegius mentions the *Unterricht* in his discussion of schools in the Hannover church order; see *Kirchenordnung,* pt. 6/1, vol. 2, p. 1011.

59. Melanchthon, *Unterricht der Visitatoren,* in *Melanchthons Werke in Auswahl,* ed. Robert Stupperich, 7 vols. (Gütersloh: Bertelsmann/Gerd Mohn, 1951), 1:221.8–222.27, 244.1–3.

60. *Wie man fürsichtiglich,* 31.

61. *Examen,* A2 verso: "Evangelium duo tradit, Lucae ult. 1. Poenitentiam. 2. Remissionem peccatorum. In iss duabus partibus universa scriptura comprehenditur." Cf. *Abdias,* D verso: "Dein et per Apostolos lex vitae et verbum Evangelii exivit de Zion in totum orbem, quae lex est doctrina de poenitentia et remissione peccatorum sub nomine Christi in omnes gentes sparsa initio facto, ut Lucas ait, ab Ierosolymis."

62. That controversy led Melanchthon in the *Unterricht* to stress the necessity of preaching repentance. Melanchthon says that his experience in the Saxon visitation first led him to define contrition as the beginning of repentance. See *Melanchthons Briefwechsel,* vol. 1, *Regesten 1–1109 (1514–1530),* ed. Heinz Scheible (Stuttgart–Bad Cannstatt: Frommann-Holzboog, 1977), no. 604, pp. 270–71. One

can follow the beginning of the controversy in the summaries of Melanchthon's correspondence beginning with this letter to Caspar Aquila written in October 1527.

63. *Wie man fürsichtiglich,* 45–49, 58–61. *Examen,* A5 verso–A6 recto: "Quomodo de bonis operibus loquendum, ut sermo Episcopi sit conditus sale theologico. . . . Hic serio monendus Epicopus, ut sic praedicet opera, ne qua fiat contumelia gratiae CHRISTI. Rursus sic vehat magnificam CHRISTI gratiam, ne qua fiat contumelia operibus bonis, hoc est, ne contemnantur vel negligantur."

64. On his way from Augsburg to Lüneburg in 1530 Rhegius stopped at Coburg to meet Luther personally for the first time and to plead the case for concord between Bucer and the Wittenbergers. Later, Rhegius recalled the day spent with Luther as the happiest day of his life and praised Luther as a theologian without equal in any age. These comments were excerpted from letters addressed by Rhegius from Lüneburg to friends in south Germany in 1534; the excerpts were published independently in 1545 under the title *Iudicium D. Urbani Rhegii de D. Martino Luthero.* The *Iudicum* was printed at the end of a collection of patristic and theological sources used by Rhegius and published posthumously by Johannes Freder as *Loci theologici* (Frankfurt: Peter Braubach, 1545), 251 verso–252 recto.

65. *Perbrevis ratio,* XV verso.

66. This stance critical of Luther and its history at the university is discussed in detail by Inge Mager, "Reformatorische Theologie und Reformationsverständnis an der Universität Helmstedt im 16. und 17. Jahrhundert," *JGNKG* 74 (1976): 11–33.

67. *Kirchenordnung,* pt. 6/1, vol. 2, pp. 1014–15: "Ob aber unser gegenpart sagte, es werde das evangelium niemands verboten, sonders des Luthers lere, die wir angenomen haben, dazu antworten wir, das wir keins menschen lere, er habe namen, wie er wölle, angenomen haben, sondern das ware, reine evangelium Jhesu Christi, welchs durch den heiligen Geist vom himel herab gesand ist, und verstehen dasselbige evangelium in allen artikeln unsers heiligen glaubens, wie es die apostel gelert und die christliche kirche allzeit verstanden und gehalten hat. Dieweil aber D. M. Lutherus aus sonderlicher gnade Gottes dasselbige evangelium dem deudschen land rein, apostolisch, one menschenlere und verfelschung in sensu ecclesiastico, wie es sich in einem christlichen generalconcilio in der warheit erfinden wird, wider herfurgebracht und gepredigt hat, so nennen unsere widerwertigen solch evangelium des Luthers lere, auf das sie der unschuldigen lere ihr glaubwirdigkeit hinnemen und ihr menschenlere wider vertedingen mögen. . . . Darumb sagen wir also: es predige das evangelium Luther oder andere, so söllen wirs gleuben, nicht umb Luthers willen, sonder umb des willen, der gar ernstlich gebeut, Mar. 1 [15]: Bessert euch und gleubet dem evangelio."

KALMAN P. BLAND
Issues in Sixteenth-Century Jewish Exegesis

1. Gershom Scholem, "The Messianic Idea in Kabbalism," in *The Messianic Idea in Judaism,* ed. G. Scholem (New York: Schocken, 1971), 42. See also G. Scholem, *Sabbatai Sevi* (Princeton: Princeton University Press, 1973), 18–26; idem, *Kabbalah* (New York: New American Library, 1974), 71ff. For sixteenth-century messianism, see Abba Hillel Silver, *A History of Messianic Speculation in Israel* (New York: MacMillan, 1927), chap. 6 ("The Sixteenth Century"), 221–33; B. Netanyahu, *Don Isaac Abravanel* (Philadelphia: Jewish Publication Society, 1968), chap. 4 ("Messianism"); and *Samuel Usque's Consolation for the Tribulations of Israel,* trans. Martin A. Cohen (Philadelphia: Jewish Publication Society, 1965).

2. Rabbi Yizhak Caro, *Sefer Toledoth Yizhak* (Warsaw, 1877; facsimile reprint, Jerusalem: Makor Publishing, 1978), 4. Background for the lively debate in Jewish philosophy over the eternity or creation of the world is found in Julius Guttmann, *Philosophies of Judaism* (New York: Holt, Rinehart, and Winston, 1964).

3. An overview of pre-1492 Iberian Jewry may be gathered from Eliyahu Ashtor, *The Jews of Moslem Spain* (Philadelphia: Jewish Publication Society, 1961); Yitzhak Baer, *A History of the Jews in Christian Spain* (Philadelphia: Jewish Publication Society, 1961); and Salo Baron, *A Social and Religious History of the Jews,* 18 vols. (Philadelphia: Jewish Publication Society and Columbia University Press, 1965), 10:118–219 (hereinafter *SRHJ*). General trends in post-1492 history may be found in *SRHJ* 13:3–63.

4. See *SRHJ* 13:159–205; Moses A. Shulvass, *The Jews in the World of the Renaissance* (Leiden: E. J. Brill and Spertus College of Judaica Press, 1973); Cecil Roth, *The Jews of the Renaissance* (Philadelphia: Jewish Publication Society, 1959); Israel Zinberg, *A History of Jewish Literature,* 12 vols. (Cincinnati: Hebrew Union College Press, 1974), 4:3–154; David B. Ruderman, *The World of a Renaissance Jew: The Life and Thought of Abraham ben Mordecai Farissol* (Cincinnati: Hebrew Union College Press, 1981); Gérard E. Weil, *Élie Lévita: Humaniste et Massorète (1469–1549)* (Leiden: E. J. Brill, 1963).

5. See *SRHJ* 13:206–96; Haim Hillel Ben-Sasson, "Jewish Christian Disputation in the Setting of Humanism and Reformation in the German Empire," *Harvard Theological Review* 59 (1966): 369–90; and idem, "The Reformation in Contemporary Jewish Eyes," *Proceedings of the Israel Academy of Sciences and Humanities* 4 (1970): 62–116, 239–326.

6. See *SRHJ,* vol. 14, chaps. 59–60; and Kenneth R. Stow, *Catholic Thought and Papal Jewry Policy 1555–1593* (New York: Jewish Theological Seminary of America, 1977).

7. See *SRHJ* 13:64–158; Cecil Roth, *A History of the Marranos* (New York:

Harper Torchbooks, 1966); and B. Netanyahu, *The Marranos of Spain* (New York: American Academy for Jewish Research, 1966).

8. See above, n. 4; and Isaac Eisenstein-Barzilay, *Between Reason and Faith: Anti-Rationalism in Italian Jewish Thought (1250–1650)* (Paris: Mouton, 1967).

9. See Mark R. Cohen, "The Jews under Islam: From the Rise of Islam to Sabbatai Zevi," *Bibliographic Essays in Medieval Jewish Studies,* 2 vols. (New York: Anti-Defamation League of B'nai B'rith, 1976), 2:199–204, 214–29; and Zinberg, *A History of Jewish Literature,* 5:17–85.

10. See *SRHJ* 16:3–163; and Zinberg, *A History of Jewish Literature,* 6:21–68, 103–20.

11. See *SRHJ,* vol. 16, chap. 61; the references to Ben-Sasson above, n. 5; Zinberg, *A History of Jewish Literature,* 6:69–102; and the recent scholarship on the important figure of the Maharal of Prague, e.g., Andre Neher, "Copernicus in the Hebraic Literature from the Sixteenth to the Eighteenth Century," *Journal of the History of Ideas* 38 (1977): 215, and Neher's article noted there, n. 11.

12. See L. Blau, *The Christian Cabala* (New York: Columbia University Press, 1944); François Secret, *Le Zôhar chez les Kabbalistes Chrétiens de la Renaissance* (Paris: Mouton, 1964); idem, *Les Kabbalistes Chrétiens de la Renaissance* (Paris: Dunod, 1964); the articles by G. Scholem, C. Wirszubski, et. al in *Kabbalistes Chrétiens* (Paris: Albin Michel, 1979); and Ruderman, *The World of a Renaissance Jew,* 35–56.

13. See *SRHJ* 13:160–72.

14. See Alexander Altmann, *Essays in Jewish Intellectual History* ("*Ars Rhetorica* as Reflected in some Jewish Figures of the Italian Renaissance") (Hanover: University Press of New England and Brandeis University Press, 1981); Joseph Dan, *Sifruth Ha-Musar ve-ha-Derush* (Jerusalem: Kether, 1975), 183–201; Israel Bettan, *Studies in Jewish Preaching* (Cincinnati: Hebrew Union College Press, 1939), 192–226; and the sections on Moscato in I. Eisenstein-Barzilay, cited above, n. 8.

15. Caro, *Sefer Toledoth Yizhaḳ,* pp. 48ff. Like many other sixteenth-century scholars, Karo relied heavily upon the commentaries of Abraham Ibn Ezra. His fourth and fifth answers, however, were largely inspired by Gerson ben Levi (Gersonides) in his commentary to Genesis 28:12ff. See *Ralbag ʿal Ha-Torah,* reprint of the 1546 Venice edition, p. 37. For a discussion of the background to Karo's notions concerning the movers and their celestial bodies consult Charles Touati, *Le Pensée Philosophique et Théologique de Gersonide* (Paris: Les Editions de Minuit, 1973), 106ff.

16. Masoretic and philological approaches to Scripture were not ignored in the sixteenth century. See Weil, *Élie Lévita;* and the *Massoreth Ha-Massoreth of Elias Levita,* ed. C. D. Ginsburg, reprinted in *The Library of Biblical Studies,* ed. H. M. Orlinsky (New York: KTAV Publishing, 1968). In Constantinople, Rabbi Solomon ben Melekh composed his *Sefer Miḳhlol Ha-Yofi ʿal ha-Torah,* a running

grammatical commentary to the entire Bible based on the medieval classic *Sefer ha-Milchlol* by David Kimhi.

17. This is the dominant medieval philosophic reinterpretation of prophecy. The classic source is Maimonides, *Guide for the Perplexed,* book 2:32ff.

18. Caro, *Sefer Toledoth Yizhak,* p. 3.

19. Literature on the centrality of study in Jewish life is abundant. For a recent statement see Jacob Neusner, *The Glory of God is Intelligence* (Salt Lake City: Brigham Young University, 1978).

20. Here too the literature is abundant. An indication of the scope of the debate may be found in Eisenstein-Barzilay, *Between Reason and Faith;* Ruderman, *The World of a Renaissance Jew,* 109ff.; Guttmann, *Philosophies of Judaism,* 286–300; Zinberg, *A History of Jewish Literature,* 6:29–44; Ph. Bloch, "Der Streit um den Moreh des Maimonides in der Gemeinde Posen um die Mitte des 16. Jahrh.," *Monatsschrift für Geschichte und Wissenschaft des Judenthums* 11 (1903): 153–69, 263–79, 346–56; and Yosef ben Shlomo, "The Attitude of R. Moses Cordovero to Philosophy and the Sciences," *Sefunot* 6 (1962), Eng. summary, 15ff.

21. In addition to the entry and bibliography for Sforno in the *Encyclopedia Judaica,* see the representative passages from his commentary translated into English and annotated by Louis Jacobs, *Jewish Biblical Exegesis* (New York: Behrman House, 1973), 134–43. For a sketch of Meir Ibn Gabbai's repudiation of philosophy and science see Zinberg, *A History of Jewish Literature,* 5:39–49.

22. For the terms *intradeical* and *extradeical* see Harry A. Wolfson, "Extradeical and Intradeical Interpretations of Platonic Ideas," in *Religious Philosophy: A Group of Essays* (New York: Atheneum, 1965), 27–68. The philosophic notion of God's relationship to the Torah, or his Wisdom and Intellect, may be gathered from Guttmann, *Philosophies of Judaism,* esp. 201–7, 218–21, 228–30, 275–99; and H. A. Wolfson, *Philo,* 2 vols. (Cambridge: Harvard University Press, 1948), 1:200–294; idem, *The Philosophy of Spinoza,* 2 vols. (Cambridge: Harvard University Press, 1934), 2:8–32. The kabbalistic notion of God's relationship to Torah is surveyed by Gershom Scholem, "The Meaning of the Torah in Jewish Mysticism," in his *On the Kabbalah and Its Symbolism* (New York: Schocken Books, 1969), 32–86.

23. See Haim Bentov, "Methods of Study of Talmud in the Yeshivot of Salonica and Turkey after the Expulsion from Spain," *Sefunot* 13 (1971–77), Eng. summary, 7–9. On Taitazak and his hermeneutics, see Shimon Shalem, "The Exegetic Method of R. Yosef Taitazak and His Circle: Its Nature and Its Form of Inquiry," G. Scholem, "The *Magid* of R. Yosef Taitazak and the Revelations Attributed to Him," and Joseph B. Sermonetta, "Scholastic Philosophic Literature in Rabbi Yoseph Taitazak's *Porath Yosef,*" *Sefunot* 11 (1971–77), Eng. summaries, 18–14.

24. See Shimon Shalem, "The Exegetical and Homiletical Method of R. Moses

Alsheikh's Commentaries to the Bible," *Sefunot* 5 (1961), Eng. summary, 8ff.; idem, "Thought and Morals in the Commentaries of R. Moses Alsheich," *Sefunot* 6 (1962), Eng. summary, 17–19; idem, "The Life and Works of Rabbi Moses Alshech," *Sefunot* 7 (1963), Eng. summary, 14–17; J. Dan, *Sifruth Ha-Musar ve-ha Derush* (Jerusalem: Kether, 1975), 225ff.

25. The literature on the community of Safed is abundant. In addition to the articles found in *Sefunot* vols. 6–7, see also Solomon Schechter, "Safed in the Sixteenth Century," in idem, *Studies in Judaism* (New York: Meridian Books and Jewish Publication Society, 1958), 231–97; and R. J. Zwi Werblowsky, *Joseph Karo: Lawyer and Mystic* (Oxford: Oxford University Press, 1962).

26. A sample of Alsheikh's commentary is also provided by Jacobs, *Jewish Biblical Exegesis,* 144–52. An important study for understanding the various approaches to the Bible in Safed is M. Pachter, "The Theory of *Deveḳut* in the Writings of the Sages of Safed in the Sixteenth Century," *Jerusalem Studies in Jewish Thought* 3 (1982), Eng. summary, VIIIff.

27. See Erich Auerbach, *Mimesis* (Princeton: Princeton University Press, 1968), 3–23. The classical rabbinic motives and mechanisms for filling the "gaps" in Scripture are spelled out by Isaac Heinemann, *Darḳe Ha-Aggadah* (Jerusalem: Magnes Press of the Hebrew University and Masada, 1954).

28. Moses Alsheikh, *Maraoth ha-Zoveoth* (Offenbach, 1719), 30a.

29. Ibid., 30b.

30. Ibid

31. Ibid.

32. The conceptual tool "to see as" derives from Wittgenstein. See the helpful essay of Joseph Margolis, "The Critic's Interpretation," in *Philosophy Looḳs at the Arts,* ed. J. Margolis (New York: Charles Scribner's Sons, 1962), 106–18.

33. See Scholem, "The Meaning of Torah in Jewish Mysticism."

34. Cordovero was probably born in Safed in 1522, and he died there in the summer of 1570. In addition to the biographical and bibliographic references supplied in K. P. Bland, "Neoplatonic and Gnostic Themes in R. Moses Cordovero's Doctrine of Evil," *Bulletin of the Institute of Jewish Studies* 3 (1975): 103ff., see G. Scholem, *Major Trends in Jewish Mysticism* (New York: Schocken Books, 1960), 252–55.

35. Moses Cordovero, *Pardes Rimmonim,* 2 vols. (Munkacs, 1906), 2:59a–68b.

36. Ibid., 68b.

37. The passage from the Zohar is cited from 3:152a, according to Scholem's translation in *The Zohar: The Booḳ of Splendor* (New York: Schocken Books, 1963), 121. It is found in *Pardes Rimmonim,* 59a.

38. *Pardes Rimmonim,* 59a.

39. "Mi she-yored le-ʿomeq ha-ʿinyan ha-zeh yukhal livro ʿolamoth" (ibid., 60a).

40. In *Pardes Rimmonim,* 69a, Cordovero himself alludes to the contemplative techniques of Abraham Abulafia and his followers. See Scholem, *Major Trends in Jewish Mysticism,* 119–55; and "The Idea of the Golem," in his *On the Kabbalah and Its Symbolism,* 158–204. See also Pachter, "The Theory of *Deveḳut.*"

41. See the provocative essay by Andrew T. Weil, "The Marriage of the Sun and Moon," in *Alternate States of Consciousness,* ed. Norman E. Zinberg (New York: The Free Press, 1977), 37–52, for psychological and epistemological considerations helpful to the historian of exegesis. See also E. E. HaLevi, *Sha ʿare Ha-Aggadah* (Tel-Aviv: Levinsky Seminar, 1963), 32–41, where a fruitful distinction is made between the "semantic-logical" and the "mantic-intuitive" methods in classical midrash.

RICHARD A. MULLER
Calvin's Exegesis of Old Testament Prophecies

1. T. H. L. Parker, *Calvin's New Testament Commentaries* (Grand Rapids, 1971), 26–68; on Bucer see Johannes Müller, *Martin Bucers Hermeneutiḳ* (Gütersloh, 1965); on Erasmus see John W. Aldridge, *The Hermeneutic of Erasmus* (Basel and Richmond, 1966); and John B. Payne, "Erasmus and Lefèvre d'Étaples as Interpreters of Paul," *Archiv für Reformationgeschichte* 65 (1974): 52–82.

2. Cf. Henri Strohl, "La méthode exégétique des Réformateurs," in *Le probléme biblique dans le Protestantisme,* ed. J. Boisset (Paris, 1955), 98.

3. Parker, *New Testament,* 55–56.

4. Ibid., 65–67.

5. Henri Clavier, "Calvin commentateur biblique," in *Études sur le calvinisme,* ed. H. Clavier (Paris, 1936), 99–144.

6. Hans Joachim Kraus, "Calvins exegetische Prinzipien," *Zeitschrift für Kirchengeschichte* 79 (1968): 329–41; "Calvin's Exegetical Principles," trans. Keith Crim, *Interpretation* 31 (1977): 8–18.

7. Wilhelm Vischer, "Calvin exégète de l'Ancien Testament," *La Revue Reformée* 18 (1967): 1–20.

8. Benoit Girardin, *Rhétorique et Théologique. Calvin: Le Commentaire de l'Epître aux Romains* (Paris, 1979), 76–81. Since the presentation of this essay in 1982, several studies of Calvin's exegesis and hermeneutics have appeared which, for the most part, argue in the same direction as the earlier scholarship noted above: Alexandre Ganoczy and Stefan Scheld, *Die Hermeneutiḳ Calvins: Geistesgeschichtliche Voraussetzungen und Grundzüge* (Wiesbaden, 1983), is a major study noteworthy for its setting of Calvin into the context of early-sixteenth-century hermeneutics. The authors emphasize Calvin's interest in historical explanation (144–54) and its importance for his sense of the relationship of the Old and New

Testaments, specifically for the typological and exemplary relation of events and persons in the Old Testament to the proclamation of salvation in the New. The point is similar to Kraus's sense of "kerygmatic analogies" ("Exegetical Principles," 12) and, I believe, consonant with the findings of this essay. T. H. L. Parker, *Calvin's Old Testament Commentaries* (Edinburgh, 1986), is a sequel to Parker's book on the New Testament commentaries that surveys Calvin's writings and then offers a theological overview of his work, emphasizing Calvin's interest in the "purpose" of the biblical authors and the shadow-promise relation of the two Testaments. A series of articles by Richard Gamble emphasize Calvin's interest in clarity and brevity of exposition as they lead toward the exposition of the author's intention. See "*Brevitas et facilitas:* Toward an Understanding of Calvin's Hermeneutic," *Westminster Theological Journal* 47 (1985): 1–17; "Exposition and Method in Calvin," *Westminster Theological Journal* 49 (1987): 153–65; and "Calvin as Theologian and Exegete: Is There Anything New?" *Calvin Theological Journal* 23 (1988): 178–94. An entirely different approach with little relevance to this essay is evident in Thomas F. Torrance, *Calvin's Hermeneutic* (Edinburgh, 1988), which attempts to explain Calvin's early hermeneutic in terms drawn from Scotist and nominalist epistemology—all on the assumption, long since exploded by Ganoczy's *Le Jeune Calvin* (Wiesbaden, 1966), that Calvin imbibed Scotism at Paris under John Major.

9. Kraus, "Exegetical Principles," 12–17 (following Crim's translation).

10. Ibid., 12.

11. Strohl, "Méthode exégétique," 102–3.

12. Henri de Lubac, *Exégèse médiévale: les quatre sens de l'écriture,* 2 pts. in 4 vols. (Paris, 1959–64).

13. Beryl Smalley, *The Study of the Bible in the Middle Ages* (Oxford, 1952).

14. James Samuel Preus, *From Shadow to Promise: Old Testament Interpretation from Augustine to the Young Luther* (Cambridge, Mass., 1969).

15. Cf. de Lubac, *Exégèse,* pt. 1, vol. 2, pp. 425–87; pt. 2, vol. 2, pp. 291–92, 344–49; Smalley, *Study,* 97–106, 214–42, 297–308; Preus, *From Shadow to Promise,* 28–36, 51–57, 81–105, 133–39.

16. Kraus, "Exegetical Principles," 18. The term "scope of Christ" used by Kraus is not cited by him from Calvin but is used to explain Calvin's sense of the way in which Christ is the focal point of Scripture toward whom exegesis is directed. The term *scopus* was strongly favored by Erasmus (cf. the discussion in Marjorie O'Rourke Boyle, *Erasmus on Language and Method in Theology* [Toronto, 1977], 72–81), and it entered Reformed theology as early as the *Confessio Helvetica Prior* (1536), chap. 5: "*Scopus Scripturae*"; chap. 12: "*Scopus evangelicae doctrinae*"—in both cases translating the German *Zweck* and pointing to Christ and his work. The relationship of the Reformed use of the term (and the idea) to Erasmus is a subject for further inquiry.

17. For the Latin text of Calvin's commentaries I have consulted *Ioannis Calvini Opera quae supersunt Omnia,* ed. Baum, Cunitz, and Reuss (Brunswick, 1863–1900), hereinafter cited as *CO;* I have also consulted *Commentaries of John Calvin,* 46 vols. (Edinburgh, 1843–55; reprint, Grand Rapids, 1979), hereinafter referred to by prophet, volume, and page (e.g., *Daniel* I:35). On this point see Joel 3:1 in *CO* 42:580 (*Minor Prophets* II:112–13); Isaiah 17:9, 11; 19:18, 19; 22:12; 26:1; 28:5 in *CO* 36:316, 317–18, 340–43, 373–74, 424–26, 464–65 (*Isaiah* II:27, 30, 68, 71, 123, 208, 273); Jeremiah 48:41; 49:22, 26 in *CO* 39:341, 373–74, 377 (*Jeremiah* V:45–46, 95–96, 101).

18. Cf. Amos 8:9, 10, 13 in *CO* 43:149–51, 154–55 (*Minor Prophets* II:372–73, 381) with Zechariah 14:8–9 and Malachi 3:17 in *CO* 44:371–74, 483 (*Minor Prophets* V:422–25, 605–6).

19. *CO* 43:169: "ut Deus colligeret dispersa membra sub unum caput."

20. *CO* 43:170–71 (*Minor Prophets* II:405); cf. Micah 4:1–2 in *CO* 43:339–40 (*Minor Prophets* III:250–51).

21. Cf. Amos 9:11 and Micah 4:3 in *CO* 43:171, 347–48 (*Minor Prophets* II:406; III:265) with Isaiah 65:17 and Psalm 2:8 in *CO* 37:428–29; 31:47–48 (*Isaiah* IV:398; *Psalms* I:20).

22. Heinrich Bullinger, *In Apocalypsim Iesu Christi, revelatam quidem per angelum Domini* (Basel, 1557), 174–75 on the identification of Antichrist with the papacy; cf. 172, 191–93, 231, where the "little horn" is identified with the papacy. Bullinger is particularly interested here in identifying the kingdoms of Daniel 7 with post-Constantinian kingdoms in the West.

23. Ioannes Oecolampadius, *Commentariorum in Danielem Prophetam, libri duo* (Geneva, 1567), 92–93. Oecolampadius argues that "Antichrist" is anyone who sits in the seat of God, blasphemes the name of God, and persecutes the church of Christ: thus the pope's impiety is surely of Antichrist, but so also is the blasphemy of the Mohammedans.

24. Cf. Martin Luther, "Das zwölfte Capitel Danielis," in *Dr. Martin Luthers sämmtliche Werke,* 2d ed., 66 vols. (Erlangen, 1832–85), 41:294–324. This commentary, on only one chapter, was written in 1541 and inserted in some of the later sixteenth-century editions of Luther's introduction to Daniel. It does not appear in the Weimar edition.

25. Cf. Thomas Müntzer, "An Exposition of the Second Chapter of Daniel," in *Spiritual and Anabaptist Writers: Documents Illustrative of the Radical Reformation,* ed. Williams and Mergal (Philadelphia, 1957), 62–63. Müntzer understands the "fourth kingdom" of iron (v. 40) to be Rome and the divided kingdom of iron and clay (v. 41) to be the "fifth monarchy"—the last to be broken before the end of the world.

26. Note in particular the analysis of the "little horn" in *CO* 41:49–50 (*Daniel* II:26–27).

27. *CO* 42:516 (*Minor Prophets* II:15).

28. *CO* 42:516, 533–58 (*Minor Prophets* II:15, 46–54).

29. *CO* 42:571 (*Minor Prophets* II:90–93).

30. Ibid.

31. *CO* 42:565–69 (*Minor Prophets* II:90–93); and note that even this directly attested prophecy is treated largely in terms of Old Testament history, the corporate Israel, and as having multiple referents, one of which is the Christ event.

32. *CO* 42:571.

33. Ibid.

34. *CO* 42:572; cf. Isaiah 33:2 in *CO* 36:558–59 (*Isaiah* III:2).

35. *CO* 42:573–74: "*dies Iehovae magnus et terribilis.* Quaeritur nunc quem diem his propheta notet. Nam hactenus loquutus est de priori Christu adventu. Videtur etiam hoc loco esse quaedam species repugnantiae. Respondeo prophetam comprehendere totum Christi regnum ab initio usque ad finem: et hoc satis tritum est: et aliis etiam locis diximus prophetas communiter ita loqui, Quum ergo sermo de Christi regno habetur, interdum attingunt princicpium duntaxat, interdum etiam loquuntur de ipso fine. Sed saepe uno complexu designant totum cursum regni Christi ab initio usque ad finem. Talis est huius loci ratio."

36. *M. Fabi Quintilliani Institutionis oratoriae, libri XII,* ed. Radermacher (Leipzig, 1908), I.5.46, III.5.7; cf. I.5.3.

37. Quirinus Breen, "John Calvin and the Rhetorical Tradition," in idem, *Christianity and Humanism* (Grand Rapids, 1968), 114.

38. "Calvinus Piis Gallis," in *CO* 18:614–24 (letter 3485); the letter appeared as the preface to the 1561 edition of Daniel (also see *Daniel* I:64–75). The above citation is from *CO* 18:620: "sed facit temporum similitudo, ut nobis eadem conveniant, ac proinde aptanda sint in usum nostrum."

39. *CO* 42:581: "Dicit autem propheta, *diebus illis et tempore illo quum Dominus converterit captivitatem Iehuda et Ierusalem.* Tempus hoc Iudaei restringunt ad reditum: quum ergo permissa illis fuit libertas redeundi in patriam a Cyro et Dario, putant tunc completum fuisse quod docet hic propheta. Christiani doctores trahunt hoc vaticinum ad Christi adventum. Sed utrique detorquent alio verba prophetae quam postulet circumstantia loci. Neque enim dubium est quin propheta hic loquutus fuerit de redemptione illa, quam diximus: et tamen complexus simul fuerit regnum Christi. Atque hoc, quemadmodum alibi vidimus, satis tritum est. Dum igitur prophetae testantur Deum fore redemptorem populi sui, et promittunt liberationem ab exsilio babylonico, quasi continuo tractatu et tenore deducunt fideles ad Christi regnum. Quid enim aliud fuit restitutio illa, quam praeludium verae et solidae redemptionis, quae vere etiam exhibita fuit in persona Christi?" (Cf. *Minor Prophets* II:113).

40. *CO* 37:428–29 (*Isaiah* IV:398); cf. Isaiah 33:6 and 66:15–16 in *CO* 36:563; 37:447–48 (*Isaiah* III:18; IV:428–29) for similar sets of multiple referents.

41. *CO* 36:441–42 (*Isaiah* II:236–37).

42. *CO* 36:442–43 (*Isaiah* II:238–39).

43. *CO* 36:444–45 (*Isaiah* II:237).

44. Malachi 3:2 in *CO* 44:463: "Hic synecdochia est locutio: sed tamen extenditur promissio haec ad totam ecclesiam, quoniam filii Levi erant quasi primitiae." (*Minor Prophets* V:572).

45. Ibid.

46. *CO* 44:466: "Quoniam autem hodie etiam grassantur in mundo tales blasphemiae, locus hic accommodatus est nobis in usum." (*Minor Prophets* V:577).

47. *CO* 44:170: "Iubet igitur propheta esse bono animo fideles, quamvis species sacerdotii tunc vilis esset ac sordida, quoniam Deus non ignoret contemptum illum sacerdotii, sed nondum advenerit remedii tempus: quia tunc reddetur pristina dignitas sacerdoti, ita ut appareat in specie nova." (*Minor Prophets* V:86).

48. *CO* 44:168: "Etsi autem visio haec prophetae oblata fuit in usum suae aetatis, non dubium tamen est quin ad nos quoque pertineat. Nam sacerdotium illud umbratile, imago fuit sacerdotii Christi et Iehosuah, qui tunc reversus est ab exsilio, etiam gestavit Christi filii Dei personam." (*Minor Prophets* V:86).

49. *CO* 44:172: "Hic autem primo loco expendere convenit zelum prophetae et piam sollicitudinem, quam gerebat pro sacerdotii praestantia et honore. . . . Et hoc exemplum nobis ad imitationem proponitur, ut scilicet optemus augescere Dei gratias, quibus sacerdotium Christi insignitur, donec ad solidam perfectionem adscendat. Videmus autem multos huic voto obsistere: quia hodie qui profitentur aliquod studium sincerae pietatis, contenti essent umbra aliqua: vel saltem, modo viderent dimidia ex parte purgatam ecclesiam, hoc illis abunde sufficeret. . . . Atqui longe alio nos propheta vocat." (*Minor Prophets* V:89–90).

50. Zechariah 3:6 in *CO* 44:173; cf. the dedicatory letter to the commentary on Isaiah, "Calvinus Eduardo Regi," *CO* 13:672: "imo Deus ipse per os Iesaiae servi sui te compellat."

51. *CO* 31:663–64 (*Psalms* III:100).

52. Kraus, "Exegetical Principles," 17.

53. Ibid., 18.

54. Ibid., 15.

55. Cf. Jacobus Faber Stapulensis, "Introduction to Commentary on the Psalms," in *Forerunners of the Reformation,* ed. with introduction by Heiko A. Oberman (New York, 1966), 297–305.

56. *CO* 31:664 (*Psalms* III:100).

57. Ibid.

58. *CO* 31:746 (*Psalms* III:280).

59. *CO* 31:745.

60. *CO* 31:666–67: "postulat David ut Deus nominis sui ac gloriae respectum habeat in rege conservando. . . . Iam ubi ad Christum venitur, hoc longe verius in eum competit. . . . Docet ergo David, non aliter Deum consulere ecclesiae suae saluti, sub regis terram ab aestu defendit. Hoc vero praecipue in Christo videmus impleri, qui arcanam gratiam stillando facit ecclesiam suam pullulare. . . . precatus est David, regem ornari iustitia et iudicio. Solomonis quidem officiumfuit iustor tueri: sed proprium Christi est iustos facere: quia non tantum ius suum cuique reddit, sed spiritu animos reformat." (*Psalms* III:107–8).

61. The emphasis on multiple fulfillment of prophecy tied to a single, literal sense of the text correlates neatly with Calvin's view of the perpetuity of the law and of prophecy as an exposition of the law. In his preface to Isaiah, Calvin argues that the law is "a perpetual rule for the Church" interpreted by the prophets. This law is threefold, containing "the doctrine of life," "threatenings and promises," and "the convenant of grace . . . founded on Christ" and its "special promises" (*CO* 36:19; *Isaiah* I:26–27). With this threefold law as a constant, the movement from promise to fulfillment in Christ does not result in the relativization of the address of prophesy to any situation either prior to or following the moment of fulfillment in Christ: The law, as a constant, addresses each situation equally as a doctrine of life, as threat and promise, and as gracious covenant. This in no way contradicts the fact that the promise of salvation in Christ grows more distinct as the Old Testament history progresses (cf. *CO* 36:22; *Isaiah* I:29) because the foundation and substance of the promise, like the standard of the law within which the promise has been made, cannot change (cf. Jeremiah 33:9 in *CO* 39:57–58; *Jeremiah* IV:239).

62. Psalms 2:1–3 in *CO* 31:43 (*Psalms* I:11).

63. *CO* 31:42.

64. *CO* 31:43.

65. *CO* 31:43: "Iam ex hoc loco duplex consolatio elici potest, nam quoties mundum tumultuari continget, ut Christi regnum turbet vel moretur, si nobis occurrat in momoriam, impleri quod iam olim praedictum est, nulla novitas nos percellet. . . . Sequitur altera consolatio. . . . Quare dum videmus hostium copia et viribus Christum.

66. Cf. Vischer, "Calvin exégète," 15.

67. Cf. "Calvinus Piis Gallis," in *CO* 18:622: "Nec vero illorum modo temporum ad spem et patientiam nos animavit propheta: sed exhortationem a spiritu dictatam, quae ad totum Christi regnum extenditur nobisque propria est, adiunxit" (*Daniel* I:72–73); also Isaiah 2:2 (*CO* 36:59–60; *Isaiah* I:91), Jeremiah 33:7, 9, 14, 16 (*CO* 39:55, 57, 62–64, 67–69; *Jeremiah* IV:238–39, 247–49, 253–54); Joel 3:17–19; Haggai 2:20–24; Zechariah 2:11; 4:11–13; 9:16; Malachi 3:2, 17; 4:1, 3 (*CO* 42:596–99; 44:116–24, 164, 192–94, 281–83, 462–63, 482–83, 487–88, 492–93; *Minor Prophets* II:137–40; IV:384–86; V:76–77, 156–60, 275, 570–72, 605–7, 613–14, 623).

68. *Praelectiones in prophetas minores* (1524–26); *In Iohelem D. Martinus Lutherus,* in *WA,* 13:111–14. Note the hermeneutical comment in the preface: "Omnium prophetarum una est sententia: hic enim unus est scopus, ut in futurum Christum seu in furutum regnum Christi respitiant. Huc omnes eorum spectant prophetiae nec alio sunt referendae. quanquam varias intermisceant historias sive rerum praesentium sive futurarum, tamen eo omnia pertinent, ut regnum Christi futurum declarent. Itaque quandocunque sive mala sive prospera annunciaverunt prophetae, in regnum Christi respici voluerunt" (*WA* 13:88).

69. Ibid., 113, ll. 14–15: "cur signa omnia intelligi velim de die revelati evangelii, quae valde est reverenda et magna."

70. Ibid., 113, ll. 32–33: "regnum Christianum nihil aliud est quam regnum fidei in verbo Dei."

71. David C. Steinmetz, *Luther and Staupitz: An Essay in the Intellectual Origins of the Protestant Reformation* (Durham: Duke University Press, 1980), 63. Cf. the *In Esaiam prophetam D. Doc. Martini Lutheri enarraciones* (1527), *WA* 31/2, p. 1, ll. 15–21, where Luther may press an analogy of message between the Mosaic preaching of future redemption and his own preaching of redemption, Moses looking toward the First Coming of Christ, Luther toward the Second. This comes closer to the dynamic we have found in Calvin, though it remains within the literal-prophetic paradigm—showing perhaps a relation between Calvin's model and the literal-prophetic model.

72. Cf. Strohl, "Methode exégétique," 97.

73. Ibid.

74. Joannes Oecolampadius, *In minoros, quos vocant prophetas, Ioannis Oecolampadii . . . lucubrationes* (Geneva, 1558), 58: "Quomodo versandum sit in Prophetis, ita ut cognitionem Christi feliciter perveniatur, cognoscaturque verum regnum illius, satis praefatus in Hoseam. Et ut paucis repetam solent Prophetae populo improperare principio peccata, deinde, praedicere poenam peccatis debitam, cum admonitione ad poenitentiam, et postremum subdere promissiones illas Evangelicas, in quibus Christus ipse agnoscitur et regnum eius." Cf. the preface to Hosea in ibid., fol. 5r–6v, where Oecolampadius discusses briefly the times in which the prophets wrote, but his emphasis is clearly on the fulfillment in Christ as the literal and essential meaning of the text.

75. Ibid., 72–76. Note (p. 76): "Multa bona praedicta sunt iis, qui Deum et Christum recepturi erant: sic nunc praedicuntur adversa iis, qui Christum non erant recepturi. Hisce verbis, ut paucis dicam, Iudaeis grave exitium minatur, in perditionem civitatis et gentis suae. . . . Nam Petrus ut terreret Iudaeos, magna tamen modestia proposuit eis ista prodigia, quae quotidie visebantur, quibus protendebatur exterminium Hierusalem. Iosephus testis est, qui scribit armatasacies disuurrisse in aere, praecedebant terrae motus, fames et alia mala. . . . Simul et salvatio Iudaeorum bonorum et perditio malorum praedicitur. Unica

ratio salvandi est, in nomine Iesu Christi. . . . Eo scilicet tempore quo iudicaturus erat Dominus, non repudiavit ita Iudaeos, quasi non essent salvandi, si poenitentiam egissent. Paulus Christum intelligi vult cum dicit, in nomine Domine. Qui vero in Christum non crediderit, ille condemnatus est."

76. Joannes Oecolampadius, *In Jesiam prophetam, hypomnematon, hoc est, commentariorum . . . libri sex* (Geneva, 1558), 315: "Saepe et alias dictum est, in regno Christi, hoc est, vera Dei Ecclesia, abolenda et defutura idola, et sola Dei dandam gloriam: sicut Paulus clambat, Regi autem seculorum, immortali, invisibili, soli sapienti Dei honor, gloria in secula seculorum." There is no mention here of the Old Testament restoration of Israel, as in Calvin's commentary on the text.

77. *Commentarius Philippi Melanthonis in prophetam Zachariam,* in *Omnium operum,* 4 vols. (Wittenberg, 1562–64), 2:533.

78. Ibid., 2:531: "Nominantur autem Prophetae in politia Mosi, qui immediatem a Deo missi sunt ad illustrandum promissionem Messia. . . . Tales fuerunt Moises, Samuel, Nathan, David, Elias, Elisaeus, Esias, Hieremias, Daniel, Haggaeus, Zacharias et alia *politeumata* habuerunt. Sed doctrina est eadem, concio poenitantiae et repetitio ac illustratio pr missionis." Cf. the *Argumentum concionum prophetae Haggai,* in ibid., 527–31.

79. *Argumentum concionum prophetae Haggai,* 529–30: "Haec historia in Prophetis primum consideranda sunt, et in partibus historiae tamen Ecclesia omnium temporum intuenda est, et considerandum. Quomodo inde usque ab initio, quo genere doctrinae, ubi collecta sit, quae fuerint pericula, et aerumnae, quomodo liberata et servata sit, quae vox, quae virtutes eam a caeteris gebtibus discernant, quas ob causas cruci subiecta sit, et quis sit autor, quis finis liberationum.

80. Ibid., "Huic verae Ecclesiae nos adiungamus, dicamus eius doctrinam, Exempla intueamur et quae timorem excitant, et quae fidem et spem confirmant. . . . Postquam haec historia de totius Ecclesiae doctrina, periculis, liberationibus et de causis poenarum et liberationum consideravimus."

R. GERALD HOBBS
Hebraica Veritas *and* Traditio Apostolica
Sources

The code used here for easy reference is that employed in the edition of the biblical commentaries of Martin Bucer, in the *Martini Buceri Opera Latina,* Studies in Medieval and Reformation Thought (Leiden: E. J. Brill).

The first unit identifies the biblical unit of reference, the second the author, publisher, or title; the third adds, where necessary, the date of publication (used only to distinguish otherwise similar works from the same source). Where the work is in a European vernacular, this is indicated by the addition of a single letter to the first unit of the code: F = French; D = German; E = English; I = Italian.

Thus Ps Pel 1527 stands for the volume on the Psalms issued by Konrad Pellican in 1527; BiF Oli for the French Bible of Pierre Robert Olivétan.

Bi Bra 1502	*Biblie iampridem renovate pars prima (-sexta) . . . una cum glosa ordinaria: et litterali moralique expositi Nicolai de Lyra: necnon additionibus Burgensis: ac replicis Thoringi* . . . (Basel, 1502); reedition of the 1498 Bible edited by Sebastian Brant and published by Petri and Froben.
Bi Cas	Sebastian Castellio, *Biblia, interprete S"o C"e. Una cum eiusdem annotationibus* (Basel, 1551). A separate Psalter had been issued in 1547.
Bi Cla 1542	Isidoro Clarius [Chiari], *Vulgata aeditio Veteris ac Novi Testamenti, quorum alterum ad Hebraicam, alterum ad Graecam veritatem emendatum est diligentissime . . . adiectis ex eruditis scriptoribus scoliis,* 3 vols. (Venice, 1542). A second edition of 1557 (1564) was emended in response to censure.
Bi Mun	Sebastian Münster. *En tibi lector Hebraica Biblia Latina planeque nova* (Basel, 1534–35).
Bi Pag	Sanctes Pagnini. *Biblia. Habes in hoc libro . . . utriusque instrumenti novam tranlationem* (Lyon, 1527–28).
Bi Pel	Konrad Pellican. *Commentaria Bibliorum,* 7 vols. (Zurich, 1532–39). Psalms in vol. 4, published in 1534.
Bi Tre	Ioannes Tremellius, François du Jon et al. *Testamenti Veteris Biblia sacra . . . quibus etiam adiunximus Novi Testamenti libros* . . . (Geneva, 1617). First appeared in 1575–80.
Bi Tri	*Biblia sacrae vulgatae editionis Sixti Quinti Pont. Max. iussu recognita* (Antwerp, 1608); reprint of the Sixtine-Clementine Vulgate.
Bi Zur	[Leo Jud, K. Pellican, et al.], *Biblia Sacrosancta testamenti veteris et novi e sacra Hebraeorum lingua Graecorumque fontibus* . . . (Zurich, 1543). The Psalms are the work of Leo Jud and Theodore Bibliander.
BiD Dtb	Johannes Dietenberger. *Biblia beider Allt unnd Newen Testamenten, fleissig, treulich und Christlich . . . neu verdeutscht* (Mainz, 1534).
BiE Gen	*The Bible: That is, the Holy Scriptures Conteined in the Old and New Testament* (Geneva, 1561).

BiE Gre	*The Byble in Englyshe . . .* (London, 1541). The Great Bible.
BiF Ham	*La Bible, qui est toute la saincte Escriture* (Geneva, 1556). Edition by the French printer and colporteur Philbert Hamelin.
BiF Oli	[Pierre Robert Olivétan], *La Bible, Qui est toute la saincte escripture* (Neuchatel, 1535).
BiI Bru 1539	Antonio Brucioli, *La biblia quale continiene i sacri libri . . . tradotti de la hebraica verita in lingua toscana* (Venice, 1539). Brucioli's Psalms appeared in 1531, the first full edition of the Bible in 1532.
Ps Bel	Robert Bellarmine, *In omnes psalmos dilucida expositio* (Cologne, 1611).
Ps Buc 1529	Aretius Felinus [Martin Bucer] *Sacrorum Psalmorum libri quinque* (Strasbourg, 1529; 2d ed., 1532).
Ps Bug	Johannes Bugenhagen, *In librum Psalmorum interpretatio* (Basel, 1524). Cf. also infra, PsD Wvt.
Ps Caj	Thomas de Vio Cajetanus, *Psalmi Davidici ad Hebraicam veritatem castigati et iuxta sensum quem literalem vocant enarrati* (Venice, 1530).
Ps Cal	Jean Calvin, *In librum Psalmorum commentarius* (Geneva, 1557), as reprinted in *Corpus Reformatorum* 13:1017–1472.
Ps Cam	Jan van Campen, *Psalmorum omnium iuxta hebraicam veritatem paraphrastica interpretatio* (Nuremberg, 1532).
Ps Cen	Richard of Le Mans [Cenomanus], *Collationes in Psalmos* (Paris, 1541). Appended to the commentaries of Peter Lombard and reprinted with these in *MPL* 191:1–1296.
Ps Dtr	Veit Dietrich [*Annotationes,* appended to the Ps Eob; published as *Psalterium Davidis, carmine redditum per E. H. Cum annotationibus Viti Theodori Noribergensis, quae commentarii vice esse possunt* (Frankfurt, 1538).
Ps Eob	Helius Eobanus Hessus. *Psalterium universum carmine elegiaco redditum atque explicatum . . .* (Marburg, 1537). Editions of this work from 1538 on carry the annotations of Veit Dietrich. Cf. Ps Dtr.
Ps Est 1556	*Liber Psalmorum Davidis* (Geneva, 1556). A reedition by Robert Estienne of Ps Vat 1546, with significant revisions introduced after the death of Vatable.
Ps Fex	Felix Pratensis. *Psalterium ex hebreo . . . ad verbum fere tralatum* (Venice, 1515; 2d ed., Hagenau, 1522). The third edition (Basel, 1524) omits the notes.

Ps Giu	Agostino Giustiniani, *Psalterium Hebraeum, Graecum, Arabicum, et Chaldaeum cum tribus latinis interpretationibus et glossis* (Genoa, 1516). The seven versions of the text are identified as follows: H = Hebrew; Hl = Giustiniani's Latin translation of the Hebrew; G = Greek; Gl = Gallican Psalter; A = Arabic; T = Targum; Tl = Giustiniani's Latin translation of the Targum.
Ps Lef	Jacques Lefèvre d'Étaples, *Quincuplex Psalterium,* 2d ed. (Paris, 1513). (1st ed., Paris, 1508). Reprinted in Travaux d'Humanisme et Renaissance 170 (Geneva: Droz, 1979) (hereinafter abbreviated THR). The five different Latin versions are identified as follows: r = romanum; g = gallicanum; h = hebraicum; v = vetus; c = conciliatum.
Ps Lut 1513	Martin Luther, *Dictata super Psalterium.* MS lectures, 1513–15, printed in *WA* 3.
Ps Lut 1519	Martin Luther, *Operationes in Psalmos* (Wittenberg, 1519–21). Contains only Psalms 1–22. Reprinted in *WA* 5; and in *Archiv zur Weimarer Ausgabe der Werke Martin Luthers* (Cologne and Vienna, 1981–) (hereinafter *AzWA*). At present only volume 2 of the latter is available.
Ps Mar	Augustin Marlorat. *In CL. Psalmos Davidis et aliorum prophetarum explicatio ecclesiastica* (Geneva, 1562).
Ps Mel 1528	Philip Melanchthon, *In Psalmos aliquot Davidicos enarrationes doctissimae* (Hagenau, 1528). On selected psalms (1–4, 120–33).
Ps Mel 1555	Philip Melanchthon, *Commentarii in Psalmos* (1553–55), as in *Corpus Reformatorum* 13:1017–1472.
Ps Pag	Sanctes Pagnini, *Psalterium nuper translatum ex Hebraeo. Chaldaeo et Graeco . . . cum commentariis Hebraeorum . . . translatis et scholiis cum orthodoxa atque Catholica expositione* (Rome, 1520). Incomplete, halting abruptly in the last verse of Psalm 29.
Ps Pel 1516	Konrad Pellican, *Appendici huic inest Quadruplex Psalterium* (Basel, 1516). Published first as a supplement to the Erasmus/Froben edition of Jerome. The four versions of the text are identified as follows: H = Hebrew; Hl = Jerome's Latin *Iuxta Hebraeum;* G = Greek; Gl = Gallican Psalter.
Ps Pel 1527	Konrad Pellican, *Psalterium Davidis* (Strasbourg, 1527).

Issued without Pellican's approval; reissued in 1532 with his emendations.

Ps Sno — Reignier Snoy Goudanus, *Psalterium paraphrasibus illustratum. servata ubique ad verbum Hieronymi translatione* (Paris, 1551); a reprint, first issued in Cologne in 1536.

Ps Vat 1546 — [François Vatable], *Liber Psalmorum Davidis. Annotationes in eosdem ex Hebraeorum commentariis* (Paris, 1546). See also Ps Est 1556.

Ps Zwi — Huldreich Zwingli, *Enchiridion Psalmorum* (Zurich, 1532); reprinted in *Corpus Reformatorum* 100:467–836. A posthumous publication through the efforts of Leo Jud.

Ps1[2 . . .] Era — Desiderius Erasmus, *Enarratio primi psalmi . . .* Treatises on a number of individual psalms published between 1515 and 1536. Reprinted in *Desiderii Erasmi Roterodami opera omnia,* ed. J. Leclerc, 10 vols. (Leiden, 1703–6), vol. 5, cols. 171–556 (hereinafter cited as *LB*).

PsD Lut 1524; 1532 — Martin Luther, *Der Psalter.* First published in 1524, revised in 1531 and 1545. All in *WA, Bibel,* vol. 10, pt. 1.

PsD Wvt — Johannes Bugenhagen [and Martin Bucer] *Psalter wol verteutscht* (Basel, 1526). Purportedly a German translation of Ps Bug; in fact, a major revision by Bucer. Uses PsD Lut 1524 for text.

PsE Joy 1530 — [Martin Bucer, trans. George Joye], *The Psalter of David in Englishe Purely and Faithfully Translated aftir the Texte of Ffeline . . .* (Antwerp, 1530). First of three printings of parts of Ps Buc 1529.

PsF Lef — Jacques Lefèvre d'Étaples, *Le psautier de David* (Paris, 1524).

Liturgical and Paraliturgical Texts

Baïf — Jean Antoine de Baïf, *Le psautier de 1587.* Texte inédit. Critical edition by Yves Le Hir (Paris, 1963)

BCP — The Book of Common Prayer . . . (London, 1549). Reprinted in *The First and Second Prayerbooks of Edward VI* (London: Everyman's Library, 1910).

Marot — *Les Psaumes de Clément Marot. Edition critique du plus Ancien texte . . . accompagnée du texte définitif de 1562,* by Samuel Lenselink; *Le Psautier Huguenot,* vol. 3 (Assen-Kassel, 1969).

Primer — *A Primer in Englysshe with Dyvers Prayers,* by Thomas Godfray [London, 1534 or 1535].

Sternhold & Hopkins — Thomas Sternhold, John Hopkins, et al. *The Whole Book of Psalms. Collected into English Meeter* (London, 1622).

1. Published in Pforzheim by Thomas Ashelm; photoreprint, Hildesheim and New York: Olms-Verlag, 1974. See Lewis W. Spitz, "Reuchlin—Pythagoras reborn," in *The Religious Renaissance of the German Humanists* (Cambridge, Mass.: Harvard University Press, 1963), 61–80.

2. Pellican's *De modo legendi et intelligendi Hebraeum* (Strasbourg, 1504) seems, however, to have had little contemporary impact. It was reprinted by Eberhard Nestlé, *Deutschlands erstes Lehr-, Lese- und Wörterbuch der hebräischen Sprache* (Tübingen, 1877). On Konrad Pellican see C. Zürcher, *Konrad Pellikans Wirken in Zürich 1526–1556.* Zürcher Beiträge zur Reformationsgeschichte 4 (Zurich, 1975).

3. *In septem psalmos poenitentiales . . . interpretatio* (Tübingen, 1512).

4. On Münster see Jerome Friedman, *The Most Ancient Testimony Sixteenth-Century Christian-Hebraica in the Age of Renaissance Nostalgia* (Athens: Ohio University Press, 1983). On Pagnini see T. M. Centi, "L'attività letteraria di Santi Pagnini (1470–1536) nel campo delle scienze bibliche." *Archivum Fratrum Praedicatorum* 15 (1945): 5–51. An introduction to the editing of Hebrew grammars by Renaissance Christians is in Louis Kukenheim, *Contributions à l'Histoire de la Grammaire grecque, latine et hébraïque* (Leiden: Brill, 1951).

5. *De rudimentis,* 547–49.

6. The *De rudimentis* is probably the first Latin work to be printed Hebrew fashion, from right to left. The unalerted reader, turning to the accustomed title page, reads: "Finis libri. Canon: Non est liber legendus hic ceu caeteri. Faciem sinistra dextera dorsum tene, et de sinistra paginas ad dexteram quascumque verte. Quae latina videris legito latine, hebraea si sint insita, a dextera legenda sunt sinistrorum"—an omen of even more unsettling changes to come.

7. An issue discussed in this paper. For Jerome, see *Corpus Christianorum Series Latina,* 72:193 (hereinafter cited as *CCSL*). Here and throughout this paper I use the Hebrew numbering of the Psalms, a convention generally accepted today, though a point of contention in the sixteenth century.

8. Jerome, *Epistulae,* letter 120, sec. 11, *MPL,* vol. 22, cols. 1001–2.

9. *Commentarioli, CCSL* 72:181. See similarly his comment on Amos 9:11–12 (quoted in Acts 15): "ubi apostolorum praecedit auctoritas . . . ibi omnis variae explanationis tollenda suspicio est, et quod a tantis viris exponitur, hoc sequendum" (*CCSL* 76:345–46).

10. See the evidence assembled in Henri de Lubac, *Exégèse Médiévale: les Quatre Sens de l'Ecriture* (Paris: Aubier, 1959–63), vol. 2/1, chap. 3/4.

11. *De Civitate Dei,* bk. 17, sec. 11, *CCSL* 48:513.

12. See Beryl Smalley, *The Study of the Bible in the Middle Ages* (Notre Dame, Ind.: University of Notre Dame Press, 1964), chap. 4; Raphael Loewe, "Herbert of Bosham's Commentary on Jerome's Hebrew Psalter," *Biblica* 34 (1953): 44–77, 159–92, 275–98; Herman Hailperin, *Rashi and the Christian Scholars* (Pittsburgh: University of Pittsburgh Press, 1963).

13. *The Greek New Testament,* 3d ed., ed. K. Aland, M. Black, et al. (New York: American Bible Society, 1975), 897–903.

14. The Sixtine Vulgate itself, the commentaries of Robert Bellarmine, and the metrical Psalms of Jean-Antoine de Baïf.

15. A direction of research to which Pierre Fraenkel pointed in his conclusion to the Geneva congress in 1976: *Histoire de l'Exégèse au XVIe Siècle.* Études de Philologie et d'Histoire 34 (Geneva: Droz, 1978), 10–11.

16. Since the conference for which this paper was prepared, Guy Bedouelle and Bernard Roussel have completed their encyclopedic study of the Bible in the sixteenth century. Their volume will be the basic reference in this field for years to come: *Le temps des Réformes et la Bible.* La Bible de Tous les Temps 5 (Paris: Beauchesne, 1989). I gratefully acknowledge the value of their earlier work for my own studies.

17. For example, in Ps Buc 1529 Martin Bucer adopts one interpretation of Psalm 51:6 (which is quoted at Romans 3:4), reconciling it carefully with its Pauline use. In his Romans commentary of 1536, however, he reinterprets at some length, disagreeing with his earlier exegesis: *Metaphrases et enarrationes in Epistolam ad Romanos* (Strasbourg, 1536), 148–50.

18. Compare the not altogether flattering image at Amos 6:5 with the detailed priestly accounts of the chronicler (1 Chronicles 23:5; 2 Chronicles 7:6; etc.). Both the inclusion of versions of psalms at 2 Samuel, chaps. 22 and 23, and the "historical" prefaces to thirteen psalms relating them to incidents in the life of David (of which the best known is Psalm 51) attest the growing tradition.

19. See *Babylonian Talmud,* Pesahim 117a, Bababathra 14b; and *Midrash Rabbah* on Ecclesiastes 7:19, 4.

20. E.g., Matthew 22:43; Acts 1:16; Romans 4:6.

21. Augustine, *De Civitate Dei,* bk. 17, sec. 14, *CCSL* 48:578–79; and Jerome, *Epistulae,* letter 140 ad Cyprianum, sec. 4, *Corpus Scriptorum Ecclesiasticorum Latinorum,* 56:273 (hereinafter cited as *CSEL*). Both Jerome and Origen (*MPG* 12:1055) depend upon the dissenting midrashic sources.

22. Bi Bra 1502, ad Psalm 1:1.

23. For the Davidic: Ps Sno, Ps Cen. Ps Bel. The latter's statement that this view is "probabilior" reflects the cautious designation by the Council of Trent of the Psalter as "Davidicum." For multiple authorship, see especially Bucer, who adds this to Bugenhagen in PsD Wvt and writes a section "de scriptoribus" in Ps Buc 1529; see also Ps Cal, Ps Mar, Bi Cla, Bi Tre, and BiE Gen.

24. Bi Pel, preface to the Psalms.

25. For Psalm 2, a Davidic superscription occurs in Ps Lef, r, g, v, and c; and in Ps Giu G and Gl. For Psalm 95, in Ps Lef, r and g; Ps Giu G and Gl; Ps Pel 1516 G and Gl.

26. Bi Mun, ad loc. For Münster and his colleagues in Basel and Strasbourg, the opinion of rabbinic commentators carried considerable weight. See my article "Bucer on Psalm 22," in *Histoire de l'exégèse au XVIe Siècle,* 144–63, for a study of how one such Hebraist reconciled conflicting Christian and Jewish authorities in a psalm of traditional christological significance.

27. Ps Lef, Ps Fex, Ps Giu, Ps Bug, PsD Wvt, Ps Buc, Bi Mun, Bi Pel, and Ps Mel 1555.

28. Ps Pag 1520, Ps Caj, Bi Pel, and Bi Tre.

29. Ps Pel 1516 G reads: Ανεπίγραφος παρ' ἑβραίοις. Cf. Erasmus in Ps2 Era; *LB* 5:200–202.

30. Ps Bel, both in the preface and ad loc.

31. Ps Lut 1519, *AzWA* 2:66–67; see also Ps Pag 1520, Ps2 Era, Ps Caj, Ps Cal, Ps Mar, and Bi Tre.

32. *MPL* 191:38.

33. See *Midrash Tehillim: The Midrash on the Psalms,* ed. W. G. Braude, Yale Judaica 13 (New Haven: Yale University Press, 1959), 2:87–88. The tradition is, however, much older than this late midrash. Origen reports it from Jewish sources (*MPG* 12:1055–58), thence it passes through Hilary of Poitiers (*CSEL* 72:4–5) and Jerome (*Epistulae,* letter 140, sec. 2, *CSEL* 56:270–71).

34. Ps Buc 1532, sign. [a7]r, and ad Psalm 90:1. Kimhi's commentary—one of Bucer's principal sources—was available in the *Miqraot Gedolot,* the so-called Biblia Rabbinica, edited by Daniel Bomberg in Venice in 1517. On Kimhi, see *Encyclopedia Judaica 2,* vol. 10, cols. 1001–4.

35. Ps Cal ad loc., *CR* 60:29.

36. *CR* 83:46–47.

37. By Herbert Buffum, copyright Haldor Lillenas Publishing Company, 1951.

38. *Epistulae,* letter 23 ad Marcellam, sec. 1, *CSEL* 54:211.

39. Münster adopts the division in his Hebrew text but ignores it in the parallel Latin column.

40. B Ps 1532, sign. [a7]r.

41. Luther, for example, uses the Septuagint/Vulgate system in Ps Lut 1513, the Masoretic in PsD Lut 1524, and in between, in Ps Lut 1519, gives both numberings. Amongst our sources, those who retain the old are Ps Bug, Ps Era, Ps Zwi, Ps Sno, Ps Cen, Bi Cla, Ps Bel, Bi Tri, PsF Lef, and BiD Dtb. Those who give both: Ps Lef, Ps Pel 1516, Ps Giu, Ps Caj, Ps Vat, and Bi Pag.

42. See the discussion of this text in F. Jackson and K. Lake, *The Beginnings of*

Christianity, part 1, *The Acts of the Apostles,* ed. J. H. Ropes (London, 1920–33), 3:263–65.

43. Amongst those who explicitly cite the text, "in secundo ps.": Ps Lef, Ps Caj; "in psalmo": Ps Bug, PsD Wvt.

44. *LB* 5:197–200, here quoting 197F–98E.

45. Ps Buc 1529, f. 18r. This is probably the same tradition upon which Jerome depends, albeit by a different channel.

46. See L. A. Keck, "The Function of Rom. 3:10–18," in *God's Christ and His People.* Studies in Honour of Nils Alstrup Dahl, ed. Jacob Jervell and Wayne A. Meeks (Oslo, 1977), 141–57.

47. W. Sanday and A. C. Headlam, *A Critical and Exegetical Commentary on . . . Romans.* International Critical Commentary (Edinburgh: T. and T. Clark, 1907), 77–78.

48. *CCSL* 72:193, where he argues that Paul himself is the author of the catena.

49. On Lefèvre as text editor and his *conciliatus,* see Guy Bedouelle, *Le Quincuplex Psalterium de Lefèvre d'Étaples: un guide de lecture,* THR 171 (Geneva: Droz, 1979), 49–53.

50. Although Luther is not certain of this. He repeats this argument from Lefèvre but adds other options, including the possibility that Paul invented the catena under the inspiration of the Spirit (*WA* 5:415).

51. Sanday and Headlam (*Commentary on Romans,* n. 64) observe that Coverdale, like Origen and his imitators, set the passage aside with diacritical marks, but these rapidly disappeared in subsequent reprintings.

52. The commentary of the latter was available in the second Bomberg Rabbinic Bible (Venice, 1524–25). On Ibn Ezra, see *Encyclopedia Judaica 2,* vol. 8, cols. 1163–70.

53. See Hobbs, "Zwingli and the Study of the Old Testament," in *Huldrych Zwingli (1484–1531): A Legacy of Radical Reform.* Papers from the 1984 International Zwingli Symposium, McGill University, ed. E. J. Furcha (Montreal: McGill University, 1985), 144–79.

54. Note that Giustiniani gives the Masoretic punctuation in his Hebrew (Ps Giu H), but in his parallel translation (Ps Giu Hl) punctuates with the New Testament.

55. Also Ps Lef, Ps Sno, Bi Cla, Bi Tri, BiD Dtb.

56. See also Ps Mar, Bi Tre, BiE Gen, PsD Wvt.

57. See similarly the Latin paraphrastic translation of Castellio.

58. The Romans lectures of 1515–16, *WA* 56:414.

59. Augustine, *CCSL* 38:102–13; *Codex Iuris Canonici,* Ia pars., d.19, c.7; Friedberg 1, 62.

60. See H. A. Oberman, *Forerunners of the Reformation* (London: Lutterworth,

1967), esp. chap. 6, "Exegesis," for a useful presentation of the state of this question.

61. Ps Lef, Ps Lut 1513, Ps Bug, Ps Sno, Bi Tri, PsF Lef, BiE Gre, BiD Dtb, BCP.

62. Ps Zwi "oratio"; Ps Cam "doctrina"; Sternhold "theyr knowledge is conferred."

63. Ps Fex, Ps Giu, Ps Pag 1520, PsD Lut, PsD Wvt, Ps Pel 1527, Ps Buc, Ps Caj, Bi Pel, Bi Mun, Bi Pag, Ps Eob, Ps Vat 1546, Ps Cal, Ps Mar, Bi Zur, Bi Tre, BiI Bru, BiF Oli, BiF Ham, PsE Joy, BiE Gen, Bi Cas, Marot, Baïf, Prymer.

64. Ps Lut 1519; *WA* 5:547–48. See also Ps Giu, Ps Pag 1520, PsD Wvt, Ps Pel 1527, Ps Bel.

65. Apparently in his *Enarrationes in Psalmos . . . Opera Omnia* (Venice, 1591), vol. 2, fol. 60C. Amongst the explicit targets of Richard of Le Mans's wrath: Münster. Cajetan, Pagnini, Felix Pratensis, and Pellican (*MPL* 191:214–15).

66. Ps Lef pref., sign. A iir, as translated by Paul Nyhus in Oberman, *Forerunners,* 299–300.

67. Ps Cen, Ps Dtr, Ps Mel 1555. The others who concur: Ps Lut 1513, Ps Giu, Ps Lut 1519, Ps Pag 1520, Ps Bug, PsD Wvt, Ps Pel 1527, and Ps Sno. Giustiniani attaches a lengthy note asserting the completion of the fulfillment of this prophecy in his day by the exploits of his fellow Genoan, Columbus.

68. Ps Buc, Ps Caj, Bi Mun, Bi Pel, Bi Cla, Ps Vat 1546, Ps Bel.

69. For a wider discussion see Hobbs, "How Firm a Foundation: Martin Bucer's Historical Exegesis of the Psalms," *Church History* 53 (1984): 477–91.

70. *CR* 59:197–98.

71. Thus in respect to Psalm 19, which Hessus had taken in a creation sense, Dietrich's annotation says: "Poeta Iudaeorum sententiam secutus est . . ." and goes on to show that, in fact, the psalm points to God's glory in the gospel.

72. The alliance with Zwingli is made simple by the fact that he read him in one of the several Paris, Lyon, and Antwerp editions that set Zwingli (unidentified) alongside van Campen.

73. Bedouelle, *Le Quincuplex,* 113–20.

74. *Erasmus and the Jews* (Chicago: University of Chicago Press, 1986).

75. See Friedman, *Most Ancient Testimony,* chap. 9; and Hobbs, "Monitio amica: Pellican à Capiton sur le danger des lectures rabbiniques," in *Horizons Européens de la Réforme en Alsace,* ed. M. de Kroon and M. Lienhard (Strasbourg: Istra, 1980), 81–93.

76. Ps Mel 1555, on Psalm 19; but see also his preface to Ps Eob: "Ineptissimum genus est illorum, qui quadam Iudaica superstitione addicti glossematis Iudaeorum, cum figuras non intelligant, nec sententiarum ordinem animadvertant, saepe absurdas interpretationes . . . affingunt."

77. Richard of Le Mans, Ps Cen on Psalm 19:4.
78. *CCSL* 97:128.

DAVID C. STEINMETZ
Calvin and the Patristic Exegesis of Paul

1. T. H. L. Parker, *Calvin's New Testament Commentaries* (Grand Rapids: Eerdmans, 1971), 88.

2. Luchesius Smits, *Saint Augustine dans l'oeuvre de Jean Calvin,* 2 vols. (Assen: Van Gorcum, 1957–58).

3. John R. Walchenbach, "John Calvin as Biblical Commentator: An Investigation into Calvin's Use of John Chrysostom as an Exegetical Tutor" (Ph.D. diss., University of Pittsburgh, 1974).

4. E. P. Meijering, *Calvin wider die Neugierde: Ein Beitrag zum Vergleich zwischen reformatorischem und patristischem Denken* (Nieuwkoop: B. De Graaf, 1980).

5. *Iohannis Calvini Commentarius in Epistolam Pauli ad Romanos,* ed. T. H. L. Parker. Studies in the History of Christian Thought 22 (Leiden: E. J. Brill, 1981), 2 (hereinafter cited as *Calvini Commentarius*). Translations are taken from *Calvin's Commentaries: The Epistle of Paul the Apostle to the Romans and to the Thessalonians,* trans. Ross Mackensie (Grand Rapids: Eerdmans, 1961).

6. In this connection see Alexandre Ganoczy and Klaus Müller, *Calvins Handschriftliche Annotationen zu Chrysostomus: Ein Beitrag zur Hermeneutik Calvins* (Wiesbaden, 1981).

7. Karl Hermann Schelkle, *Paulus, Lehrer der Väter: Die altkirchliche Auslegung von Römer 1–11* (Düsseldorf, 1956).

8. Maurice F. Wiles, *The Divine Apostle: The Interpretation of St. Paul's Epistles in the Early Church* (Cambridge: Cambridge University Press, 1967). See particularly the summary of Wiles's conclusions on pp. 132–39.

9. For a detailed survey of the commentators of the Latin and Greek churches see Wiles, *Divine Apostle,* 3–13; Schelkle, *Paulus,* 11–14.

10. On Ambrosiaster, the older works of Alexander Souter are still important. See A. Souter, *A Study of Ambrosiaster* (Cambridge: Cambridge University Press, 1905); and *The Earliest Latin Commentaries on the Epistles of St. Paul* (Oxford: Oxford University Press, 1927), esp. 39–95.

11. Chrysostom is cited in the edition of J. P. Migne, *Patrologia Graeca,* 161 vols. (Paris, 1857–1912), vol. 60 (hereinafter abbreviated as *PG*).

12. Ambrosiaster is cited in the critical edition prepared by H. J. Vogels, *Ambrosiastri qui dicitur Commentarius in Epistulas Paulinas; Pars Prima, In Epistulam ad Romanos, CSEL* 81 (Vienna, 1966).

13. Ambrosiaster, "Ad Romanos," in Vogels, *Ambrosiastri,* 251.
14. Ibid., 251.
15. Ibid., 251.
16. Ibid., 253, 255.
17. Ibid., 263.
18. Ibid., 257.
19. Ibid., 269.
20. Ibid., 269.
21. Ibid., 269.
22. Ibid., 269.
23. Ibid., 265.
24. Ibid., 261.
25. Ibid., 261.
26. Ibid., 261.
27. Ibid., 261.
28. Ibid., 261, 263.
29. Ibid., 263.
30. Ibid., 263.
31. Ibid., 263.
32. Ibid., 265.
33. Ibid., 255.
34. Ibid., 255.
35. Ibid., 255.
36. Ibid., 255.
37. Ibid., 255.
38. Ibid., 257.
39. Ibid., 259.
40. Ibid., 259.
41. Ibid., 257.
42. Ibid., 265.
43. Ibid., 267.
44. Ibid., 267.
45. Ibid., 267.
46. Ibid., 255.
47. Ibid., 265.
48. Chrysostom, "Homilia 13," *PG* 60:507–8.
49. Ibid., 507–8.
50. Ibid., 510–11.
51. Ibid., 510–11.
52. Ibid., 510–11.
53. Ibid., 511–12.

54. Ibid., 511.
55. Ibid., 513.
56. Ibid., 515.
57. Ibid., 517.
58. Ibid., 515.
59. Ibid., 515.
60. Ibid., 515–16.
61. Ibid., 517–18.
62. Ibid., 519.
63. Ibid., 513–15.
64. Ibid., 513–15.
65. Ibid., 513–15.
66. Ibid., 513–15.
67. Ibid., 513.
68. Ibid., 513.
69. Ibid., 515.
70. Ibid., 512–13.
71. Ibid., 520–24.
72. Ibid., 513.
73. The 1536 *Institutes* was edited by Peter Barth, *Joannis Calvini, Opera Selecta,* vol. 1 (Munich: Christian Kaiser Verlag, 1926). For the English translation, see John Calvin, *Institution of the Christian Religion,* ed. and trans. Ford Lewis Battles (Richmond: John Knox Press, 1975). The standard English translation of the 1559 *Institutes* is by John T. McNeill, ed., and Ford Lewis Battles, trans., *Calvin: Institutes of the Christian Religion,* 2 vols. (Philadelphia: Westminster Press, 1960).
74. *Institutes* (1536), 3.6.
75. Ibid., 2.7.
76. Ibid., 1.26.
77. Ibid., 5.38.
78. Ibid., 5.36.
79. *Institutes* (1559), III.xx.24.
80. Ibid., II.i.9.
81. Ibid., II.iii.1.
82. Ibid., III.iii.8.
83. Ibid., II.xiii.4.
84. Ibid., II.xiii.1, II.xvi.6, III.iv.27.
85. Ibid., II.xii.4.
86. Ibid., IV.xvii.12.
87. Ibid., II.i.6, II.ii.16, III.i.3, III.ii.39, III.xxv.3, III.xxv.8, IV.xvii.12.
88. Walchenbach, "Calvin as Biblical Commentator," 148–49.

89. See the footnote to *Institutes,* III.ii.39, in the McNeill and Battles translation of the *Institutes.*

90. *Calvini Commentarius,* 158. Oecumenius (Pseudo-), *Commentaria Luculentissima vetustissimorum Graecorum in Omnes D. Pauli Epistolas ab Oecumenio exacte et magna cura ad Compendium Collecta: Interprete vero Johanne Hentenio Nechliniensis Hieronymiano* (Paris: Jean Foucher, 1547). The real Oecumenius lived in the first half of the sixth century.

91. Origen, *PG* 14:1091–92.

92. Lanfranc, *MPL* 150:130.

93. Haymo of Auxerre is incorrectly published under the name Haymo of Halberstadt (*MPL* 117:426). Haymo's commentary on Paul was readily available in the early sixteenth century in the edition *Haymonis Episcopi Halberstatten in D. Pauli Epistolas Omnes Interpretatio* (Cologne: Eucharius Cervicornus, 1539).

94. Lanfranc is careful to attribute this view to Ambrose (Ambrosiaster) in *MPL* 150:130.

95. Augustine, "Expositio Quarundam Propositionum ex Epistola ad Romanos," *CSEL* 84:21–22.

96. *Pelagius's Expositions of the Thirteen Epistles of St. Paul, II,* ed. Alexander Souter. Texts and Studies 9 (Cambridge: Cambridge University Press, 1926), 60–61.

97. *Calvini Commentarius,* 156.

98. Ibid., 156.

99. Ibid., 156.

100. Ibid., 157.

101. Augustine, "Expositio," 21.

102. *Petri Abelardi Opera Theologica,* ed. E. M. Buytaert. Corpus Christianorum, Continuatio Mediaevalis 12 (Turnhout: Brepols, 1969), 2:249–51.

103. Hervaeus of Bourg-Dieu, *MPL* 181:697–98.

104. William of St. Thierry, *MPL* 180:624–25.

105. Pseudo-Bruno the Carthusian, *MPL* 153:70–71.

106. Hugh of Saint Cher, *Tomus Septimus in Epistolas D. Pauli, Actus Apostolorum, Epist. septem canonicas, Apocalypsim B. Joannis* (Venice, 1732), 45v.

107. St. Thomas Aquinas, *Opera Omnia,* 25 vols. (Parma, 1862), 13:74–75.

108. Martin Bucer, *Metaphrases et Enarrationes perpetuae Epistolarum D. Pauli Apostoli. Tomus Primus continens Metaphrasim et Enarrationem in Epistolam ad Romanos* (Strasbourg: Wendelin Rihel, 1536), 331: "Istuc D. Ambrosius legit, Damnavit peccatum de peccato, hoc est, peccatum proprio peccato damnavit. Christus enim cum a peccato crucifigitur, quod est Satanas. Peccatum peccavit in carne corporis Salvatoris. Haec Ambrosius, cum quo consentit Chrysostomus."

109. *Calvini Commentarius,* 156.

110. Ibid., 156.

111. Ibid., 163.
112. Ibid., 159.
113. Ibid., 151.
114. Ibid., 166.
115. Ibid., 151.
116. Ibid., 151.
117. Ibid., 166.
118. Ibid., 167.
119. Ibid., 162.
120. Ibid., 163.
121. Ibid., 159.
122. Ibid., 159.
123. Ibid., 160.
124. Ibid., 164–65.
125. Ibid., 166–67.
126. Ibid., 165.
127. Ibid., 156.
128. Ibid., 157.
129. Ibid., 156.
130. Ibid., 156.
131. Ibid., 156.

JOHN B. PAYNE
Erasmus on Romans 9:6–24

1. For Origen and the Fathers, see Karl H. Schelkle, *Paulus Lehrer der Väter. Die altkirchliche Auslegung von Römer 1–11* (Düsseldorf, 1956), 336ff.; Maurice F. Wiles, *The Divine Apostle. The Interpretation of St. Paul's Epistles in the Early Church* (Cambridge, 1967), 98ff. For a survey of the connection of Romans 9–11, especially Romans 9, to the problem of predestination, see Otto Kuss, *Der Römerbrief,* 3 vols. (Regensburg, 1978), 828–934.

2. *Paraphrasis in Epistolam Pauli Apostoli ad Romanos* (Louvain: T. Martens, 1517), li verso: "Nec est, quod haec quae diximus quisque impius eo detorqueat, quasi iam culpa non sit penes homines, sed penes deum, qui nihil commeritos aut promeritos pro sua libidine reiiciat aut asciscat." Cf. Origen, *PG* 14:1144A–B; and Schelkle, *Paulus,* 341ff.

3. *Paraphrasis . . . ad Romanos,* li recto; *Collected Works of Erasmus,* vol. 42: *Paraphrases on Romans and Galatians,* ed. Robert D. Sider, trans. and annot. John B. Payne, Albert Rabil, Jr., and Warren S. Smith, Jr. (Toronto, 1984), 56 (hereinafter cited as *CWE*).

4. Ibid., lii verso. Cf. Origen, *PG* 14:1147B–48A; Chrysostom, *PG* 60:559–60.

5. Ibid., lii verso; *CWE* 42:56.

6. Ibid., lii recto.

7. Ibid., lii verso; *CWE* 42:53.

8. Origen, *PG* 14:1142A.

9. *Ambrosiaster, Ambrosiastri Qui Dicitur Commentarius in Epistulas Paulinas, Pars I, In Epistulam ad Romanos, CSEL,* ed. H. J. Vogels (Vienna, 1966), vol. 81, pt. 1, 308, ll. 23ff.; 309, ll. 21ff.

10. A Souter, *Pelagius' Expositions of Thirteen Epistles of Paul: Texts and Studies,* ed. J. A. Robinson, 10 vols. (Cambridge, 1922), 9:74, ll. 4–6. Even though Erasmus included the commentaries on the thirteen epistles of Paul bearing the name of Jerome as author in the ninth volume of his Jerome edition of 1516, he was already aware that they were pseudonymous, as his preface to that portion of his work indicates. See Souter, *Pelagius' Expositions,* 6, where he quotes from this preface. Likewise, in the annotations he shows that he knows that this commentary is not by Jerome. See *Novum Testamentum, in LB* 6:584C, 586C. Souter (*Pelagius' Expositions,* 277) proves that the manuscript then housed at the Echternach Abbey near Freiburg (now Paris, BN.9525) "is the very MS from which and from which alone Erasmus derived the text of Pseudo-Jerome." However, Erasmus gives no indication that he knew that the author of this work was Pelagius.

11. Ibid., li verso; Origen, *PG* 14:1145.

12. See below, p. 132.

13. *Paraphrasis . . . ad Romanos,* li recto; *CWE* 42:55.

14. Ibid., lii verso; *CWE* 42:56–57.

15. In his letter to Hedibia concerning twelve questions, Jerome likewise makes sure to give a place to free will in his exegesis of Romans 9. *Epistulae,* letter 120, sec. 10, *MPL,* 22:999.

16. *Opus Epistolarum Erasmi,* ed. P. S. Allen and H. M. Allen (Oxford, 1924), letter 1342, ll. 926ff.

17. My analysis is based primarily on the Latin text in *LB* 9:1230A–34A. I have made use of the translation of E. G. Rupp and A. N. Marlow in *Luther and Erasmus: Free Will and Salvation,* in *Library of Christian Classics,* 26 vols. (Philadelphia, 1969), 17:64–72. Unless otherwise indicated, the translations are mine.

18. Karl Zickendraht, *Der Streit zwischen Erasmus und Luther über die Willensfreiheit* (Leipzig, 1909), 39.

19. André Godin, "Une lecture sélective d'Origène à la Renaissance: Erasme et le Peri Archon," in *Origeniana (Premier Colloque international des études origéniennes), Vetera Christianorum* (Bari, 1975), 12:87ff.

20. *LB* 9:1230C; cf. Origen, *Peri Archon,* III.1.10; *PG* 11:263.

21. *LB* 9:1230C–E; *Peri Archon,* III.1.10–14; *PG* 11:266–78.

22. *LB* 9:1230D; cf. Origen, *Peri Archon,* 3.1.11; *PG* 11:267C, 270A. Erasmus somewhat modifies Origen's simile here from master-servant to father-son.

23. *LB* 9:1230D; Origen, *Peri Archon,* III.1.12; *PG* 11:270B; Jerome, *Commentariorum in Esaiam,* 63:17–19, *Corpus Christianorum,* 73A:731, ll. 27–36.

24. *LB* 9:1230E; Origen, *Peri Archon,* III.1.12; *PG* 11:270C–271B.

25. *Peri Archon* III.1.14; *PG* 11:278A.

26. *PG* 14:1146B–C; Godin, "Une lecture," 88.

27. *LB* 9:1230F.

28. *LB* 10:1231C.

29. *LB* 9:1232E–F.

30. *LB* 9:1233A–B; Origen, *Peri Archon,* II.9.7; *PG* 11:231A–32B. See also Jerome, *Commentariorum in Malachiam Prophetam* 1:2–5, *Corpus Christianorum,* 76A:906, ll. 126–27, who also argues that the love and hatred is on the basis of foreknowledge of future works.

31. *LB* 9:1233C; translation by Rupp and Marlow, *Luther and Erasmus,* 71.

32. *Peri Archon,* III.1.22; *PG* 11:302B–C; *Commentariorum in Epistolam B. Pauli and Romanos,* 7.16, *PG* 14:1149A–B.

33. *LB* 9:1220F; translation by Rupp and Marlow, *Luther and Erasmus,* 47.

34. *LB* 9:1234A.

35. *LB* 9:1233F. The translation of Rupp and Marlow, *Luther and Erasmus,* 72, is faulty. The text I have paraphrased is: "Figulus hic facit vas in contumelian, sed ex meritis praecedentibus quemadmodum rejecit Judaeos quosdam, sed ob incredulitatem. Rursus ex Gentibus facit vas honorificum ob credulitatem." Rupp and Marlow translate: "This potter makes a vase for dishonor not on account of preceding merits, just as he rejects some Jews, but on account of unbelief. Again, of the Gentiles he makes a vessel of honor on account of their belief." Here *sed* is not a negative but is used to heighten the affirmative in a kind of ascent or climax. "This potter makes a vessel for dishonor, but in fact on account of preceding merits, just as he rejects some Jews, but on account of unbelief."

36. *Peri Archon,* III.1.21; *PG* 11:299C, 300C, 301A–B, 302A.

37. *LB* 9:1231A; *Peri Archon,* III.1.18; *PG* 11:291A; cf. *Comment. in Epist. ad Rom., PG* 14:1145B.

38. *LB* 10:1396–1451.

39. Ibid., 1412A–B. For this view in the paraphrase of Romans see John B. Payne, "Erasmus: Interpreter of Romans," in *Sixteenth Century Essays and Studies,* ed. Carl S. Meyer II (St. Louis, 1971), 17–20.

40. *LB* 10:1412B–C.

41. Ibid., 1412F.

42. Ibid., 1412D.

43. Ibid., 1413A–B.

44. Ibid., 1413D.
45. Ibid., 1413D–E.
46. Heiko A. Oberman, "A Nominalistic Glossary," in *The Harvest of Medieval Theology,* 3d ed. (Durham, 1983), 468. On the relation between the *fides acquisita* and *fides infusa* in Occam see R. Seeberg, *Dogmengeschichte,* 5 vols. (Darmstadt, 1959), 3:719; and for the same in Biel, see Oberman, 71–74.
47. See below, p. 129.
48. *LB* 10:1413F, 1418C.
49. Ibid., 1419B–D. See Origen, *Peri Archon,* III.1.18; *PG* 11:290A, 291A, who makes reference to the same corroborating passages of Scripture. In his rush Erasmus passes over the first half of Psalm 127:1 quoted by Origen, which would have been especially pertinent: "Unless the Lord builds the house, those who build it labor in vain."
50. *De servo arbitrio* (ed. A. Freitag), in *WA* 18:730, ll. 6–9; translation by P. S. Watson and B. Drewery in *Luther and Erasmus: Free Will and Salvation,* 258.
51. *LB* 10:1447C.
52. Ibid., 1442C. Though in his paraphrase of Romans 9–11 Erasmus interprets Paul as being harsh in his criticism of the Jews as he refers to their puerile ceremonialism, "impiety," "envy," "arrogance," "blindness," "stubbornness," and "malice," nevertheless he understands 11:26 as teaching without qualification that the entire people of Israel will be saved; and here he varies from most of his favorites, all of whom, except for Augustine and Ambrosiaster, seek to qualify Paul's statement. *Paraphrasis . . . ad Romanos,* niii recto. That Erasmus was no lover of the Jews is well known. Guido Kisch describes Erasmus as characterized by "der tiefverwurzelte, masslose Judenhass," in *Erasmus' Stellung zu Juden und Judentum, Philosophie und Geschichte. Eine Sammlung von Vorträgen und Schriften aus dem Bebiet der Philosophie und Geschichte* (Tübingen, 1969), 83–84:29. Kisch's judgment must be balanced by the more charitable one of Shimon Markisch, *Erasmus and the Jews* (Chicago, 1986).
53. *LB* 10:1430F–35B.
54. The added annotations on Romans in 1527 show also the prominence of Chrysostom for the first time; he is cited, often at length, over seventy times. A manuscript of the Homilies on Romans was in Erasmus's hands in 1526. See *Opus Epistolarum Erasmi,* vol. 6, letter 1736, ll. 23–24. He had hoped to have it translated at Louvain by Goclenus or Cranevelt or at Ghent by Levinus Ammonius in time to be included in his 1530 edition of Chrysostom, but his hopes were not realized because the manuscript was returned to him only after several months' delay. He sent it off this time to Germanus Brixius, who accomplished the translation in 1532; Froben printed it in 1533. The translation reappeared in the full edition of Chevallon at Paris in 1536. See *Opus Epistolarum Erasmi,* 8:327, n. 6.

55. *LB* 10:1448C.

56. Whereas Scotus presupposed special grace for the *meritum de congruo,* Occam and Biel posited this merit on a purely naturalistic basis. See Oberman, *Harvest,* 164, 210–11; Seeberg, *Dogmengeschichte,* 3:666, n. 1.; and P. Minges, *Die Gnadenlehre des Duns Scotus auf ihren angeblichen Pelagianismus und Semipelagianismus Geprüft* (Münster, 1906), 45ff., 69.

57. *LB* 9:1222F–24D; X:1327B–E.

58. *LB* 9:1224C.

59. *Hyperaspistae I, LB* 10:1327D–F, 1330E; *Hyperaspistae II, LB* 10:1339C–D, 1356E–F, 1358A, 1457B, 1472B–C, 1473F, 1476D–E.

60. *Hyper. II, LB* 10:1487A–B: "Iam saepius testatus sum Scholasticorum opinionem, quod liberum arbitrium suis viribus possit promereri, saltem de congruo, gratiam iustificantem, me nec probare nec improbare: *proclivior tamen ad probandum quam ad improbandum*" (my italics).

61. E. W. Kohls aligns Erasmus with Thomas in arguing that Erasmus's position in the *Diatribe on Free Will* is that of "ein durch die Gnade befreiter Willen." *Die Theologie des Erasmus,* 2 vols. (Basel, 1966), 2:24, n. 154, and 64, n. 78. Kohls here follows Ole Modalsi, *Das Gericht nach den Werken* (Göttingen, 1963), 181ff. For a critique of Kohls, see my book, *Erasmus: His Theology of the Sacraments* (Richmond, 1970), 264, n. 18, and 266, n. 30. In this study (pp. 80ff.) I had argued that in the *Hyperaspistae II* Erasmus shows that he had moved into the Occamist, which I call there, rather too imprecisely, the "Scotist-nominalist" camp. H. Humbertclaude long ago noted that during the course of the *Hyperaspistae* Erasmus became "more and more" favorable to the Scotist position. *Erasme et Luther leur polémique sur le libre arbitre* (Paris, 1909), 220. Marjorie O'Rourke Boyle has argued that Erasmus in the *Diatribe,* "while suspending a judgment of absolute certainty" and after balancing both sides of the question, "calculated that mean to coincide with Augustine's moderate theory." See "Erasmus and the "Modern" Question: Was He Semi-Pelagian?" *ARG* 75 (1984): 76. She gives little attention to the *Hyperaspistae.*

62. Harry J. McSorley thinks Erasmus hovers "between Neo-Semi-Pelagianism and Augustine," in *Luther: Right or Wrong? An Ecumenical-Theological Study of Luther's Major Work, the Bondage of the Will* (New York, 1969), 288–93. Charles Trinkaus, though noting Erasmus's use of the "nominalistic" *meritum de congruo* even when he does not mention the term, does not firmly align him with the nominalists but seems instead to think he steers an independent middle course between the nominalists and Augustine, "in partial agreement and disagreement with both." See Charles Trinkaus, "Erasmus, Augustine, and the Nominalists," *ARG* 67 (1976): 6ff. Similarly, James Tracy in a recent essay concludes that Erasmus's view on this subject is double-sided, that "he did not necessarily succeed in bringing the warring impulses of his own mind into harmony." See

"Two Erasmuses, Two Luthers: Erasmus' Strategy in Defense of *De libero arbitrio*," *ARG* 78 (1987): 56.

63. B. A. Gerrish, "*De Libero Arbitrio* (1524): Erasmus on Piety, Theology, and the Lutheran Dogma," in *Essays on the Works of Erasmus,* ed. Richard L. DeMolen (New Haven, 1978), 198.

64. See *Opus Epistolarum Erasmi,* vol. 7, letter 1815, ll. 52–59, and letter 1853, introduction.

65. Ibid., letter 1804, ll. 75–95.

66. *LB* 10:1396D, 1401A.

67. *Paraphr. in epist. . . . ad Romanos in Paraphrasis in omneis epistolas apostolicas* (Basel, 1532), fol. 44; *CWE* 42:55.

68. Ibid., fol. 45; *CWE* 42:56. Harry McSorley fails to note that this passage was added in 1532 when he quotes the first part of it as evidence that Erasmus correctly understands the Pauline theory. See *Luther: Right or Wrong,* 285, n. 35.

69. *LB* 6:582D. For the Fathers see Schelkle, *Paulus,* 150.

70. *LB* 6:601E; Origen, *PG* 14:1098B; Ambrosiaster, *CSEL* 81(1):264, ll. 12ff.; 265, ll. 13ff.; Chrysostom, *PG* 60:518. However, in spite of this correct perception of the Pauline sense in his annotation, his own paraphrase follows Origen and Ambrosiaster in adopting the conditional meaning. *Paraphrasis . . . ad Romanos,* (1532), fol. 37–38.

71. *LB* 6:606B–C; Origen, *PG* 14:1125D–26B; Ambrosiaster, *CSEL* 81(1):288, ll. 21ff.; 289, ll. 20ff. Other Fathers, in order to stress human responsibility even more, interpreted the term as meaning exclusively the human will. However, again as opposed to the annotation, the paraphrase follows Origen and Ambrosiaster in insisting that Paul does not intend here to deny free will. *Paraphrasis . . . ad Romanos* (1532), fol. 40: "Noster conatus est, caeterum eventus pendet a decreto dei."

72. *LB* 6:608B. For the Fathers see Schelkle, *Paulus,* 320ff.

73. *Paraphrasis . . . ad Romanos* (1532), fol. 45; *CWE* 42:56.

74. Ibid.; *CWE* 42:56.

75. Ibid., fol. 44; *CWE* 42:55. See above, n. 71, for an indication that he has not relinquished his synergistic interpretation of the Pauline doctrine of grace.

76. John B. Payne, "The Significance of Lutheranizing Changes in Erasmus' Interpretation of Paul's Letters to the Romans in his *Annotationes* (1527) and *Paraphrases* (1532)," in *Histoire de l'exégèse au XVIe siècle,* ed. O. Fatio and P. Fraenkel (Geneva, 1978), pp. 314–30.

77. Melanchthon, *Römerbrief-Kommentar 1532, Melanchthons Werke,* ed. R. Stupperich and R. Schäfer (Gütersloh, 1965), esp. vol. 5, p. 250, ll. 10–11, 19–25; p. 254, ll. 8–12; p. 257, ll. 22–258, l. 2. Melanchthon had already modified his position on free will in 1527 in the *Scholia in Epistulam ad Colossenses,* and *Articuli Visitationis.* See *Melanchthons Werke,* ed. R. Stupperich and P. Barton (Gütersloh:

1963), 4:222ff., 238ff.; and *Corpus Reformatorum,* 26, 26ff. Cf. Melanchthon, *Annotationes in epistolam ad Romanos.* (Wittenberg, 1522), 50 recto, 51 verso, 54 verso-recto, and *Loci Communes* (1521), *Melanchthons Werke,* ed. H. Engelland (Gütersloh, 1952), 2(1):8ff. Cf. Wilhelm Maurer, *Der junge Melanchthon,* 2 vols. (Göttingen, 1969), 2:481ff.

78. *Römerbrief-Kommentar* 1532, 29, ll. 7ff.

JEAN-CLAUDE MARGOLIN
Valla, Colet, Lefèvre, and Erasmus

1. John B. Payne, "Erasmus and Lefèvre d'Étaples as Interpreters of Paul," *Archiv für Reformationsgeschichte* 65 (1974): 54–83.

2. Jerry H. Bentley, "Biblical Philology and Christian Humanism: Lorenzo Valla and Erasmus as Scholars of the Gospels," *Sixteenth Century Journal* 8, no. 2 (1977): 9–28.

3. See the text of his essay in this volume.

4. See, for instance, John B. Payne, "Erasmus, Jean Le Clerc, and the Principle of the Harder Reading," *Renaissance Quarterly* 31, no. 3 (1978): 309–21; and Jerry H. Bentley, "Interpretations of Paul in the Reformation," *Encounter* 36 (1975): 196–211.

5. R. Padberg, "Zur heutigen Erasmus-Interpretationen," *Theologische Revue* 59, no. 3 (1963): 149–54; "Reformation catholica: Die theologische Konzeption der erasmischen Erneuerung, 'Volk Gottes,'" in *Festgabe für Josef Höfer* (Basel, 1973), 293–305; *Erasmus von Rotterdam: Seine Spiritualität Grundlage seines Reformprogramm* (Paderborn, 1975); Albert Rabil, *Erasmus and the New Testament: The Mind of a Christian Humanist* (San Antonio, 1972); Bo Reicke, "Erasmus und die neutestamentliche Textgeschichte," *Anlässlich der Erasmus-Ausstellung in der Universitätsbibliothek zu Basle* (February–March 1966), *Theologische Zeitschrift* (1966): 254–65; C. A. L. Jarrott, "Erasmus' *in principio erat sermo:* A Controversial Translation," *Studies in Philology* 61, no. 1 (1964): 35–40; "Erasmus' Biblical Humanism," *Studies in the Renaissance* 17 (1970): 119–52; M. A. Anderson, "Erasmus the Exegete," *Concordia Theological Monthly* 60, no. 11 (1969): 722–33; W. Kohls, *Die Theologie des Erasmus,* 2 vols. (Basel, 1966); G. Chantraine, *"Mystère" et "Philosophie du Christ" selon Erasme* (Namur, 1971); idem, *Erasme et Luther, libre et serf arbitre* (Paris, 1981); M. A. Screech, *Ecstasy and the Praise of Folly* (London, 1980). See also more recent works, e.g., Jerry Bentley, *Humanists and Holy Writs,* (Princeton, 1983), this study contains also a section on Lorenzo Valla; Friedheim Krüger, *Humanistische Evangelienauslegung* (Tübingen, 1986), and esp. *Paraphrases on Romans and Galatians,* vol. 42 of *Collected Works of Erasmus* (Toronto, 1984). This translation and annotation is by John B. Payne,

Albert Rabil, Jr., and Warren S. Smith, Jr. At the time of the Duke University conference that book was not yet published; however, the readers can see the preface (xi–xxix), pp. 63–69 (chap. 11), and notes, pp. 155–56. Also see Eugene Rice, Jr., *Saint Jerome in the Renaissance* (Baltimore, 1985).

6. "Les *Annotations* de Valla, celles d'Erasme et la grammaire," in *Histoire de l'exégèse au XVIe siècle* (Geneva, 1978), 202–28.

7. *Grammaire et Rhétorique chez Erasme* (Paris: Belles-Lettres, 1981), *passim.*

8. *Humanisme et Patristique: Erasme, lecteur d'Origène* (Geneva: Droz, 1982).

9. See especially *Lorenzo Valla, Umanesimo e Teologia* (Firenze, 1972).

10. See especially *Il pensiero cristiano di Lorenza Valla* (Rome, 1969).

11. *Humanists and Holy Writs,* which also contains a section on Valla.

12. Sears Jayne, *John Colet and Marsilio Ficino* (Oxford, 1963).

13. Eugene R. Rice, "The Humanist Idea of Christian Antiquity: Lefèvre d'Étaples and His Circle," *Studies in the Renaissance* 9 (1962): 126–60; "Jacques Lefèvre d'Étaples and the Medieval Christian Mystics," in *Florilegium Historiale* (Toronto, 1971), 99ff.; *The Prefatory Epistles of Jacques Lefèvre d'Étaples and Related Texts* (New York, 1972). See also his book on Saint Jerome in the Renaissance, cited in n. 5, above.

14. See especially his edition of the *New Testament,* 2 vols. (Paris, 1970).

15. Guy Bedouelle, *Lefèvre d'Étaples et l'Intelligence des Ecritures* (Geneva: Droz, 1973).

16. See n. 1.

17. Helmut Feld, "Der humanisten Streit um Hebräer 2, 7 (Psalm 8, 6)," *Archiv für Reformationsgeschichte* 61 (1970): 5–33.

18. See Catherine A. L. Jarrott, "Erasmus's Annotations and Colet's Commentaries on Paul: A Comparison of some Theological Themes," in *Essays on the Works of Erasmus,* ed. Richard L. DeMolen (New Haven, 1978), 125–44.

19. This expression was coined by F. Seebohm, *The Oxford Reformers: John Colet, Erasmus, and Thomas More* (London, 1867).

20. In his famous letter portrait of 13 June 1521 (Allen, *Opus Epistolarum Erasmi,* vol. 4, ep. 1211), translated and discussed by André Godin in *Vies de Jean Vitrier et de John Colet* (Angers: Editions Moreana, 1982).

21. That is, Good Friday. See "The Sermon of Doctor Colete, Made to the Convocacion at Paulis," in J. H. Lupton, *Life of John Colet* (1887; reprint, 1961), 293–304.

22. Actually, the founding of Saint Paul's School extended from 1509 to 1512.

23. See M. F. J. MacDonnel, *History of St. Paul's School* (London, 1909); and also Lupton, *Life of John Colet.*

24. Thanks especially to a painstaking study by Margaret Mann Phillips, "The Mystery of the Metsys Portrait," *Erasmus in English* 7 (1975): 18–21.

25. It was Alessandro Perosa who rediscovered and published the first version

of the text of Valla's *Collatio Novi Testamenti,* completed with a preface by Valla himself. But Erasmus was not aware of this version.

26. Paris: Bade Ascensius, 1505, fol.; other editions include Basel: A. Cratander, 1526, in octavo; Basel, 1541, in octavo.

27. For the French editions of the New Testament by Lefèvre, see Rice, *Prefatory Epistles,* 563–65, nos. 271–311.

28. *Les épîstres S. Pol. xiii* . . . (Paris: Simon de Colines, 1523).

29. The number of commentaries on the Epistle to the Romans, and especially on the historical and theological problems posed by the eleventh chapter, is quite impressive. Here we refer to the most recent bibliographies of Pauline studies and to several important works by contemporary exegetes. First of all, consult Bruce M. Metzger, *Index to the Periodical Literature on the Epistles of Paul* (Leiden: Brill, 1960); Dom Paul Delatte, *Les Épîtres de saint Paul replacées dans le milieu historique des Actes des Apôtres,* 2 vols. (Tours, 1938); J. Cantinat, *Les Épîtres de saint Paul expliquées* (Paris, 1960); P. Beda Rigaux, *St. Paul et ses Lettres, état de la question* (Paris, 1962); Joseph Turmel, *Nouvelles recherches sur les Épîtres pauliniennes et sur le 4e Evangile* (Paris, 1966); Augustin George, *L'Evangile de Paul* (Paris, 1966); T. W. Manson, *Studies in the Gospels and Epistles* (Manchester, 1982); S. Lyonnet, *Le message de l'Épître aux Romains* (Paris: 1971); F. Godet, *Commentaire sur l'Épître aux Romains,* 3d ed. (Geneva, n.d.); G. Schneider, *Kernprobleme des Christentums, eine Studie zu Paulus, Evangelium und Paulinismus* (Stuttgart, 1959); J. Cambier, *L'Evangile de Dieu selon l'Épître aux Romains* (Paris, 1967); H. W. Schmidt, *Der Brief des Paulus an die Römer* (Berlin, 1962); Karl Barth, *L'Épître aux Romains,* trans. from the German by P. Jundt, along with the text of the epistle (Geneva, 1972); W. Lindemann, *Karl Barth und die kritische Schriftauslegung* (Hamburg, 1973); A. Thomas-Brès, *La vie chrétienne victorieuse selon l'Épître aux Romains* (Lyon, 1974); A. Viard, *St. Paul, Épître aux Romains* (Paris, 1975), with a translation of the text and a bibliography, 29–31; F. Cordero, *L'Epistola ai Romani, anthropologia del cristianesimo paolino* (Turin, 1972); W. Nee, *La vie chrétienne normale* (Fontenay, 1975), which essentially bears on chapters 1–8 of the Epistle to the Romans. In spite of the fact that the following work is somewhat dated, it is still worth consulting: C. Gore, *St. Paul's Epistle to the Romans, a Practical Exposition,* 2 vols. (London, 1900–1). See also H. Schlier, *Der Römerbrief. Kommentar* (Friburg, 1977). On chapter 11, "which is the focus of the present study, and on the chapters immediately preceding it, see Christian Müllet, *Gottes Gerechtigkeit und Gottes Volk* (Göttingen, 1964); Christoph Plag, *Israels Wege zum Heil* (Stuttgart, 1969), an exegesis of chapters 9 through 11. In relation to the Reformation, it will be sufficient to mention the name of Luther and Dorothea Demmer's study in Luther's exegesis of the Epistle to the Romans: *Lutherus interpres, der theologische Neuansatz in seiner Römerbriefexegese* . . . (Witten, 1968).

30. See, for example, Cecil Roth, *The Jews in the Renaissance* (Philadelphia, 1959).

31. In addition to the dated but still useful monograph by Ludwig Geiger, *Johann Reuchlin, sein Leben und seine Werke* (Leipzig, 1871), see François Secret, Les kabbalistes chrétiens de la Renaissance (Paris, 1964); and Lewis W. Spitz, *The Religious Renaissance of the German Humanists* (Cambridge, Mass., 1963); idem, "Pythagoras and Cabala Christ," *Archiv für Reformationsgeschichte* 47 (1966): 1–20.

32. See Nikolaus Paulus, *Die deutschen Dominikaner im Kampfe gegen Luther, 1518–1563* (Freiburg, 1903).

33. This difficult problem of historical appreciation, which renders every assessment of objective intention fragile and even debatable, has been examined honestly by Simon Markish in *Erasme et les Juifs* (Lausanne, 1979). I myself approach this problem at points in my article "Antisémitisme d'hier et d'aujourd'hui: Antisémitisme éternel?" *Temps Modernes* (September 1980): 429–43. See also the English translation of Markish's book: *Erasmus and the Jews,* trans. Anthony Olcott, with an afterword by Arthur A. Cohen (Chicago: 1986).

34. See in this regard Andrew J. Brown, "The Date of Erasmus' Latin Translation of the New Testament," *Transactions of the Cambridge Bibliographical Society* 8, pt. 4, (1986): 351–80 (criticizing with good arguments Henri Gibaud's assumption in his book, *Un inédit d'Erasme: la première version du "Nouveau Testament" copiée par Pierre Meghen 1506–1509 d'après les manuscrits de Londres, Cambridge et Hatfield,* [Angers: Editions Moreana, 1982]).

35. *Epistolae B. Pauli ad Romanos Exposito Literalis,* ed. J. H. Lupton (London, 1876), with the Latin and English texts.

36. *Enarratio in Epistolam Primam S. Pauli ad Corinthios,* ed. J. H. Lupton (London, 1874), with the Latin and English texts, and R. Bernard O'Kelly, *John Colet's Enarratio in Primam S. Pauli Epistolam ad Corinthios* (unpublished Harvard thesis, 1964, Latin and English).

37. *Enarratio in Epistolam B. Pauli ad Romanos,* ed. J. H. Lupton (London, 1873), with the Latin and English texts. We owe to Sears Jayne (*John Colet,* bibliography, 149ff.) the most recent and complete attempt—following the work of J. H. Lupton and especially that of E. W. Hunt, *Dean Colet and His Theology* (London, 1956)—to put together both a bibliography of Colet, including unpublished and unedited works, and a plausible chronology of his life and work. This chronology is particularly useful in helping us to reconstruct the development of his exegetical thought with regard to Saint Paul.

38. During that same year a corrected edition with annotations and expurgations was published by the same printer. This is the edition that I have consulted for the most part, using the copy that is available in the National Library of Paris, along with a facsimile of the copy that is held in the Bayerische Staatsbibliothek

of Münich, reproduced by Friedrich Fromman Verlag (Stuttgart–Bad Cannstatt, 1978). See Rice, *Prefatory Epistles,* 558–59, no. 245.

39. See especially in Allen, *Opus Epistolarum Erasmi,* vol. 1, letters 108 (Erasmus to Colet), 109 (Erasmus to Colet), 123 (Erasmus to Batt), 164 (Erasmus to an unknown party), 165 (to a certain Franciscan by the name of Edmond), 180 (to Jean Desmarez), 181 (to Colet), 225 (to Colet), 237 (to Colet), 260 (to Colet), and 296 (to Roger Servais). In this sampling of Erasmus's correspondence (up to mid- 1514) one notes that a significant proportion of the letters are addressed to John Colet.

40. Erasmus recounts the discovery in a letter dedicated to Christopher Fisher (an Englishman in service to the pontifical court in France and the future secretary to the Sacred College in Rome) written in Paris around March 1505 (Allen, *Opus Epistolarum Erasmi,* vol. 1, letter 182): "Last summer, while I was conducting an investigation in a very old library (that of the Abbey of the Premonstratensians of the Park, near Louvain)—the hunt may be more pleasant where the woods are not so thick!—by chance there fell into my hands an uncommon prize: the notes by Lorenzo Valla on the New Testament." Trans. M. Delcourt, *La Correspondance d'Erasme,* 12 vols. (Brussels, 1967), 1:381.

41. See Rice, *Prefatory Epistles,* no. 247.

42. Ibid., nos. 245 and 246.

43. Erasmus edited and annotated them (in the authorized version published in Fribourg in 1531 by Jo. Faber Emmeus) under the title *Paraphrasis in Elegantias Laur. Vallae.* See the critical edition by C. L. Heesakers and J. H. Waszink in *Opera Omnia Des. Erasmi* (Amsterdam [*ASD*]: 1–4, 1973), 187–351 (hereinafter cited as *ASD*).

44. See the translation cited in A. Godin, *Vies de Jean Vitrier.*

45. See especially Bedouelle, *Lefèvre,* 191–96.

46. Note especially the exegetical debate between the two men during the period from 1516 to 1518 (Bedouelle, ibid., 218–23). For instance, they strongly disagreed about the interpretation of Hebrews 2:6, 9, where in the Vulgate it was said that "Christ had been made *a little lower than the angels,*" or that (in Lefèvre's reading of Psalm 8:6) "Thou hast made him a little less than a god." Erasmus is moving in the direction of an extreme "humanization" of Christ, and he finds philological reasons for supporting his interpretation.

47. *Index expurgatorius hispanicus et romanus,* cols. 1781–1844. For the materials relating to the Epistle to the Romans, see cols. 1827–28. Yet we should note that chapter 11 was never the object of such censure.

48. See O. Scheel, *Martin Luther, Vom Katholisismus zur Reformation,* 2 vols. (Tübingen, 1916–17), and the already cited study by Dorothea Demmer on Luther's exegesis of the Epistle to the Romans (1968).

49. See J. Chomarat, "*Annotations* de Valla"; as well as Heinz Holecsek, *Humanistische Bibelphilologie als Reformproblem* (Leyden, 1975), 79–100.

50. *Collatio Novi Testamenti,* ed. Perosa (Firenze, 1970).

51. *Spiritus* in the *Collatio* was replaced by *species* in the *Annotationes.*

52. See the article, "Massa" by Forcellini, *Lexicon totius latinitatis:* "farina subacta, unde fit panis" (Greek: μάζα).

53. "Si les premices sont saintes, la masse l'est aussi, et si la racine est sainte, les branches aussi le sont" (Viard, *St. Paul*).

54. Forcellini: "Instrumentum quo frumenta aliaeque fruges conteruntur et in farinam rediguntur" (sense no. 1); "ipsum far tostum, molitum et sale sparum" (sense no. 2).

55. It is in this sense that classical authors such as Plautus, Cicero, Tibullius, and Valerius Maximus often understood the term.

56. The texts of the *Annotationes,* with just cause, has the Greek verb preceded by the negation (μὴ).

57. In the *Annotationes,* the three Greek words are placed *after* sentiatis.

58. "Novum Testamentum a nobis versum. De essentie van Erasmus' uitgave van het Nieuwe Testament," *Lampas* 15, no. 3 (1982): 231–48.

59. Notation 626D–27D.

60. The text of the *Annotations* added, after the Latin, the Greek ἀνεξιχνίαττο.

61. *Annotationes:* in *quo* omnia.

62. *Annotationes:* Καὶ εἰς αὐτὸν.

63. Especially in his thesis (Godin, *Humanisme*).

64. See above, p. 138 in this volume, and n. 40, above.

65. The *Antidota* are included in the personal library of Erasmus. (In this regard, see the article on the catalog on this library in *Gedenkschrift zum 400. Todestage des E.v.R.* [Basel, 1936], 228–59).

66. *Antidotum,* book 4, in Valla, *Opera omnia* (Basel, 1540; reprint, Turin, 1962), 1:268.

67. Chomarat, "*Annotations* de Valla," 264.

68. Trans. Chomarat, ibid., 224–25.

69. See n. 39, above, and more generally the index to the *Opus Epistolarum,* Paul (Saint).

70. See Sears Jayne, *John Colet,* "Bibliographical Appendix."

71. See Lupton, *A Life of Colet,* 85.

72. Anvers: Mart. Caesar; esp. Basel: Frobenius and Episcopius, 1535.

73. See Lupton, *A Life of Colet,* chap. 10, 178ff.

74. Ibid., 189ff. ("Good Friday," 27 March 1513).

75. Ibid., 69.

76. Ibid., 66–67. In general, Colet tends to cite Greek words in Latin. The only point at which he dares to *write* in Greek is in his *Expositio* of 1 Corinthians 8:1.

77. See ibid., 67–68. Colet must have borrowed this etymology from Nicolas Perotti (*Cornucopiae*), although Perotti is usually more circumspect.

78. *LB* 6:622A (at the beginning of the commentary on Romans 11).

79. See his colloquium *Epicureus* (crit. ed. Halkin [*ASD* 1–3, 1972], 720–33).

80. See Lupton, *Life of Colet,* chap. 6, 101ff. (which deals with controversies concerning the agony of Christ). See also F. Seebohm, *Oxford Reformers,* 116, and Allen, *Opus Epistolarum Erasmi,* vol. 1, letter 181, which is a letter from Erasmus to Colet (December 1504) corresponding to a small work which he would later publish under the title *Disputatiuncula de tedio, pavore, tristitia Jesu* (Anvers: T. Martens, 1503) and which he placed as an appendix to the 1515 edition of the *Enchiridion.* See also the article by James Tracy on the *De tedio Jesu* and the relationship between Colet and Erasmus in *Erasmus of Rotterdam Society Yearbook* 5 (1965): 30–59.

81. See the letter portrait addressed to J. Jonas (cf. n. 20, above).

82. On the Erasmian *copia* and, more generally, on the rhetorical and philosophical issues posed by this concept, see Terence Cave, *The Cornucopian Text* (Oxford, 1979); and J. Chomarat, "*Annotations* de Valla," 711–61, 962–66.

83. See the titles mentioned in n. 29, above, in particular the volume by Dom Paul Delatte.

84. See J. B. Trapp, "Peter Meghen, 1466/67–1540, Scribe and Courier," *Erasmus in English* 11 (1981–82): 28–35; and, above all, Andrew J. Brown, "Date of Erasmus' Translation."

85. See J.-C. Margolin, critical edition of *De ratione studii* (*ASD* 1–2, 1971), 79–151.

86. See above references to the two editions of 1512 (Rice, no. 45) and 1515 (Rice, no. 246). The copies to which I refer are found in the Bibliothèque Nationale.

87. Ed. F. Regnault and Jean de la Porte, fol. (Rice, no. 248).

88. This copy is not included in Rice's listings of the locations of the various manuscripts of Lefèvre's works.

89. Once more we refer to his excellent pioneering article that was mentioned at the beginning of this essay: "Erasmus and Lefèvre d'Étaples as Interpreters of Paul."

90. We will leave to one side Colet, who, as we have seen, lacked any deep learning in Greek.

91. See Jean Céard, "Les transformations du genre du commentaire," in *L'Automne de la Renaissance, 1580–1630* (Paris: Vrin, 1961), 101–15, esp. 102–3.

92. See J.-C. Margolin, "La fonction pragmatique et l'influence culturelle de la *Cornucopiae* de Niccolo Perotti," *Res Publica Litterarum* 4 (1981): 123–71, esp. 146–48.

93. See the article "Commentarius," by Dolet, vol. 1, cols. 1702r–1703r.

94. In the *Thesaurus,* fol. 343 (1v)–344(1r).

95. Already in April 1505 he had offered to Briçonnet his edition of the Pimander, and in August 1506 his edition of Aristotle's *Politics.* On the connections between Lefèvre and Bishop Briçonnet, see esp. Bedouelle, *Lefèvre,* chap. 3, 57–60.

96. "Nonnulli etiam forte mirabuntur . . . ecclesiae lumen Hieronymum" (*Epistola,* a2r).

97. Payne, "Erasmus and Lefèvre," 68.

98. See notes 2, 8, and 11; *LB* 6:621–22.

99. This second kind of interpretation begins on fol. 95v and occupies a space that is roughly half of the space devoted to the first (i.e., "spiritual") kind of exegesis.

100. See above, n. 78 (*LB* 6:622A).

101. Erasmus, *LB* 6:621A–24A; *Annotationes* 1–18; Lefèvre, [m5]v–[m6]r, three lines before the end, and [m7]v–[m8]r.

IRENA BACKUS

Bucer's Interpretation of John 6:52, 53, and 64

This article is a by-product of my critical edition of Bucer's commentary on the Fourth Gospel: *Martini Buceri Enarratio in Evangelion Iohannis* (1528, 1530, 1536). Studies in Medieval and Reformation Thought 40 (Leiden, 1988). Hereinafter *Buceri Enarratio.*

1. Cf. *Buceri Enarratio,* xlvii.

2. Cf. R. Stupperich, *Bibliographia Bucerana,* no. 14, [14a]. *Schriften des Vereins für Reformationsgeschichte* 169, Jhrg. 58 (1952).

3. Cf. Stupperich, no. 17, 18.

4. *Buceri Enarratio* (1528), 13.

5. Cf. *Handlung oder Acta gehaltner Disputation zů Berñ in ůchtland* (Zurich: Chr. Froschouer, 23 April 1528), vr: "Das der lyb und das blůt Christi /wasenlich unnd lyblich / in dem brot der dancksagung empfangen werd / mag mit Biblischer gschrifft nit bybracht werden." Ibid., 115v–192r, for acts of the debate. The Lutheran side was represented notably by Benedictus Burgauer of Saint Gallen and Andreas Althamer of Nuremberg.

6. *Enarrationes perpetuae in sacra quatuor Evangelia, recognitae nuper et locis compluribus auctae . . . per Martinum Bucerum. Epistola eiusdem nuncupatoria ad Academiam Marpurgensem de servanda unitate ecclesiae, in qua excutiuntur et articuli conventus Marpurgi Hessorum celebrati* (Argentorati apud Georgium Ulricherum Andlanum, mense martio, 1530). Cf. Stupperich, no. 28; *Buceri Enarratio,* xlviii–ix.

7. *Enarrationes* (1530), A5r–v. The chief point of contention was the question

of "manducatio corporalis," which the Lutherans admitted could take place through faith.

8. *In sacra quatuor Evangelia enarrationes perpetuae, secundum recognitae, in quibus praeterea habes syncerioris Theologiae locos communes... adiectis etiam aliquot locorum retractationibus* (Basel: Ioannes Hervagius, 1536). Cf. Stupperich, no. 28a; *Buceri Enarratio,* l–li.

9. For a purely theological analysis of Bucer's interpretation of the whole of John 6 see Ian Hazlett, "Zur Auslegung von Johannes 6 bei Bucer während der Abendmahlskontroverse," in *Bucer und seine Zeit,* ed. M. de Kroon and F. Krüger (Wiesbaden, 1976), 74–87.

10. *De captivitate, WA* 6:502.

11. Rome: Guillireti, 1521; reprint, Ridgewood, N.J.: Gregg, 1966, c2r–h2r.

12. *Assertionum regis Angliae de fide catholica adversus Lutheri babylonicam captivitatem defensio* [1525], in *I'is Fischerii* [!] *Roffensis in Anglia episcopi opera, quae hactenus inveniri potuerunt omnia...* (Wirceburgi, 1597; reprint, Farnborough, 1967), 101–271.

13. *Defensio,* cap. 4, para. 17, in ibid., 172–73.

14. Cf. *LB* 6:366.

15. *Theophylacti archiepiscopi Bulgariae in quatuor Evangelia enarrationes* (Basel: Andreas Cratander, 1524). Cf. E. Staehelin, *Briefe und Akten zum Leben Oekolampads* (Leipzig, 1927), vol. 1, no. 187, 268–69.

16. Cf. Theophylactus, *In Ioh.,* ad loc., *PG* 123:1307–10.

17. Chrysostom's commentary (cf. *PG* 59:259–60) is ambivalent in identifying *panis* in 52a with faith in Christ but referring 52b to the Eucharist. Most other commentaries interpret the verse as referring to the Eucharist (transsubstantiation) and adopt the reading with only one *dabo.* Cf., e.g., Augustine, *In Ioh.,* tract. 26, ad loc., *MPL* 35:1612–13, *CCL* 36:266–67; Aquinas, *In Ioh.,* ad loc., *Piana* 14:2, 41v, cols. A–B.

18. How well? Cf. contemptuous reference in 1528 version of preface to the Bernese ministers (*Buceri Enarratio* [1528], 11), where "Roffensis" is named together with Eck as author of pamphlets against the Berne disputation. The reference is removed in 1530.

19. *Buceri Enarratio* (1536), 255.

20. *Divi Cyrilli patriarchae Alexandrini in Evangelium Iohannis commentaria... opus insigne quod Thesaurus inscribitur... Georgio Trapezontio interprete... insuper in Leviticum libri 16...* (Basel: Andreas Cratander, 1524).

21. This is emphasized in the Trebizond translation; *Cyril* (1524), ad loc., 72r–73v. Cf. *PG* 73:563–72.

22. *PG* 73:563–67.

23. *De vera et falsa religione commentarius* (1525), *Corpus Reformatorum* 90:779–80.

24. "Panis de quo multa loquor, quem et vobis daturus sum, caro mea est, quam ego pro mundi vita expendam" (*Commentarius, Corpus Reformatorum* 90:779.

25. *In divi Iohannis Evangelion I'is Br'ii exegesis, per autorem diligenter revisa ac multis in locis locupletata* (Haganoe: Iohannes Secer, 1528). Bucer throughout uses Brenz's commentary as a source, which does not stop him from criticizing it vigorously on certain points, notably Christology and the Eucharist.

26. Brenz, *In Ioh.* (1528), 112v.

27. Brenz, *In Ioh.* (1528), 121r.

28. Bucer was using the Latin translation (by Franciscus Aretinus) of Chrysostom's homilies on the Fourth Gospel printed as part of his *Opera* by Andreas Cratander in Basel in 1522 and 1525. References here are to the 1522 edition. Cf. Dom Chr. Baur, *S. Jean Chrysostome et ses oeuvres dans l'histoire littéraire* (Louvain/Paris, 1907), nos. 76 and 86, pp. 152–53. Cf. Bucer's preface to the Bernese ministers: "Non quod mea haec cupiam praeferri iis quae tam veteres, praecipue Chrysostomus et Augustinus, quam recentes quidam, praecipue Erasmus Roterodamus et Philippus Melanchthon in hunc Evangelistam praeclare scripserunt." In 1536 the name of Brenz was added to the list. The acknowledgment of Melanchthon is surprising as Bucer makes very little use of his *Annotationes* (1523) on the Fourth Gospel (*Buceri Enarratio* [1528], 13).

29. Chrysostom, *In Ioh.*, hom. 46 (45), ad loc. (*PG* 59:260), Latin ed. (1522), 118. Cf. Melanchthon, *Sententiae veterum . . . de coena Domini,* 23:737–38, where the passage is cited in full.

30. Cf. Zwingli, *Commentarius, Corpus Reformatorum,* 90:779: "Nam hactenus tantum est nobis salutaris, quatenus pro nobis mactatus est; at secundum carnem mactari tantum potuit, et secundum divinitatem tantum salutaris esse. Sic ergo Christus est animae cibus, quod ea, dum videt Deum Filio suo unigenito non pepercisse, sed in contumeliosam mortem tradidisse, ut nos vitae restitueret, certa fit gratiae Dei salutisque."

31. Paschasius Radbertus, *Ex vetustissimorum orthodoxorum Patrum . . . de genuino eucharistiae negocii intellectu et usu libellus,* ed. Hiob Gast (Haganoae: Ioh. Secer, 1528) (=*Liber de corpore et sanguine Christi, MPL* 120).

32. "Et per sacramentum corporis ac sanguinis Christus in nobis non solum fide, sed etiam unitate carnis et sanguinis manere probatur. . . . Iteratur autem hoc mysterium et ob commemorationem passionis Christi, sicut ipse ait. . . . Non itaque sit accipiendum *donec mors Christi veniat* [1 Corinthians 11:26], qui iam ultra non moritur, sed donec ipse Dominus ad iudicium veniat" (*Liber de corpore et sanguine Christi* 9, *MPL* 120:1297).

33. Cf. n. 30, above.

34. Bugenhagen, *Epistola,* 3v; Brenz; *In Ioh.* (1528), ad loc., 112r–v.

35. *Buceri Enarratio* (1536) ad 6:53, 259ff.

36. Cf. Chrysostom, *In Ioh.,* hom. 47 (46), *PG* 59:264–65.

37. *Buceri Enarratio* (1536) ad 6:53, 263: "Idem sensit divus Chrysostomus ut legis in homilia 46 in Ioannem."

38. Augustine, *In Ioh.,* tract. 26 ad 6:53, *MPL* 35:1613; *CCSL* 36:267.

39. Augustine, *In Ioh.,* tract. 27, ad 6:63ff., *MPL* 35:1617; *CCSL* 36:272.

40. *In Ioh.,* ad loc., *Piana* 14:2, 41v, col. B.

41. *Paraphrasis* (1524), ad loc., *LB* 7:549.

42. *Wider die himml. Propheten* (1525), *WA* 18:193; *Vom Abendmahl Christi Bekenntnis* (1528), *WA* 26:367.

43. *De genuina verborum Domini hoc est corpus meum . . . expositione liber* (Basel, 1525), K5r.

44. *Über Bekenntnis* (1528), *Corpus Reformatorum* 93:188.

45. *In Ioh.* (1528), ad loc., 112v.

46. Lactantius, *Div. inst.* 4:18, *CSEL* 19:348: "Sic universa praecepta Iudaicae legis ad exhibendam iustitiam spectant, quoniam per ambagem data sunt ut per carnalium figuram spiritalia noscerentur."

47. Ibid., 4:16, *CSEL* 19:341.

48. Albert, *In Ioh.,* ad 6:41ff.; *Opera omnia,* vol. 24, ed. Aug. Borgnet (Paris, 1899), 265, col. B.

49. Brenz, *In Ioh.,* (1528), ad 4:11, 62r–v.

50. Cf. *Buceri Enarratio* (1528, 1530), 281.

51. Cf. A. Hahn and G. L. Hahn, *Bibliothek der Symbole und Glaubensregeln der alten Kirche* (Breslau, 1897; reprint, Hildesheim, 1962), para. 143, p. 162.

52. Brenz, *In Ioh.,* (1528), ad 6:63–64, 123r.

53. *Buceri Enarratio* (1528, 1530), 281.

54. *WA* 19:491, 500.

55. *Buceri Enarratio* (1528, 1530), 281.

56. *MPL* 38:184; *CCSL* 41:369–70.

57. 4:27; *MPL* 217:875.

58. Quarta pars, quintum confortativum. Cf. Johannes von Paltz, *Werke,* vol. 1, *Coelifodina,* ed. C. Burger and F. Stasch in collaboration with B. Hamm and V. Marcolino (Berlin, 1982), 282–83. *De coelifodina* would certainly have been known to Luther. Cf. Ernst Schäfer, *Luther als Kirchenhistoriker* (Gütersloh, 1897), 154.

59. *WA* 19:500.

60. Cf. *Corpus Reformatorum* 92:661–62.

61. *Summa Theologiae,* 3a q. 75 a 1, ed. P. Caramello (Turin: Marietti, 1962), 3:446–47.

62. *Summa Theologiae,* 3a q. 75 a 2, ed. P. Caramello 3:448.

63. *Handlung oder Acta: die vierdt Schlussred,* 178v–79r.

64. *Buceri Enarratio* (1528, 1530), 281: "Deo sunt omnia possibilia, libenter

fatemur, sed Deus simul verax est, is testatur nobis Filium suum verum hominem fecisse, verum corpus illum assumpsisse et humanum corpus."

65. *WA* 19:487ff.

66. *De coelifodina,* quarta pars, quintum confortativum, *Werke,* 1:282.

67. Cf. Zwingli, *Amica exegesis* (1527), *Corpus Reformatorum* 92:671.

68. *Buceri Enarratio* (1528, 1530), 282.

69. Cf. Brenz, *In Ioh.* (1528), ad loc., 126v; Luther, e.g., *Bekenntnis* (1528), *WA* 26:367.

70. *In Ioh.,* hom. 47 (46), ad loc., *PG* 59:265.

71. Augustine, *In Ioh.,* tract. 27, ad loc., *MPL* 35:1617–18; *CCSL* 36:272. Thus also: Cyril, *In Ioh.,* ad loc., *PG* 73:602–3. Bucer refers to Cyril in his rejection of Augustine in 1536.

72. *Bucer Enarratio* (1536), 283.

73. Cf. *Wittenberg Concord,* arts. 1–2, *Corpus Reformatorum* 3:75: (1) "Itaque sentiunt et docent cum pane et vino vere et substantialiter adesse exhiberi et sumi corpus Christi et sanguinem." (2) "Et quanquam negant fieri transsubstantiationem, nec sentiunt fieri localem inclusionem in pane, aut durabilem aliquam coniunctionem extra usum sacramenti."

74. *WA* 26:367.

75. This was remarked on by Caspar Schwenckfeld in his letter to the duke of Liegnitz, 23 May 1540: "Ich hab auch jnn sonnderheit des Martin Butzers Leere vom gepredigtenn wort, Tauff, Nachtmall dienst unnd aller zugehorung auss seinem Commentaria übern Johannen in ainem aignen buechlin muessenn mittschickhenn [no longer extant]. . . . Denn solchs noch fur unnd fur in vil buchladenn funden. Unnd doch nicht mit der Augspurgischen Confession, wie auch nit mit dem Luther gleichstymmet. Wie woll Butzer wider solche sein aigne vorige leere unnd gewissenn ytz mit ihm Concordirt unnd dennoch da auch wider jhn schreibt" (*Corpus Schwenckfeldianorum* 7 [1926], doc. 318).

KENNETH HAGEN
Niels Hemmingsen's De Methodis *(1555)*

Gratefully acknowledged for their research support for 1982 are the following: Herzog-August-Bibliothek, Wolfenbüttel, and its Geschäftsstelle für das Forschungsprogramm; Norges almenvitenskapelige forskningsråd for the Hemmingsen project at the Royal University Library, Oslo; and Marquette University and its sabbatical program.

1. John Benson, "The History of the Historical-Critical Method in the Church: A Survey," *Dialog* 12 (1973): 98.

2. Günter Moldaenke, *Schriftverständnis und Schriftdeutung im Zeitalter der Reformation,* pt. 1, *Matthias Flacius Illyricus* (Stuttgart: Kohlhammer, 1936), 558.

3. *De methodis libri duo, quorum prior quidem omnium methodorum universalium et particularium, quarum usus est in Philosophia, brevem ac dilucidam declarationem: posterior vero ecclesiasten sive methodum theologicam interpretandi, concionandique continet. Authore Nicolao Hemmingio* (Rostock, 1555; Wittenberg, 1559, 1562; Leipzig, 1565, 1570, 1578; Geneva, 1586). The *Dansk bibliographi 1551–1600,* ed. Lauritz Nielsen (Copenhagen, 1931–33), does not list the editions of Wittenberg 1559, or Geneva 1586.

4. Kjell Barnekow, *Niels Hemmingsens Teologiska Åskådning* (Lund, 1940); reviewed by B. Kornerup, "En svensk disputats om Niels Hemmingsen," *Dansk teologisk tidsskrift* 4 (1941): 57–66 (hereinafter *DTT*); and J. O. Anderson, "Om Niels Hemmingsens teologi," *Kyrkohistorisk årsskrift* 41 (1942): 108–31; E. M. Madsen, "Om Forholdet mellem Niels Hemmingsens Enchiridion theologicum og Melanchthons Loci Communes," *DTT* 5 (1942): 137–51, 215–32; Madsen, "Er Calvin Niels Hemmingsens eksegetiske Forbillede?" *DTT* 9 (1946): 1–10. For various studies on Niels Hemmingsen, cf. the overview of nineteenth- and twentieth-century literature by Jens Glebe-Møller, "Socialetiske aspekter af Niels Hemmingsens forfatterskab," *Kirkehistoriske samlinger* (1979): 7–11.

5. Carl von Kaltenborn, *Die Vorläufer des Hugo Grotius auf dem Gebiete des Ius naturae et gentium, sowie der Politik im Reformationszeitalter* (Leipzig: Mayer, 1848), 237–38, VII.

6. Trygve Skarsten, "The Reception of the Augsburg Confession in Scandinavia," *Sixteenth Century Journal* 11 (1980): 96.

7. M. E. Schild, "Leading Motifs in some Western Bible Prologues," *Journal of Religious History* 7 (1972): 107.

8. "As the method of teaching is the *opus* in other disciplines, the *ratio docendi* is to be established especially in the Queen of the Disciplines, Theology," *Enchiridion theologicum* (1559), in *Opuscula theologica* (1586), 324. "*Exegesis*" is also used in his three works on the Psalter (1567, 1569, 1592) and throughout his commentaries on the Epistles, gathered together in *Commentaria in omnes epistolas apostolorum* (1586).

9. Reinhard Kirste, "Massstäbe und Methoden biblischer Hermeneutik in der altprotestantischen Orthodoxie," *Bijdragen: Tijdschrift voor philosophie en theologie* 36 (1975): 290.

10. Johannes Altenstaig, *Vocabularius theologie* (Hagenau, 1517), "Interpretatio."

11. I consulted the *Vocabularia* by Reuchlin (1478), Calepino ([1510], 1542, 1598, 1647), Altenstaig (1517), *Dictionaire en Theologie* (1560), Arguerio (1567), Chaulmer (1672), Magri (1677), Du Cange (1688), and the *Thesaurus linguae Latinae* by Estienne (1543, 1740), Burer (1576), Pareus (1645), Morel (1657). *Exegesis* does

exist in Zwingli's title, *Amica Exegesis, id est expositio Eucharistiae* (1527). *Exegematicum* is in Budé (*De Asse, Opera Omnia,* 1557, 2:8; *Exegetes,* p. 149), as is ἐξηγήσεως (*Commentarii linguae graeize, Opera Omnia,* 4:1062.34). *Exegetei, exegematicus,* and *exegeticon* appear in some sixteenth-century lexicons.

12. N. W. Gilbert, *Renaissance Concepts of Method* (New York: Columbia University Press, 1960), 108.

13. Hemmingsen, *Opuscula theologica,* 332.

14. Madsen, "Er Calvin Niels Hemmingsens eksegetiske Forbillede?"

15. Ibid., 2, 4–5.

16. Nils K. Andersen, "De teologiske Fakultet, 1479–1597," *Københavns universitet 1479–1979* (Copenhagen, 1980), vol. 48.

17. Gilbert, *Renaissance Concepts,* 127.

18. Wilhelm Risse, *Die Logik der Neuzeit,* vol. 1, *1500–1640* (Stuttgart, 1964).

19. Barnekow, *Teologiska Åskådning,* 34, n. 3.

20. *Dansk Biografisk Leksikon* (1895): 326 (hereinafter *DBL*); *DBL* 2 (1936): 55; *DBL* 3 (1980) does not mention it.

21. Risse, *Die Logik,* 1:120.

22. Ibid., 1:111–12.

23. Gilbert, *Renaissance Concepts,* 92–100. Gilbert knows only of the 1570 edition of Hemmingsen's *De methodis,* and "unfortunately" has not consulted it. Also unfortunately, he places it after works on theological method by Zanchi (post-1568), Strigel (1581), Flacius (1567), and Melanchthon (Gilbert, 107–12).

24. Flacius, *Clavis Scripturae Sacrae* (Basel, 1567), pt. 2, pp. 41–45.

25. "Quapropter constitui Methodum Theologicam conscribere, in qua rationem et interpretandi scripturam, et formandi sacras conciones complectar, quorum prius faciet, ut facilius alios interpretes intelligamus, et ipsi interpretandi formas teneamus, quas sequi utile erit. Posterius vero, ut citra garrulitatem, dextre et copiose de re proposita disserere incoetu Ecclesiastico valeamus" (Hemmingsen, pp. 120–21).

26. J. H. Paulli, *Dr. Niels Hemmingsens Pastoraltheologie* (Copenhagen, 1851); P. G. Lindhardt, "Til belysning af Niels Hemmingsens indflydelse på dansk praediken omkring 1600," in *Festskrift til Jens Nørregaard* (Copenhagen: Gads, 1947).

27. *Commentaria in omnes epistolas apostolorum* (Leipzig, 1572), 7.

28. Ibid., 921.

29. Ibid., 315.

30. Benson "History," 98.

31. Basil Hall, *The Cambridge History of the Bible,* 3 vols. (Cambridge: University Press, 1963), 3:50–51.

32. Brevard Childs, *Introduction to the Old Testament as Scripture* (Philadelphia: Fortress, 1979), 32.

33. H. J. Kraus, "Calvin's Exegetical Principles," *Interpretation* 31 (1977): 14.

34. "Ratio sev compendium verae theologiae," in *Novum Testamentum* (Basel: Froben, 1519), 17.

35. Otto Kaiser, *Introduction to the Old Testament,* trans. John Sturdy (Minneapolis: Augsburg, 1977), 7.

36. Kraus, *Geschichte der historisch-kritischen Erforschung des Alten Testaments,* 2d ed. (Neukirchen: Neukirchener Verlag, 1969), 28–29.

37. In: Karl Credner, *Zur Geschichte des Kanons* (Halle, 1847), 327.

38. Theodor Zahn, "Einleitung in das Neue Testament," *Realencyklopädie für protestantische Theologie und Kirche* (1898), 5:263.

39. Pagnino, *Isagogae ad sacras literas, liber unicus. Eiusdem Isagogae ad mysticos sacrae scripturae sensus* (Lyon: Hugo à Porta, 1536), 51–818.

40. Flacius, *Clavis scripturae sacrae, seu de sermone sacrarum literarum, plurimas generales regulas continens altera pars* (Basel: Eusebius Episcopius, 1581 [prefaced 1567]).

41. Werner Kümmel, *The New Testament: The History of the Investigation of Its Problems,* trans. S. McLean Gilmour and Howard Kee (New York: Abingdon Press, 1972), 27.

42. Kraus, *Edition,* 28–29.

43. Hans Frei, *The Eclipse of Biblical Narrative: A Study in Eighteenth and Nineteenth Century Hermeneutics* (London: Yale University Press, 1974), 37.

44. Olivier Fatio, "Hyperius plagié par Flacius. La destinée d'une méthode exégétique," *Histoire de l'exégèse au XVIe siècle* (Geneva: Droz, 1978), 375–79.

45. K. A. von Schwartz, "Die theologische Hermeneutik des Matthias Flacius Illyricus," *Lutherjahrbuch* 15 (1933): 149.

46. *Glossa compendiaria M. Matthiae Flacii Illyrici Albonensis in novum Testamentum* (Basel: P. Perna and T. Dietrich, 1570).

47. Kümmel, *New Testament,* 20; Hendricus Boers, *What Is New Testament Theology? The Rise of Criticism and the Problem of a Theology of the New Testament* (Philadelphia: Fortress, 1979), 17.

48. *DBL.* 1.

Index

Library of Congress Cataloging-in-Publication Data
The Bible in the sixteenth century / David C. Steinmetz, editor.
p. cm.
"Essays in this volume were written for the 2nd International Colloquy on the History of Biblical Exegesis in the Sixteenth Century, held at Duke University, September 23–25, 1982"—Introd.
ISBN 0-8223-1012-0
1. Bible—Criticism, interpretation, etc.—History—16th century—Congresses. 2. Bible. O.T.—Criticism, interpretation, etc., Jewish—History—Congresses. I. Steinmetz, David Curtis. II. International Colloquy on the History of Biblical Exegesis in the Sixteenth Century (2nd : 1982 : Duke University)
BS500.B548 1990
220.6′09′031—dc20 89-27910
CIP